Intelligent Policing

How Systems Thinking Methods Eclipse

Conventional Management Practice

Simon Guilfoyle

Published in this first edition in 2013 by:
Triarchy Press
Station Offices
Axminster
Devon. EX13 5PF
United Kingdom

+44 (0)1297 631456
info@triarchypress.com
www.triarchypress.com

A catalogue record for this book is available from the British Library.

Cover design by James Castleden
www.jamescastleden.com
Photograph by Tom Guilfoyle

Print ISBN: 978-1-909470-05-7

Contents

Preface

This book is about applying systems thinking to policing. It is the culmination of five years' research into systems thinking and related theories, combined with 18 years of policing experience. It outlines a methodology for building a more effective policing system that will enhance organisational effectiveness, cut costs and improve service delivery.

The book is intended for police and public sector leaders at all levels and for people who care about how the police service is run. It will also be of interest to people who want to learn about systems thinking, organisational improvement, leadership and management, or who want to read about the unintended consequences of some conventional management practices. Despite this, there is no prerequisite for the reader to have any prior knowledge of systems theory, management or even policing.

Whilst the concepts discussed in this book are very much rooted in theory, I deliberately haven't written the text in a formal academic style. This, I hope, will make it more accessible and interesting. I have focused a lot of the examples on frontline operational policing because it is the area of policing that enjoys the greatest direct contact with the public and where the systemic effects of police operating models are most profound. I hope this approach will help managers understand how system design and decisions taken at the strategic level affect ground-level activity.

The underlying philosophy of the book is based on analysis of the work of W. Edwards Deming, Taiichi Ohno, Donald Wheeler, Russell Ackoff, Myron Tribus, Brian Joiner and John Seddon, as well as other associated authors. You will see some of these names pop up time and again throughout the book. John Seddon is also credited with applying and adapting much of Deming's philosophy to the service industry and public sector. Direct quotes and specific points are referenced in the footnotes, with a comprehensive bibliography for readers who are bitten by the systems bug and want to read further. I have used practical real-life examples to illustrate the concepts that are discussed – many are from personal experience and therefore cannot be referenced but, trust me, I was there.

My research and writing has been conducted away from work and came about due to a personal interest in this field of study. It just so happened that the more I learnt about systems thinking, the more I noticed areas where it could be applied in the workplace. Within my sphere of influence, I have been able to implement systems thinking practices and this has had a sustained beneficial effect. Not all UK police forces have embraced systems thinking principles, although I have detected a real undercurrent of interest recently. Therefore, I want to emphasise that this piece of work is entirely independent of my employers, West Midlands Police.

Apart from the review and analysis of existing literature, the book draws upon exploratory research that I conducted with 30 officers from 12 UK police forces during 2012. It is acknowledged that the scale of the research is small and its findings should be considered in this context – what is remarkable, however, is the consistency of the views presented by those who participated. It is also notable that their views largely reflect evidence from the wider literature, as well as my own experiences.

I would suggest that further, larger-scale research of a similar nature would add significant empirical evidence to existing knowledge within this field.

Simon Guilfoyle

Foreword

When I met Simon Guilfoyle I was hugely impressed. Under his own steam he had transformed policing in his area, achieving outstanding improvements in terms of preventing and detecting crime and, moreover, had massively improved officer morale. More than that: to step outside of convention is especially difficult in an organisation like the police service.

As you will see, his strength to challenge management norms was rooted in unequivocal evidence. While, no doubt, some would regard him as a maverick, a non-conformist, he should be seen as a pioneer and thought leader. What he has achieved in one area should open the minds of police leaders everywhere.

John Seddon

Introduction

Best Intentions Aren't Enough

When I was a Sergeant I devised a method of performance measurement to assess the quality of ongoing criminal investigations. The method involved evaluating relevant paperwork and awarding a percentage score based on a number of factors. At the time, my approach was heralded as innovative because it concentrated purely on aspects of quality and what mattered to victims of crime. This, at least, I had got right.

The assessment was conducted on a monthly basis and included a comparison to the previous month's score for each team. Team scores were shown in green (improving) or red (deteriorating). However, I decided that it would be unfair to brand a team as 'deteriorating' if they had achieved a high score that was marginally less than last month's, so I chose 90% as a threshold – as long as a team scored more than this, their result would be shown in green. This would categorise them as having achieved the defined standard. Each month, the divisional management congratulated those teams that showed improvement or consistent achievement, whilst those that didn't were asked difficult questions.

Everyone seemed to think that this method of assessment was a good idea, and I put a lot of effort into it. I devised the process purely out of a desire to improve standards and ensure that the public received a better service. I had done everything for the right reasons. However, what I had unwittingly achieved was dysfunctional team versus team competition through a statistically baseless methodology in comparing 'this month versus last month' and, worst of all, I had introduced an arbitrary numerical target of 90%. Where had 90% come from? I just thought it seemed 'about right'. People were praised or admonished based on whether they had met my arbitrary target, or shown subjective 'improvement'.

Unfortunately, I had blundered into performance measurement blindly, without proper knowledge or understanding, and created a system of assessment that was meaningless and harmful. I didn't know about binary comparisons, or variation, or tampering, or gaming, or Statistical Process

Control charts. I didn't understand the importance of purpose, or the interdependencies that comprise the foundation of an effective system. I didn't appreciate the outcomes generated by internalised competition or sub-optimisation. I didn't know about waste or flow, perverse incentives, or the behaviours likely to be initiated by disproportionate audit and inspection. I had never heard of a lot of things that are critical for building a stronger system and improving service delivery.

The lesson I learnt was this – there are a lot of good people out there with good intentions who inadvertently cause worse problems than the ones they are trying to solve. Now that I understand where I went wrong I can make amends. Only when you know *how* to do something properly can you achieve what you set out to. Hold that thought.

The Importance of Theory

This book aims to blend the understanding that is gained from theory with putting that theory into practice. When designing systems to ensure organisational effectiveness, it is essential that underlying theories are properly understood before attempting to apply them. Experience is not enough in itself – learning depends on a combination of experience and relevant theory.

Deming taught us the following:

> Theory is a window into the world. Theory leads to prediction. Without prediction, experience and examples teach nothing. To copy an example of success, without understanding it with the aid of theory, may lead to disaster.[1]

There are many real life examples and case studies in this book which I hope you will find interesting and enlightening in their own right. Moreover, I hope that by understanding them in conjunction with the relevant theory, they will prove useful.

Let's Have a Debate

Captain Leslie E. Simon of the US Army stated in 1936, "If you cannot argue with your boss, he is not worth working for",[2] and this holds as true

---

1   Deming (1994) p.103

2   *ibid* p.121

today as it did then. The statement is not a call to arms for disgruntled workers to confront their bosses and spread disharmony in the workplace, but an exhortation to constructive dialogue that is geared towards improving the system. Sharing ideas and different perspectives can lead to the development of new concepts and approaches, and this pulls the organisation toward continuous improvement. In the police service, officers have a huge variety of skills and different areas of expertise; some are developed whilst in post, some have been brought to the table from previous life experience, personal interests or external qualifications. Just because someone is your boss, it doesn't mean that their ideas are better than yours. Likewise, just because you are someone's boss doesn't mean that you automatically have better ideas than your staff.

Some of the best ideas come from frontline officers. Although I am now an Inspector, I still proudly class myself as frontline, yet it is the Constables and Sergeants who *really* know what is going on. That is why I am not offended or defensive when one of them suggests an alternative way of tackling a problem. Often it is a better option than the one I had proposed. If I were to suppress this type of constructive dialogue, staff would feel devalued and potentially brilliant ideas would never see the light of day. An ego is never an excuse to restrict others' creativity. The system always pays the price.

Of course, in some circumstances a debate is not always possible – for example, if I am in the middle of a riot and I want my highly trained public order unit to disperse the rioters, the command "Advance!" should be enough. The style of leadership is adapted to the situation.

Nevertheless, in the right circumstances there is a case for 'arguing' with your boss and questioning the *status quo*, on condition that it is done with the aim of improving the system. Bosses at all levels should consider such debate as an opportunity rather than a threat. The alternative is a stagnant organisation where fresh ideas are stifled and anyone who asks why we do something in a particular fashion is met with the response, "Because the boss said so", or "Because that's the policy". This type of reply misses the point – after all, the real 'boss' is the service user.

What's In A Name?

Taiichi Ohno, the man largely responsible for the renowned Toyota Production System[3] adamantly refused to give his systems based methods a name. He feared that to do so would result in codification of his methododologies, thereby restricting innovation and inadvertently encouraging imitation without understanding.

With due regard to Mr Ohno, I use the terms 'systems thinking', 'the systems approach', 'systems philosophy', 'systems-orientated' and 'pro-systemic', relatively interchangeably. This is deliberate. You will notice a common theme amongst these phrases – they revolve around the word *systems*. That is the important thing. Whatever you wish to call the approaches outlined in this book, they are all based on an understanding of the *systems* context and associated theories.

It is not important what label you prefer to give the philosophy – what I'm talking about is simply good management.

---

3   Ohno (1988)

CHAPTER ONE

Systems and Processes

Systems...

Much of the systems philosophy in this book is derived from the work of W. Edwards Deming, who urged managers to consider their organisations as *whole systems*, to use straightforward statistical methods to ascertain how processes actually perform and, through the intelligent interpretation of data, to establish an evidence base that provides a mandate for action. The approach is much more than just a set of tools that can reduce waste in disparate processes; it is a *philosophy* that challenges the dominant mode of management thinking. It rejects coercive managerial control, along with assumptions that workers cannot be trusted or require extrinsic motivators.

The systems approach fosters clear continuous improvement through a programme of innovation, meaningful performance measurement and worker engagement. It promotes evidence-based priorities, devolved responsibility, organisational trust and a culture of ongoing learning to engender an organisational climate where energy is focused on achieving overall purpose from the customer's or service user's perspective.

In short, the adoption of systems principles results in a superior model of policing that eclipses conventional management practice in every respect.

Spot The Difference

You might have heard managers or colleagues confidently talking about 'systems and processes'. But do those who routinely trot out this phrase really understand what they are talking about? As this book is about building effective systems it makes sense to start with a few straightforward definitions, key concepts and examples, and 'system' is a good place to start.

Deming defines a system as:

> ...a network of interdependent components that work together to try to accomplish the aim of the system.[1]

Police forces are made up of many components such as 24/7 response teams, CID, Counter Terrorism Units, as well as planning and administration departments. However, before we examine the interplay between these components, police forces need to be clear about their aim or purpose. As Deming says, "A system must have an aim. Without an aim there is no system".[2] The aim of a system may also be described as its *purpose*.[3]

Police forces try to capture an overarching corporate aim in a mission statement, such as the famous motto of the LAPD – "To protect and to serve". Closer to home, West Midlands Police's current mission statement is, "Serving our communities, protecting them from harm". Other UK police forces use similar mottos, such as "Keeping our communities safe and reassured" (Staffordshire Police) and "Serving – protecting – making a difference" (West Mercia Police). There is not a great deal of difference between any of these slogans – each is a clear outline of what the purpose of the police service is, i.e. *to serve and protect*. The public also expect the police to prevent and detect crime, be polite, professional and caring, to arrive at emergency incidents quickly and respond effectively to public concerns. Deming also asks, "By what method?"[4] By this he means that it is all well and good to state an aim, such as to catch burglars, but without a considered method for actually doing it, the aim will not be realised. It is only when the extent of a perceived burglary problem is understood, through intelligent interpretation of the available information, that an evidence-based response can be formulated to tackle it.

---

1   Deming (1994) p.50
2   *ibid*
3   Throughout this book you will encounter overlapping terms synonymous with 'aim'. Whilst 'aim' and 'purpose' have specific meanings within the systems context, others such as 'goals', 'objectives' and even 'targets' are sometimes used in everyday parlance when describing similar concepts. For the purposes of clarity, my interpretation of these terms in this book can be visualised on a sliding scale, with 'purpose' and 'aim' at one end (describing the broad, overarching aim or purpose of a system); next, you have 'goal', which takes on its everyday meaning, followed by 'objective' (more prescriptive and often linked to hard targets), and then 'target', taken to mean numerical target.
4   *ibid*

Components of a System

The key principle of systems philosophy is that every element of a system must work together to achieve the overall aim of the system. A simple analogy might be to consider the human body – all the major organs and the trillions of cells have a distinct and important role to play. None can thrive independently of the others, and each performs a function that contributes to the overall system. The result is that the aim (or purpose) of the system – life – is achieved.

In an organisation, components of a system could be departments, functions and individual processes. To illustrate what a policing system looks like at the organisational level, I have put together a simple representation of some main departmental functions. Of course, there are many other components that exist within a police force, but it would be impossible to fit them all on the page. The purpose of the diagram is to demonstrate the interdependencies that exist between the individual parts.

Figure 1.1: Components of a policing system

Now imagine that each of these departments is connected to every other one by a connecting line. It would look like a bowl of spaghetti, which is why I haven't tried to draw it. Next, imagine that some strands of spaghetti are thicker than others, to show that some departments are more reliant on each other and work closely together. For example, the control room is strongly linked to both the call handlers and the 24/7 response units. The call handlers generate much of the work subsequently conducted by the control room staff (i.e. they will take calls about incidents, and send electronic incident logs to the control room staff who prioritise incidents and despatch 24/7 response units).

There would also be a strong link between the control room staff and the 24/7 response units, as radio messages are sent and received between the two. Response units also rely on the control room to perform actions on their behalf, such as to conduct PNC (Police National Computer) checks on vehicle registration numbers and people, or record updates about incidents they have attended. On the other hand, there would be little direct interaction between the response units and the call handlers, so the strand of spaghetti that connects them is much thinner.

Similarly, there will be stronger connections between the response units and the traffic department than there would be between them and the licensing department. Likewise, the CID and firearms department may not routinely mix, but would certainly come together for high profile operations that require both sets of expertise. Everyone relies on the admin and finance department to ensure wages are paid on time. In fact, each department is directly or indirectly linked at different times and to varying degrees. In other words, all the components of the system are required to work together to achieve the policing aims set out above. As with the human body analogy, the system is adaptive and fluid and each component has an important part to play to achieve purpose.

Systems in organisations begin to collapse if one or more components act in a self-interested way, such as maximising their own outputs (or profit, test scores, vehicle fleet, budgetary savings, etc.), and they become directionless and ineffective when management methods interfere with or obscure the system's aim or purpose.

Conventional Management Practice

Conventional management practices are often at odds with systems principles. The established model is usually hierarchical, reliant on prescriptive doctrine and focuses its attention on parts of the system. This type of model has a number of drawbacks, yet is commonplace in what John Seddon calls Command and Control organisations.[5]

When one part of a system or process is optimised at the expense of other parts of the system, or when individual components of the system maximise their own utility, this is known as *sub-optimisation*. Moving people from one department to boost staffing levels in another is an example of this. Individual departments operating in such a parochial fashion give rise to the phrase 'working in silos', and ensure that inter-departmental cooperation is damaged and unhealthy competition prevails. Tools of the trade include the yearly performance review, disproportionate audit and inspection regimes, and blaming individuals for systemic failings. Departments and individuals are pitted against each other and ranked according to performance as measured against targets, standards, or management expectations, all of which damage systemic interrelations and break down the very cohesion that the system relies upon.

Apart from the terrible human cost of adversarial relationships within the organisation, silo working and inter-departmental competition sounds the death knell for achieving organisational purpose. Each department will often act to protect itself in order to survive in what can be a very hostile working environment. Such behaviour can manifest itself in subterfuge aimed at achieving performance targets; this includes the passing on of defective work to other departments or a reluctance to cooperate in case someone else gets the credit.

It is well known that excessive and inappropriate interference from management causes these sorts of reactions. As far back as the 6th Century BC, the Chinese philosopher Lao Tzu wrote:

> *When a nation is ruled*
> *With a light touch,*
> *People lead simple lives.*
> *When a government*
> *Is harsh and demanding,*
> *People will spend their time*
> *Trying to outsmart it.*[6]

---

5   Seddon (2008) p.47
6   Loa Tzu (or Laozi). 6th Century BC.

Workers do not try to outsmart control mechanisms because they are inherently 'bad' people. Rather, it is about survival. When jobs, credibility or pay are at stake and all that management seems to care about is whether quotas have been achieved, you can rest assured – quotas *will* be achieved. This human response is practically guaranteed in any organisation that demands improvement without method, or which relies on targets, prescriptive policies or internal competition to control its staff. Whilst some departments will 'win' under this approach, many others will lose, but the absolute certainty is that the overall system will lose out, in a big way. In policing, this means that the public lose out.

Optimising the System – Looking at the Big Picture

Just sitting and hoping that the aim will be achieved (or angrily demanding it) will not make any difference. Even where there is a broad stated aim, if it is incompatible with what the customer or service user requires, or there is no defined method for achieving it, only failure can ensue.

Part of the essential bedrock of an effective system design is that it is optimised to meet predictable *demand*.[7] Demand is simply what customers or service users want or expect from the system. In manufacturing it could be metal components, cars or toasters. In policing, demand can be extremely varied, from attending crimes in progress, to directing traffic at road collisions, or finding a missing child. Nevertheless, it is essential to investigate what the main types and volumes of demand are within any organisation, as this leads to a greater understanding of how the system needs to be designed.

An effective system aligns the aim (or purpose) of the system with an understanding of what the actual demand is. For example, there is no point producing pink car tyres if no one wants them. Equally, there is no point providing a one-size-fits-all service to meet an array of similar but individualistic or unpredictable circumstances. Likewise, purpose will not be met by limiting service to times that suit the organisation rather than the service user, or by restricting access to the people who can actually help – services users are often required to jump through several hoops before they can get what they want. It is important to listen to what service users are asking for and allow them to *pull* the service they require from a responsive system, rather than shoving what you think they want in their face.

---

7   The notions of designing against demand, pulling value from the system, placing expertise at the front end, managing value and variety of demand are all integral to the work of John Seddon (2003, 2008) and are explored in more detail in subsequent chapters.

It may be necessary to allow some components of the system to operate below capacity in order to ensure that the overall system is optimised. This is counterintuitive, but it can be vital to invest what might seem to be a disproportionate amount of expertise, resources or expense into one part of the system, whilst reducing the size or role of another. One of the main tenets of the systems approach is to place *expertise at the front end.* The reason for this is that service users can usually get the help they need without being referred on to others.

Having empowered and knowledgeable front line staff who are trusted to make decisions means that the organisation can deliver a faster and better service. Not only does devolved responsibility result in greater efficiency, enhanced morale, and a much improved service, it is actually less costly than the traditional approach of making referrals or seeking permission from managers. It works because the emphasis is on managing value instead of cost. (Contrast this with the torture of being bounced from department to department whilst trying to get someone to help you with a problem – we've all been there.) Such systems principles may be shockingly contrary to conventional practice, but the overriding consideration must be how to achieve purpose from the service user's perspective, as well as improving the system as a whole. This is demonstrated below:

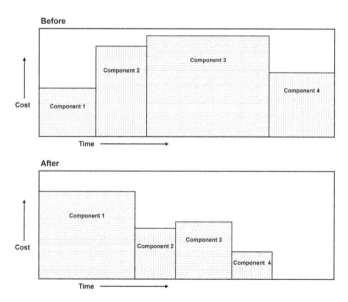

Figure 1.2: Optimising the system

These diagrams show the different components (which could be departments, activities or functions) that exist within a system. In the 'before' version, the components comprise a relatively small-scale front end activity at Component 1, followed by three further layers of subsequent activities. The activity that occurs at Component 3 happens to be particularly lengthy and costly. It doesn't really matter what these activities are, but look at what happens when the system is redesigned (i.e. the 'after' version).

By investing more resources and time in the first activity (often the one that involves the point of contact with the customer or service user), the cost and time invested in the subsequent activities can be reduced. Even at a quick glance it is obvious that the total amount of activity required to achieve purpose (i.e. the shaded areas) is much less in the redesigned system than in the original configuration. The total end-to-end time that the system requires to complete the work is shorter, and the overall cost is less. This is despite ploughing more resources and budget into Component 1.

(Note: It's so much better if more than one particular activity or function can be performed by the same individual or department – the splitting up of work into separate functions and allocating it to different people or departments is called *division of labour* and can slow things down unnecessarily. We'll look at division of labour in more detail later.)

Such a system redesign may provoke nervousness or even hostility from managers who want to keep the cost of Component 1 to a minimum. There may well be opposition to any rebalancing of resource levels from Components 2, 3 and 4 but what is important is the overall effect on the system. If it becomes more efficient and more cost-effective, no manager should be upset by that. All it takes is a holistic approach, instead of everyone fighting their own corner or management implementing structures that pit teams against each other.

Responding to Incidents

Here is a policing example of this theory in action and the effect it has on the various components. Imagine that the 'before' and 'after' configurations in *Figure 1.2* represent police operating models for responding to reported incidents. Starting with the 'before' version, Component 1 is the 24/7 response function; Component 2 represents a stage where incidents are sorted and allocated to either those officers who operate within the

Component 3 block (investigation teams that manage enquiries and attend pre-arranged diary appointments), Component 4 (neighbourhood policing teams) or, in some circumstances, both. Management's rationale for this model is that although the 24/7 response units are relatively small in size, they are only responsible for dealing with a small proportion of incidents at the time they are initially reported.

Reported incidents are classified according to seriousness and only the most serious incidents warrant a response from the 24/7 response units. All non-urgent calls will be redirected to other teams, or diarised for attendance at some point in the future. The model dictates that, following initial attendance at a serious incident, the response units will hand over the paperwork to other officers, as well as all follow-up enquiries and any prisoners before going out to other emergencies. At first this might seem logical, because, in theory, response units should not become tied up with non-urgent matters.

The flaws in this design are exposed when it is viewed as a whole system, especially when considered from the angle of achieving purpose from the perspective of the service user. Let's assume that a member of the public reports a suspicious person looking at houses in a cul-de-sac. Unless they are actually seen trying to break into a house, this is likely to be classified at a relatively low level and deemed unsuitable for the 24/7 response units. It may well be that a house is subsequently burgled before the police have followed up on the report about the suspicious character. What is the purpose of the police here? To stop burglaries happening; to catch burglars; to check out suspicious characters; to respond positively to a caller who cared enough to report the suspicious activity. In this case, preventative policing has been thwarted by rigid classifications and an inflexible operating model.

Consider another example. Someone reports anti-social behaviour committed by a group of youths. No criminal offences have occurred, so the call will not be routed to the 24/7 response units and is likely to be diarised. *"Would you like a neighbourhood officer to come and have a chat about the problem at three o'clock tomorrow, sir?"* *"No, I'd rather the police came out now and stopped it from happening."* What if, through non-attendance, the youths start fighting and someone is stabbed? The stabbing call would get a fast response, but by then it's too late. What is the purpose from the service user's perspective?

If something is very low level, involves negligible risk and the caller would genuinely prefer a visit the next day at a convenient time, then a diary appointment can be appropriate. The problems begin when matters are categorised by the organisation and the caller is unable to *pull* on the appropriate service. This approach does not actually save any time either; the officers end up dealing with the same amount of jobs. It's just that some are now a day old. They haven't gone away.

Given that some apparently innocuous incidents have the potential to escalate into something more serious, the delay caused by routinely diarising the police response increases the risk that something will go wrong in the interim. Surely it is better to nip these matters in the bud? At best, even if something doesn't degenerate into a stabbing or burglary, if the officer is attending 24 hours later, the whole purpose of attendance has gone anyway. The chance of identifying the potential burglar has been missed, and the unruly youths have not been advised about their behaviour so they will probably be back to cause more problems later.

By restricting the size and remit of 24/7 response teams, management restrict the usefulness of the entire system. Then, the next flaw kicks in. Those matters that do receive a response from the 24/7 response units must be handed over after initial attendance. This introduces a whole new function into the system that wasn't there before, i.e. the batching and sorting stage (Component 2). Someone has to review the incident to that point, as well as the associated paperwork, and then allocate it to either the investigation teams (Component 3) or the neighbourhood teams (Component 4). Some aspects of the follow up may need to be directed to more than one department. This whole stage involves additional work that would not exist if the officers who attended initially were able to retain the investigation and follow it through to conclusion. Of course this can't happen under this fragmented design, as it would keep these officers off the streets and there would be insufficient 24/7 response units left to respond to other emergencies. The operating model says 'No!'

Any handover in a process is by its very nature inefficient, no matter how well the documentation is completed. (A lot of systems literature uses the term *handoff*, but I prefer to use *handover* because it is the word commonly used in the police.) This is because it is impossible for the officers who pick up the enquiry to share the sights, sounds and experience of the original officers who attended the incident. It is impossible to convey every detail on a piece of paper. Handovers also create a delay in the process, as the receiving officers have to read the documentation and learn about the job from scratch before they can continue working on it. The entire operating model at the 'before' stage of *Figure 1.2* is fundamentally flawed and results in a slower and less effective service. Can it ever consistently achieve purpose? No.

Managers who endorse this operating model would argue that the 24/7 response units could not possibly retain their own enquiries as there aren't enough of them. They're right. So what is the solution?

It would look something like the 'after' version of *Figure 1.2,* although Component 2 wouldn't need to be there at all. An instant saving! With a larger, multifunctional 24/7 response capability, officers could be deployed to all manner of incidents, not just the most serious. They would also be able to retain their own enquiries (except in certain circumstances such as after arresting someone for murder – that person is always going to be dealt with by CID). They would be able to stop things happening at the time, rather than talk about them with an already dissatisfied caller 24 hours later. Also, they would develop investigative skills as a result of interviewing their own prisoners instead of handing them over to someone else.

This alternative operating model would involve greater investment, time and cost at Component 1, but it would totally eliminate Component 2 (sorting and allocating) and significantly reduce Components 3 and 4. Having more multi-skilled officers available in Component 1 means that there would be more expertise at the front end, thereby enabling the system to cope with greater volume and variety of demand. It would be directed towards achieving purpose. It would be cost effective and efficient. It would be more flexible and responsive to the huge variety of incidents that are reported by the public.

Contrast this with conventional management methods that emphasise functional specialisms and silos, breaking the work into parts, handovers, expertise positioned away from the front end, interdepartmental competition – all of which lead to the system being sub-optimised.

11

... And Processes

What is a process, and how does it differ from a system? A process involves a chain of activities that are required to take a product or service from 'A' to 'B'. The activity will move through a series of stages, each often dependent on the last, until the overall end-to-end activity is complete. (This movement through the stages of a process is known as *flow*). Processes can therefore feature as components of a system. Deming offers the following helpful explanation of a process:

> Every activity, every job is part of a process. A flow diagram of any process will divide the work into stages. The stages as a whole form a process. The stages are not individual entities, each running at maximum profit. Work comes in at any stage, changes state, and moves on into the next stage. The final stage will send product or service to the ultimate customer, ...[8]

To return to the human body analogy, getting oxygen to the brain could be classed as a process. Various organs and body parts are involved:

- The diaphragm contracts, causing air to be sucked into the lungs

- Oxygen is extracted from air in the lungs and enters the bloodstream

- Freshly oxygenated blood is pumped around the body by the heart

- The freshly oxygenated blood arrives at the brain.

The brain now has the oxygen it requires to function effectively, and the process is complete. (Of course, it is the brain sending impulses to the diaphragm that causes it to contract in the first place, and the actual process is more complex than described above, not least because it constantly repeats. I am not going to win a prize for human biology any time soon. I accept that).

In this (deliberately over simplified) example, the diaphragm, lungs, blood and heart are all components of the *system*, and the action of delivering oxygen to the brain is the *process*. Other parts of the human body also provide support to the main components responsible for carrying out the process (e.g. air travels to the lungs via the mouth and trachea; capillaries, veins and arteries transport blood around the body, and so on). This highlights the fact that in carrying out a process, success is often

8 Deming (1986) p.87

dependent on multiple components working together as part of an overall system. Systemic interdependencies go beyond the obvious, so if one part of the system refused to cooperate with the others, the processes that occur within the system would be rendered less effective, or even grind to a halt. (Imagine if the red blood cells wanted to keep all the oxygen for themselves, or the right leg refused to allow blood to pass through it!)

Mapping the Process

In order to improve a process, it is first necessary to understand it. A process is often easier to understand when it is visualised, and one of the best ways of doing this is by mapping it. Process mapping, or drawing a flowchart, highlights the individual stages of a process and shows the sequence of events necessary for the activity to progress from 'A' to 'B'. It also illustrates the dependency of each stage on the previous stage.

Complicated processes can be disentangled in this way and the flow of activity from one end to the other becomes clear. A good starting point can be to look at a process from a very high level. Whilst this does not expose the detailed interconnections, it will show the main stages of the process being considered. It is important to understand that what may at first appear to be a single process when viewed from this high level actually consists of a multitude of sub-processes. Starting at the top, however, makes it easy to identify the lower level processes that you are really interested in.

In order to demonstrate this, have a look at the process below, which is illustrated by a high level flowchart depicting what happens when someone is arrested as a result of a call to the police.

Figure 1.3: High level policing flowchart

Say you wanted to understand the custody procedure. Once you have identified where this stage sits in the overall process (as above), the next thing to do is to 'zoom in' to the custody procedure stage and map that individual sub-process. It would look something like this:

Figure 1.4: Custody procedure flowchart

If you were scrutinising one stage of this sub-process (e.g. the interview stage), you could then 'zoom in' and look at that part individually. It is likely that even after doing this, it would be possible to break down any of those stages into a new flowchart that depicts the stages of that 'sub-sub-process', and so on. The further you went, the more precise the activity being detailed in the flowcharts would become. It might be, however, that the level you wanted to work on was the overall custody process as shown above. In that case, there would be no need to 'zoom in' to sub-processes.

Even when dealing with a relatively simple flowchart such as at *Figure 1.4*, it can be useful to incorporate what are termed *swim lanes* into your diagram. As the name suggests, this gives the flowchart the appearance of a swimming pool viewed from above. The purpose is to show how different individuals or departments fit into the overall process. This helps us to understand who does what and how they all rely on each other. The custody procedure flowchart is reproduced below, this time with swim lanes.

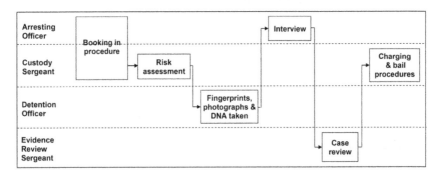

Figure 1.5: Custody procedure flowchart with swim lanes

The booking-in procedure straddles two swim lanes as it involves both the arresting officer and the Custody Sergeant. After that, each of the other parties has specific roles to play throughout the process. I have kept it simple and only shown the exact same stages as in the linear version, but in reality there would be parallel activities that occur during the process. For example, whilst the custody Sergeant is conducting the risk assessment, the arresting officer might be carrying out enquiries with witnesses elsewhere. Likewise, whilst the detention officer is taking fingerprints from the suspect, the custody Sergeant could be registering another prisoner and the Evidence Review Sergeant might be reviewing a totally unconnected case.

By depicting a process using a flowchart with swim lanes, we are able to see how processes operate *within* a system. It is possible to understand how the work moves along the process and which parts of the system are responsible for handling each stage. It also highlights the importance of inter-departmental cooperation and teamwork.

A Deeper Understanding

With this knowledge, there are opportunities for improving a process. One way of doing this is to use a technique known as *Critical Path Analysis*[9] (care must be taken of course to understand how improving one process within a system may affect other parts of the system).

The essential concept of critical path analysis is that there are some stages of a process that must happen in a particular order, whereas others can occur at any point within the process, or even run parallel to each other. All the stages shown in the example at *Figure 1.5* except the fingerprinting stage are part of the critical path. The first thing is to book the prisoner into the custody block. Nothing else can happen until this has occurred. Similarly, risk assessment, the interview, case review and charging and bail procedures must all be carried out in sequence. In contrast, the stage where the prisoner is fingerprinted and photographed can happen at any point whilst he or she is in custody, so this activity would not form part of the critical path.

If we expand the swim lanes diagram to include other activities that the parties would carry out during the process, it is easy to see the stages that must occur in sequence, and those that can occur in parallel. This is demonstrated in *Figure 1.6* below:

---

9   A straightforward text that explains critical path analysis can be found in Harrison (1997)

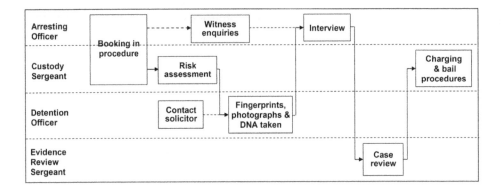

Figure 1.6: Custody procedure with parallel activities

We can now see the flow of work for everyone involved. In this example the arresting officer is carrying out further enquiries during the time that the custody Sergeant is conducting the risk assessment and the detention officer is fingerprinting and photographing the suspect. All these activities are necessary stages within the process, but none is directly dependent on the other. It makes sense, therefore, that these activities do not occur sequentially, but concurrently. In the same way, the detention officer is contacting the suspect's solicitor whilst the custody Sergeant is carrying out the risk assessment.

There is a plethora of other activities that occur within the custody environment, such as regular checks on prisoners, the provision of food and drink, and reviews at specific intervals by the Duty Inspector. Some of these stages are dependent on one or more of the previous stages; others are not. The latter have greater latitude to 'float' within the process. Obviously the diagram would become unnecessarily complicated if all these other activities were included – for the purposes of what I am trying to illustrate, the two additional activities outlined within *Figure 1.6* will suffice.

A true critical path analysis chart depicts exactly which stages of a process are contingent on earlier stages, and tracks the flow of the work through the entire process using numerically sequenced 'events' and 'nodes'. These show the duration time of the activity, as well as the earliest and latest starting and finishing times for each stage. This makes it possible to calculate the total end-to-end time (or total project time – TPT – to use the correct terminology), and to identify the critical stages.[10]

Whilst it is not always possible to determine precise timings of activities in the public services environment, the principles of critical path analysis can still be useful when trying to gain an understanding of any process.

Bottlenecks: A Deadly Enemy of the Process

Even without delving into a process to the degree involved in critical path analysis, there are some common principles that will help promote a smooth flow of work through the process. One of these is the rule of avoiding *bottlenecks*. As the name suggests, this is where the flow becomes restricted whilst passing through a particular stage of the process. The reasons for the presence of a bottleneck can be many, but common causes include having insufficient expertise or capacity at a particular stage, or an uneven flow further upstream in the process that has resulted in a glut of work arriving at that stage. It's worth remembering this maxim:

"A process is only as good as its narrowest point."

A bottleneck in a process would look something like this:

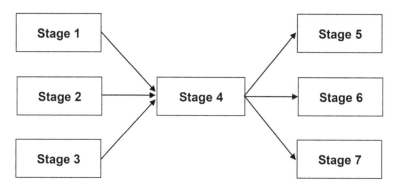

Figure 1.7: A bottleneck

Here we see that three parallel stages of the process feed into Stage 4 simultaneously, and must pass through it before continuing onto three subsequent parallel stages. (The fact that Stages 5, 6 and 7 are parallel

---

10   There are two main types of critical path analysis methods (Activity on Arrow – AoA; and Activity on Node – AoN), and whilst they are slightly different to the simple flowcharts we have looked at so far, the principles are largely the same.

is of no significance; had they been sequential, the bottleneck at Stage 4 would still have the same effect on the overall process.) This bottleneck effectively means that the entire process after Stage 4 is at its mercy – the flow of the work slows right down as it passes through this stage, and everything after it is delayed.

Assuming (for simplicity) that one work unit is handled during each stage in this process and this takes 10 minutes to complete, the work generated during the first three stages will take 30 minutes to squeeze through Stage 4. This means that after the first unit emerges from Stage Four into one of the subsequent parallel stages, only one of those three stages is actually processing work. The other two are idle, waiting for their anticipated unit of work to pass through Stage 4. By the time that all three work units leave Stages 5, 6 and 7, 50 minutes will have elapsed in total (10 minutes for parallel Stage 1, 2 and 3; 30 minutes for Stage 4, and 10 minutes for parallel Stages 5,6 and 7).

The consequences of the situation are easy to see when presented in this manner. Just one stage in what could be an extensive process effectively dictates the speed of the entire process. Solutions could include either staggering the work that arrives at Stage 4 so that it is processed evenly, or better still, increasing capacity at this point. If capacity at Stage 4 was tripled, this would ensure that work passed through this stage at the same rate as the previous and subsequent stages – a total of 30 minutes. The advantages of removing the bottleneck are clear:

- Flow is faster and smoother

- End-to-end time is reduced

- Stages are not left idle

- Costs associated with inactive stages are eliminated.

All in all, the process is now much more efficient and better geared towards meeting purpose.

Rate of Flow

A question that was posed to me about bottlenecks was, "Can the process be sped up *after* the bottleneck to compensate for the delay?"[11] The answer is twofold:

1. If it is feasible to make *any* of the stages in a process more efficient then this should be done in principle (as long as it does not cause a detrimental effect elsewhere).

2. Even if the stages after the bottleneck were streamlined and therefore faster, the rate of flow through these subsequent stages is restricted by the speed that product emerges from the bottleneck.

To explain why enhancing the post-bottleneck stages without widening the bottleneck does not speed up the overall rate, have a look at the flowchart below:

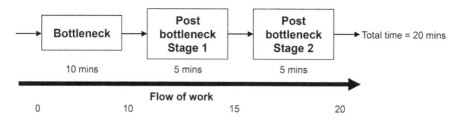

Figure 1.8: How a bottleneck restricts flow (1)

In this example, it takes 20 minutes for one unit of product to pass through the bottleneck and the two subsequent stages. As the bottleneck handles product at a rate of one unit every 10 minutes, and the subsequent stages operate at a speed of five minutes each, a unit emerges from the bottleneck at exactly the same time as the final stage completes the previous unit. This means that one unit is produced every 10 minutes after the point it emerges from the bottleneck, and that the overall *rate of flow* is one unit per 10 minutes.

---

11   My mum posed this question after reading a draft of the chapter. I answered it by demonstrating how the rate of flow is unaffected by post-bottleneck improvements, using pebbles to represent stages of a process and a different coloured pebble to represent a work unit, which then travelled along the process. The section explaining this concept was then added to the chapter (*Figures 1.8* and *1.9* are based on the impromptu pebble models).

If the two post-bottleneck stages were improved so that they could handle a unit of product in just one minute, each one unit would be produced in a total time of 12 minutes, or just two minutes after the product emerges from the bottleneck. The flowchart would look like this:

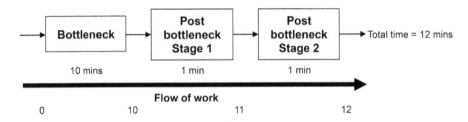

Figure 1.9: How a bottleneck restricts flow (2)

But appearances can be deceptive. True, the first unit to roll off the production line would arrive after 12 minutes, but the rate of flow is still restricted by the bottleneck. The product would whizz through the subsequent stages in just two minutes, but there would be a wait of *eight* minutes before another unit emerged from the bottleneck. Unless the processing speed of the bottleneck is increased, it will always be impossible to accelerate the overall rate of flow, no matter how efficient subsequent stages are made.

How Bottlenecks Affect Processes in Policing

In policing, bottlenecks can occur if just one custody Sergeant is on duty in a custody block when there are a number of prisoners to be processed through the booking-in procedure. One custody Sergeant can only book in one prisoner at a time, meaning others have to wait in a queue along with their arresting officers. This would have a detrimental effect on the overall system. A simple solution is to ensure that more than one custody Sergeant is available at peak times to increase throughput.

Another example could be where management decides to restrict frontline officers' ability to record certain types of crime without first referring the circumstances to a supervisor. As the ratio of supervisors to Constables could be one to ten or more, and if more than one officer seeks permission to record a crime, then there will be a bottleneck in processing these matters. Trusting the officers to do what they have been trained to do (i.e. record and investigate crime) without having to refer the circumstances to a supervisor at all is a simple solution.

Again, it is relevant here to return to the principle that adjusting one part of a system will have an effect on the overall system. For example, the bottleneck at *Figure 1.7* might have been caused by management reducing the capacity at Stage 4 as part of a cost-cutting exercise. Initially, management may have been pleased by the short-term savings. What might not have been so obvious are the consequences of the cost-cutting decision – a less efficient process, the introduction of waste (i.e. inactivity) into the stages after Stage 4 and higher overall costs. The workers who operate in Stages 5, 6 and 7 are still being paid whilst they wait around for work to come in.

By trying to 'improve' one stage of the process in isolation, the whole process has been damaged. In turn, the system that contains this process has also been damaged. Without mapping the process it might well have been impossible to see this.

An even deadlier variation on bottlenecks is where one stage of a process stalls completely. If a process is only as good as its narrowest point, it is certainly only as good as a stage that has stopped completely. Returning to the human body analogy, a heart attack caused by a blood clot blocking the flow of oxygen-rich blood to a section of heart muscle is an obvious example of this. Other examples are of a machine breaking down that forms part of a sequential manufacturing process, or being unable to find the only person in a department who is allowed to authorise something.

Examples of designing and maintaining the system in a manner that mitigates such damage could include:

- Better-trained police drivers in well-maintained and regularly serviced police vehicles will represent a lower risk of police traffic collisions.

- Comprehensive initial police training in powers of arrest will reduce the likelihood of unlawful arrests.

The cost invested in designing these features into the system before things even get the chance to go wrong is effective risk management and will save a lot of money in pay-outs at a later date. This is about taking a whole system view rather than just focusing on making short-term savings. Short-term savings always cost more in the long run.

Against the Grain

A lot of systems thinking can at first appear to run against the grain of what is accepted to be standard practice or logic. For example, it is common for products to be made in batches. This most obviously applies to manufacturing, but it is also relevant to public services. *Batching* and *queuing* occur due to the misconception that it is somehow more efficient to produce and move units of work in batches. In a similar situation to that depicted in the bottleneck diagram at *Figure 1.7*, batching causes stages in a process to experience periods of inactivity as they wait for work to arrive. Even where there is no bottleneck, delays are introduced as the process stalls waiting for the batch to be completed before being forwarded to the next stage. This is illustrated below:

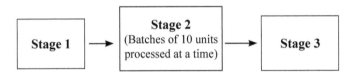

Figure 1.10: A batching stage in a process

Here, at Stage 2, product is stockpiled until it reaches batches of 10, before being processed onward to Stage 3 If you think about it, this slows the process down 10 times. Remember – a process is only as good as its narrowest point. This warning applies equally to 'narrowing' by introducing deliberate pauses, as much as it does to bottlenecks or unanticipated stoppages. Although Stage 2 can process 10 units at a time (or nine, or six, or one), the design of the process artificially holds the flow of the work in a suspended state as it waits for the magic number of 10 units to accumulate. This means that Stage 3 and any subsequent stages are under-utilised, and Stage 2 itself spends a significant proportion of its time being inactive.

Looking at this process from the customer's perspective, what is important? What is the purpose of the process? What does the service user want to pull[12] from it? When do they want it? Now! Therefore, counterintuitive as it might seem, it is more efficient to dispense with queuing and batching altogether and to send work units through at the rate of pull instead.

To demonstrate this, the two following diagrams provide visual representations of this theory in action.

12   Seddon (2003) p.138

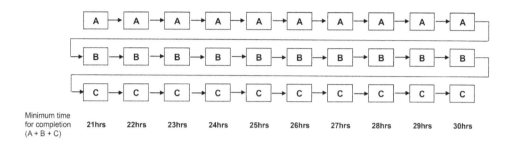

Figure 1.11 A production process: batching method

Imagine that *Figure 1.11* represents a production process where three separate components ('A', 'B' and 'C') comprise one unit of final product. This process will therefore produce a total of 10 complete units. It could be that 'A' represents a computer keyboard, 'B' represents a hard drive, and 'C' represents a monitor. Before the entire computer system can be shipped to the customer, all three components must be manufactured individually, before being despatched as a complete unit.

Alternatively, you could imagine that 'A', 'B' and 'C' are necessary stages in the production of comprehensive police documentation required for 10 separate court hearings. Either way, the same principles apply.

Assuming that the production of 10 complete units (i.e. 'A' + 'B' + 'C') is the responsibility of one person, a common approach would be to produce 10 'A' components, then 10 'B' components, then 10 'C' components. If each component takes one hour to produce, then the total time required to produce 10 complete units would be 30 hours. If the organisation that produced them wanted to be clever and not wait for all 10 completed units to be ready before despatching them together (thereby eliminating batching at the delivery stage) then the first complete unit could be shipped after 21 hours. The next would be ready after 22 hours, and so on. In effect, as soon as each 'C' component is completed, another full unit is ready to go. This means that the first complete unit is ready for the customer 21 hours after the start of production, and the tenth is ready after 30 hours.

Now, ask yourself this: "What is the purpose of this process from the customer's perspective?" It could be something along the lines of, "To produce computers (or court files) to a high quality as quickly and efficiently as possible". For the purposes of this example, let's assume that the quality of the end product is not in question. Also, no matter in which order the components are produced, each stage will always take one hour, and therefore the production of 10 complete units can never be less than 30 hours. In that respect, it might appear at first that the process can't be improved.

Think again. Look what happens if we do away with producing the components in batches, and instead redesign the operation with purpose in mind, to allow product to be *pulled* from the system. The real purpose of this example is not to demonstrate how to put computers together quickly, but to challenge conventional thinking about how things are done.

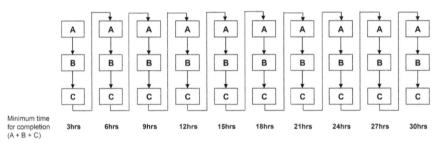

Figure 1.12 A production process: 'pull' method

Here, the process has been designed against demand. By putting the components together in this way, the earliest time a complete unit is ready for the customer is after just three hours. The next one is ready after six hours. In fact, the first seven customers will have received their product in the time it took for the first complete unit to be produced under the previous model (21 hours). Each stage still takes an hour and the total time taken to produce 10 complete units is still 30 hours, but nine of the ten customers will receive their product faster under this method than in the previous design.

This example demonstrates the value of allowing the work to flow naturally through the process, unhindered by artificial stoppages and, moreover, at the behest of the customer or service user who requires the product or service. By making a simple adjustment (i.e. avoiding batching and queuing), the redesigned version of the production model has delivered a faster and more bespoke outcome for the most important person in the process – the end user.

Clearer?

I hope this chapter has demystified some of the terms and concepts associated with systems and processes and that I have provided a basic grounding in themes that will recur as the book progresses. Although I have used some non-police examples to explain systems principles in this chapter, I have done this deliberately, as everyday case studies often serve to illustrate general points clearly. Once the principles are cemented through easily understood associations, it will be straightforward to appreciate how they can be applied to policing situations. The overriding aim (or purpose!) of the chapter has been to highlight the importance of seeing and understanding things from a systems perspective.

CHAPTER TWO

Performance Measurement and Variation

I'm going to start this chapter with a little challenge: look at the chart below.

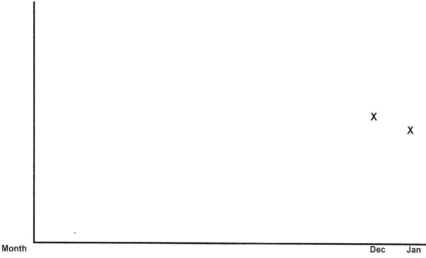

Figure 2.1: 'Performance chart. This month versus last month'

Does this appear to be a good way to measure and present performance information? Does it look useful?

Unfortunately much traditional police performance measurement involves exactly this amount of insight. During the next couple of chapters, various tables, charts and graphs will appear with explanations about which ones are useful, and why.

Performance Measurement – Good, Bad and Ugly

Performance measurement is so pervasive and influential within organisations that some argue that it can become *the* defining feature of an organisation's culture and climate.[1] Done properly, performance measurement gives leaders the data and evidence they require to improve systems and initiate effective operational responses. Done wrong, the results can be catastrophic. This chapter will look at how to do it properly, and how never to do it.

It is very important that performance measurement should always be subject to scientific rigour, and any actions resulting from its interpretation should only ever be based on proper analysis, fact and evidence. Rewards, sanctions and operational decisions often rest on management's interpretation of performance data. We will look at how police performance information is traditionally measured and presented, so you can draw your own conclusions about whether these methods are compatible with scientific principles.

Police managers place a lot of importance on being able to measure performance; their assertion is that performance measurement aids transparency and enhances accountability. I strongly agree that it is important to measure things, as long as you measure the right things and understand how to interpret what has been measured. And in all cases it is imperative that the measures are derived from purpose. This doesn't just apply to 'performance' data however – understanding the results of your measurement efforts in any area of a system can unlock hidden opportunities to improve the system.

This chapter will examine some of the pitfalls of conventional performance measurement practice, and present much more constructive and powerful alternatives. Whether you work for a police force, another public service or, perhaps, within the private sector, I suspect that some of the traditional approaches examined will be painfully familiar to you. The good news is that the alternatives have the capability to transform your organisation. The extra good news is that the techniques involved are pretty straightforward.

The key to this transformation is to understand variation, along with the application of Statistical Process Control (SPC) charts. These concepts will be explored in some detail, but if you are unfamiliar with them at the moment, or are concerned that the subject matter may be a bit dry, don't worry. Each is pivotal to intelligently interpreting performance information, indeed any type of data. The far superior performance measurement

---

1   Spitzer (2007)

alternative that I am about to explore will bring about improved service delivery, happier and more productive workers, and oddly enough, better performance.

So what is 'good performance'? It is often difficult to define and means different things to different people. For example, the Home Office defines good police performance as, "A combination of doing the right things (priorities), doing them well (quality) and doing the right amount (quantity)".[2] This is not a bad starting point, but how does a broad mission statement such as this one translate into quantifiable measures? In Chapter Four we will look at how priorities can be determined – the evidence-based method, and the 'finger in the air' method. The notion of 'quality' will be explored in Chapter Nine, where we will delve into methods for ensuring that performance measurement supports activity that meets purpose. For the purposes of this chapter we are going to focus solely on the easiest element of this definition to measure – 'quantity'.

It is always important to understand what good performance means to your organisation before you try to measure it. Too often we rush into measuring and comparing data without any appreciation of context. Counting things is relatively easy, and numerical proxy measures can be useful where it is difficult (or impossible) to quantify outcomes. Nevertheless, in situations where a causal link cannot be directly established between a unit of policing activity and an eventual outcome, numerical measures can be, at best, misleading and, at worst, counterproductive. Traditional police performance measures tend to be quantitative for reasons of expediency, and because much of the data is already routinely captured through existing recording requirements.[3]

One often-missed question to consider when measuring things is, "Why are we doing this?" The main objective should be to assist in achieving the organisational purpose from the perspective of the service user.[4] If a performance measure assists in doing this, then it increases the knowledge base necessary to foster continuous improvement and provide a better service. If it doesn't, then it should be scrapped. It's as simple as that.

I just want to point out quickly that this chapter is specifically about *using numbers objectively and understanding what they tell us*, so I need to set some parameters to stay on course. There are many appalling effects

---

2   Home Office (2008)

3   Heinrich (2008) pp.373-389

4   Seddon (2008) p.80

of badly done performance measurement and, if you are familiar with what these are, you might expect to see them in this chapter. The problem is that I could go on and on about them... so these topics will receive special attention later on in this book. For now I am going to put the following themes to one side:

- The possibility that the chosen measure may be totally inappropriate in the first place

- Unintended consequences, perverse behaviours, incentives and gaming

- External factors that affect performance.

Let's assume that there is a particular measure of policing activity that truly reflects good performance, and that all parties agree it is valuable to use this data as a barometer of effectiveness. Let's also assume that the data are impervious to tampering (see Chapter Four), contamination or errors.

A Typical Management Report

	Detected Offences
Team A	75
Team B	83
Team C	54
Team D	77
Team E	74

Figure 2.2: Table of detected offences (this month)

This simple table shows the number of detected offences recorded by each of five police teams this month. (A 'detected offence' is a crime that has been solved.) Comparisons like this are routinely made between police forces, between divisions, between teams and even between individuals from the same team. There is nothing special about using detected offences; this choice of measure serves to illustrate the following points just as well as comparing numbers of arrests, recorded crime, intelligence submissions or anything else that can be counted. Such tables are commonplace within police performance management systems and whether the data table relates to one type of 'performance indicator', or multiple rows of numbers pertaining to several different measures, the principles are the same.

What conclusions might a traditional manager draw from this set of figures? A common reaction would be to praise Team B for doing such an outstanding job, and question why Team C's figures are so poor. Teams A, D and E seem pretty similar, so their figures don't really warrant special attention. Perhaps Team B could share some good practice with Team C? Although it seems obvious that Team B is leading the way whilst Team C is struggling, some managers also like to rank teams to encourage what they term 'healthy competition'. If we were to do this here, this month the order would be as follows:

1st: Team B	*Well done. Credit where it's due.*
2nd: Team D	*Keep up the good work. Just a bit more effort required.*
3rd: Team E	*Not a bad effort. About average.*
4th: Team A	*Not too concerned at this stage, but management will be keeping an eye on future performance.*
Last: Team C	*See me. Explanation required.*

Police managers claim that the type of table at *Figure 2.2* is just 'management information' that enables them to ask questions about differentials in performance. Numbers have an allure of objectivity about them, don't they?

The table at *Figure 2.2* might seem to be a good start, but one would expect a manager to want to know more about team performance than this single snapshot can convey. This leads us to the next level of traditional methods of presenting performance data: the 'This Month versus Last Month' comparison. Comparing just two numbers with each other is known as a 'binary comparison', and occurs in many forms: this week versus last week, this quarter versus last quarter, this year versus last year, and so on. (Binary comparisons will be examined more closely in Chapter Three.)

A Typical Management Report with Extra Columns

	Detected Offences (This Month)	Detected Offences (Last Month)	Percentage Variance
Team A	75	73	2.7%
Team B	83	75	10.7%
Team C	54	71	-24.0%
Team D	77	51	51.0%
Team E	74	79	-6.4%

Figure 2.3: Table of detected offences (this month versus last month)

The 'Percentage Variance' column is an extra bonus. The table clearly shows trends, improvement and deterioration. Or does it? This type of chart is exactly the sort that some managers rely on to obtain a picture of how individual teams are performing. The 'Percentage Variance' column can also be supplemented by helpful descriptors such as 'Not meeting standard and deteriorating', along with red or green arrows pointing upwards or downwards depending on the apparent direction of travel. Important management decisions are made on the basis of this amount of information, and individuals are held to account for the numbers.

Let's see what the table at *Figure 2.3* tells us. Well, Team B is obviously going from strength to strength, building on a strong showing last month; and Team D has improved its performance by a massive 51% compared to last month's figure. Meanwhile, Team C not only has the lowest score this month, but is obviously on a downwards slide, with a 24% reduction in detected crimes compared to last month. The others are ticking along somewhere in between. Based on the percentage variances shown in *Figure 2.3*, the teams might now be ranked as follows:

Ist: Team D	*Fantastic improvement.*
2nd: Team B	*Consistently high-performing.*
3rd: Team A	*Steady.*
4th: Team E	*Slight deterioration. Need to keep an eye on this. Management expect an improvement next month.*
Last: Team C	*Significant deterioration from last month, as well as unacceptably low output this month. Explanation required!*

So there you have it. Whether you take one month's or two months' data it appears that Team C is really struggling. What is the problem? Management will expect Team C to have some answers this time. There will be demands of, "We need a plan!" and "People must be held to account!"

The First Steps To Recovery

The methods of presenting performance information outlined so far are not unusual. For the team leader whose team is at the top of the table, it is time to breathe a sigh of relief that he or she will not be on the receiving end of management scrutiny and awkward questions this time. For the team leader whose figures are at the wrong end of the spectrum, it is an uncomfortable and baffling experience to be held to account for the numbers. Someone always has to come last when using this method. For those in between, they are just glad the spotlight isn't on them.

One Inspector who took part in the research for this book describes the climate that this type of performance management creates:

> *"Blaming people for figures that are largely out of their control is unfair. The lads and lasses on my team work hard but there's no guarantee they'll have the most detections in any given month is there? Comparing teams causes unhealthy competition and people work against each other because no one wants to be bottom".*

Another Inspector wrote:

> *"I am frustrated to the point of tears by the misapplication of half-understood management methods".*

The good news is that there is a much better way. The first stage is to recognise the inbuilt limitations of the approaches described so far. To start with, let's look more closely at the rankings. In the performance assessment gleaned from *Figure 2.2*, it appeared that Team B was out in front and Team C was struggling. Looking at the additional data in *Figure 2.3*, it appeared to confirm that Team B was consistently strong and that Team C was not only underperforming, but its performance was also deteriorating significantly. What wasn't apparent from *Figure 2.2*, but which came through by looking at *Figure 2.3*, was that Team D had significantly improved its performance, increasing the total number of offences detected by 51% compared to the previous month.

The first clue about the flaws of this mode of data interpretation comes from the conflicting rankings that emerge, depending on which table you use. If the order that the teams would be ranked in each respective table is presented side-by-side this becomes apparent.

	Ranking based on *Figure 2.2*		Ranking based on *Figure 2.3*
Ist	Team B		Team D
2nd	Team D		Team B
3rd	Team E		Team A
4th	Team A		Team E
5th	Team C		Team C

Figure 2.4: Team rankings (this month versus last month)

Only Team C remains in the same position in both tables. The lesson here is that when using this method to judge performance, it is normal for teams to end up in different positions each time a snapshot is taken. It is entirely feasible that next month, 83 detected offences might be the lowest number recorded instead of the highest, leaving Team B at the bottom of the table. Any of the other teams could be at the top. Should the definition of good performance therefore be based on who is top or bottom of a table? Some managers might still argue that, whilst there are always going to be some fluctuations, the data presented so far unequivocally demonstrates that Team B consistently performs well and Team C is performing badly. Allow me to debunk that notion and demonstrate the power of something that fosters accurate and intelligent interpretation of data – Statistical Process Control.

Understanding Variation: An Introduction to Statistical Process Control

Statistical Process Control sounds daunting, but it isn't. The technique was developed during the 1920s by Dr. Walter A. Shewhart, whose work on telephone systems for Bell Laboratories led to a new paradigm in intelligent data interpretation.[5] Shewhart drew charts that plotted data over time and these enabled him to visually identify patterns and interpret the data using a much broader spectrum of information. Presenting data using graphs is

---

5   Shewhart (1939)

much more effective than looking at rows of numbers in a table (or just one row of numbers in a table!) as it instantly paints a picture that is much easier to interpret. The use of Shewhart's Statistical Process Control (SPC) charts encourages effective analysis of data and highlights the importance of understanding *variation*.

Deming taught us:

> Life is variation. Variation there will always be, between people, in output, in service, in product.[6]

Variation tells us about the capabilities of the process, and understanding variation is the key to understanding the system. Once these capabilities are understood, this knowledge unlocks powerful opportunities for continuous improvement. This applies as much to understanding and measuring performance as any other aspect of the system.

So what is variation? Building on Shewhart's work, Deming and others[7] explored the concept and found that no matter how closely we try to control outputs or events, a degree of variation is inevitable. This applies to manufacturing, service industries, the public sector, counting the number of red cars that drive past; in fact everything. Variation is inevitable, and is caused by a multitude of factors, most of which are naturally occurring and outside human control. Once managers understand and accept this fact, then progress becomes possible. Let's look at some examples:

1. The exact dimensions and characteristics of a mechanical component produced by a pressing machine in a factory are affected by the quality of raw materials, the parameters under which the machine operates, its maintenance schedule, its operating temperature, and so on. Note that the same machine being operated by the same machinist will produce components that exhibit a degree of fluctuating characteristics, regardless of the constant efforts of the operator.

2. The time it takes for a police unit to arrive at an emergency varies due to the accuracy of the information obtained by the 999 operator when taking the call, the distance travelled, traffic conditions, weather and other factors.

---

6   Deming (1994) pp.98
7   See for example: Joiner (1994); Wheeler (2000); Seddon (2003); Seddon (2008)

3. Crime rates are influenced by economic drivers (for example, the price of scrap metal affecting the rate of metal thefts), substance abuse, social deprivation, as well as personal security and a range of other factors. Policing activity does, of course, impact on crime, but research shows that the police do not have the power to influence many of the factors that affect crime rates.[8] Despite constant efforts, crime rates will always fluctuate.

If managers accept that a degree of variation is inevitable, the next stage is to discard the assumption that all variation must be attributable to individuals. Indeed, Deming asserted that the overwhelming majority of variation within any given process occurs as a result of system conditions (which he termed *common cause variation*), and only a very small proportion is as a result of *special causes*.[9]

Taking the third of the above examples for illustration purposes, a special cause could refer to a sudden rise in vehicle crime that occurs close to a football ground every time a match is played. The fact that this is a special cause, identifiable though the application of SPC, means that there is an evidence base which mandates police action. Conversely, there is no point getting excited because there were three more assaults recorded this week than there were last week, as this is likely to be the result of common cause variation that is beyond the influence of the police.

I am optimistic that anyone who makes it to the end of this chapter will resist the urge to berate Team C's leader, despite the apparent 'poor performance' uncovered earlier. In fact, if you aren't familiar with SPC charts, what follows will change the way you measure and judge performance forever. This is because when we plot a data series using an SPC chart, we are able to differentiate between common cause variation and the variation caused by more unusual events (i.e. special causes) that result in visible signals. To demonstrate this, we will now look at some SPC charts and examine the recognised patterns that constitute signals.

---

8   Loveday (2000) pp.215-237
9   Deming (1986) p.315

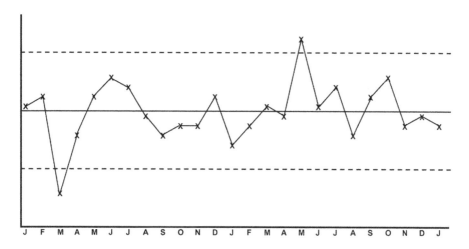

Figure 2.5: An SPC chart

What does this tell us? Well, first of all, the pattern indicates that generally the process is stable, as most of the data points fall well within the parameters determined by the upper and lower control limits (dashed lines). The upper and lower control limits represent the boundaries within which most data points will predictably fall. The control limits and centre line are set mathematically, rather than as aspirational specifications determined by a human being. This ensures that they remain objective. I will explain the method for determining the control limits in Chapter Three. For now, let the formulae worry about themselves and just listen to what the data are telling you about the capabilities of the process.

In this case, the chart runs from January two years ago to January this year. Note that the vertical axis has no numbers displayed next to it – this is not important at this stage as the idea is simply to provide a graphical representation of data over time. The pattern exhibits a steady stream of data influenced by common cause variation with a couple of data points that require closer attention. The first of these is the breach of the lower control limit during March almost two years ago, and the second is the breach of the upper control limit last May. Both these 'signals' indicate that it is highly likely that the unusual value is as a result of a special cause which will require further investigation.

The beauty of presenting the data using this method is that not only are extreme values immediately visible to the naked eye, but the calculations responsible for determining the lower and upper control limits effectively filter out the 'noise' of common cause variation amongst the data, clearly exposing these two 'signals'. This provides reassurance that there is no need to react to the other peaks and troughs present between the control limits. For example, the relatively low point last January is still well within the control limits, so should not be interpreted as a signal. It would be impossible to see this with such clarity if the data were presented as a row of numerical values in a table.

If, for the sake of argument, this SPC chart plotted recorded crime, it would be foolish to react to any of the data points except for the two signals. It is a common mistake of management to interpret every fluctuation as a signal when, in fact, it is normal variation. If resources are moved across to deal with a perceived problem that does not actually exist, this drives waste into the system and risks undermining other areas that are being effectively managed.

The spike last May will almost certainly have resulted from an identifiable special cause that needs looking into; for example, it could be a sudden increase in criminal activity in a particular locality that requires attention. The significant dip during March two years ago is also most likely to be the result of some identifiable factor. It could be that there was an IT glitch that resulted in some crimes not being properly registered onto the system before the end of the month. Alternatively, it might have been an outstanding and innovative policing operation which reduced crime so dramatically that we would not want to lose the organisational learning that can be gleaned from it. Either way, SPC provides the evidence to delve into these signals whilst preventing us from being distracted by noise.

Other Signals to Watch Out For

Breaches of the control limits are the most obvious signals that indicate the presence of special causes, but there are a handful of others that also need to be recognised. Whether or not a particular pattern or event constitutes a signal is determined by mathematics and statistical theory, and the following patterns are guidelines for other signals that practitioners need to be aware of.

Signals should be investigated as soon as they become apparent so as to prevent an unwanted trend continuing. If, however, signals are only evident amidst historic data, then it is still worthwhile to dig deeper in order to extract any learning that may help in planning for the future.

Six in a Row

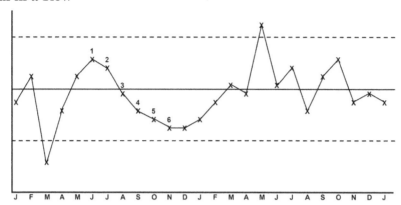

Figure 2.6: SPC chart (Run of six or more points in a row)

Here we have a run of six data points trending in one direction (trends can run in either direction). This usually indicates the pattern is not attributable to common cause variation and needs to be looked into. (Note: in the event that a point falls on the same value as the previous point, do not count it as part of the series.) The lesson here is that there is no need to react to 'trends' of less than six data points, mainly because they are NOT trends.

Eight on One Side

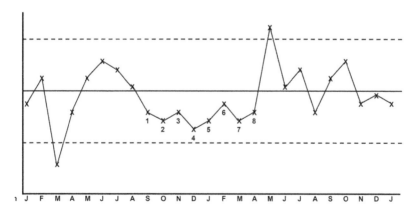

Figure 2.7: SPC chart (eight or more points on the same side of the centre line)

Here, this run of eight points on the same side of the centre line is likely to indicate the presence of something affecting the data. This can be traced and may provide useful information about the process. It's worth looking deeper…

14 or More Alternating Points

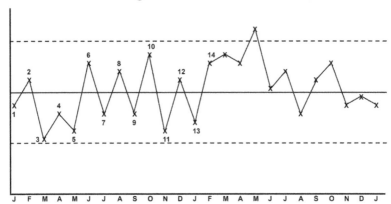

Figure 2.8: SPC chart (14 or more points alternating up and down)

This chart exhibits wild fluctuations, indicating the presence of a special cause. Wide variation gives rise to concern that the process is not as stable as it should be, but a clear run of 14 alternating data points shown in this chart warns us that there is something disrupting the process. And that something is bad.

Three Close to a Control Limit

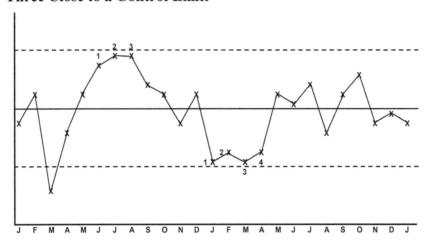

Figure 2.9: SPC chart (three or more consecutive points closer to one of the control limits than the centre line)

40

This chart contains two separate runs of three or more data points that are closer to one of the control limits than the centre line. This usually indicates the presence of a special cause. Once again, this means it's time to start looking at the story behind the pattern.

A Summary of SPC

In his essay 'Avoiding Man-Made Chaos', Donald Wheeler provides us with an excellent summary of the usefulness of SPC, which I believe should be on the wall of every manager's office:

> While all data contain noise,
> Some data contain signals.
> Before you can detect a signal within any data set
> You must first filter out the noise.[10]

In every case it is important to remember that all of the above patterns are *signals* and not cast-iron evidence of the presence of special causes. It is up to you to dig beneath the data, determine what evidence exists, then weigh it up to decide if action is necessary or whether there is any knowledge that can be gleaned from what the data are trying to tell you. Sometimes, it may be that there is no obvious special cause – false signals are not unheard of. Generally, however, the mathematics behind the construction of SPC charts means that they are sufficiently robust to distinguish between signals and noise.

The SPC method is a powerful technique that enables managers to intelligently interpret data instead of relying on simplistic binary comparisons. More importantly, it allows us to see the current capabilities of the process, and therefore predict how the process will continue to operate into the future. If the process is not altered then it will continue to operate within these parameters indefinitely.

The use of SPC is in direct contrast to the traditional method of looking at one or two rows of historical numerical data without taking context into account, then reacting to it without knowledge or insight. It is only possible to make meaningful comparisons over time, and with an understanding of the limitations and context of the data. The purpose of performance measurement must be to foster continuous improvement and to ensure effective planning for the future.

---

10   Wheeler (1998) p.31

Common Mistakes To Avoid When Using SPC Charts

It's important to understand that SPC charts are not some sort of magical quick fix tool or additional bolt-on to supplement existing organisational norms. Proper application of SPC can only occur as part of a total cultural transformation. It is also important to stress that without proper understanding of the overall system, the use of SPC is nothing more than a veneer; in the worst case scenario, improper application could even damage the system. A little knowledge is a dangerous thing.

SPC is not a substitute for applying an overall systems approach – it forms *part* of a systems approach. The pro-systems mindset has to exist first – it is about an overall philosophy, not a tool. Imagine if managers used SPC charts to rank teams against each other! We would be back to square one.

Health warning duly administered, let's continue and look at some common SPC-related mistakes. (Once you are aware they exist, you can avoid them.)

Deming draws attention to two overarching types of mistakes that occur when interpreting variation. They are:

- *Mistake One:* To react to an outcome as if it came from a special cause when, actually, it came from common causes of variation.

- *Mistake Two:* To treat an outcome as if it came from common causes of variation when, actually, it came from a special cause.[11]

In a policing context, these mistakes could manifest themselves in the examples that follow.

Mistake One

If police managers don't understand variation, or are unfamiliar with the recognised signals we have examined, mistakes are easily made. Binary comparisons are so embedded in conventional management thinking that although some police IT systems have the capacity to produce SPC charts at the touch of a button, it's common to overlay this way of thinking onto an SPC chart.

To illustrate this point, I have reproduced the first SPC chart from this chapter (*Figure 2.5*) and wish to draw your attention to the data points that relate to the three months of January.

---

11   Deming (1994) p.99

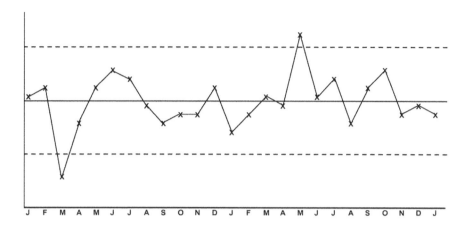

Figure 2.10: Burglaries – January vs January vs January

Let's say this SPC chart shows the burglary rate for part of a hypothetical police division. Again, the actual numbers involved that would usually appear on the vertical axis are not important for the purposes of the example. As you can see, the burglary rate this January is indeed slightly higher than it was last January. This is exactly the type of minor fluctuation that sends some uninitiated managers into a spin: "Surely if there are more burglaries now than at this time last year we must take action!"

Well, in this case, the decision to initiate an operational response is fundamentally flawed because it is based on a reaction to common cause variation *and* a binary comparison. Notwithstanding the police obligation to tackle burglaries, it is important to assess the evidence base before reacting, and in the absence of actionable lines of enquiry or identified signals, the reaction described above is wholly disproportionate.

Looking at data without understanding its meaning creates all sorts of problems. What if management were to make the comparison between this January and January two years ago, where the data point is positioned above the centre line? The number of burglaries is lower than it was two years ago. Which of these comparisons should be acted upon? The answer, of course, is neither of them. *All* of the values are subject to variation. It would be just the same as comparing the current value with *any* of the other data points on the chart. None of the values are impervious to variation so none of them can ever be used as a rock solid benchmark. Even if they could be, binary comparisons made between two values are misleading, and as seen with the January versus January comparisons, will produce different results every time.

Now let's see what happens when managers initiate an operational response based on misinterpreted data. Note the adverse effects on the overall system.

Typically, management will demand written plans about how the police are going to tackle the apparent rise in burglaries. The plan must follow a specified format – any deviation and it will be rejected and have to be rewritten. Once completed to the required standard, the plan will then be submitted for scrutiny and direction. Officers will be given specific tasks to undertake which may be merely what officers would do anyway (e.g. patrol the area), but sometimes they are removed from other priorities and redeployed. As mentioned earlier, this increases the risk that other matters (which may be genuine priorities identified through proper data analysis) become neglected and spiral out of control.

Research conducted for this book indicates that management's obsession with plans as the perceived solution to all manner of crime problems is endemic. One Sergeant described the situation as follows:

> *"The bosses are constantly designating one thing or another as a priority, then demanding plans. They want to know every detail of what my team is going to do about 'X'. I'm not convinced that some of these issues are actually backed up by data that indicates there's even a real pattern. I have to write up the plan then task my troops to patrol that area, deliver leaflets or whatever. Filling in the task 'results' takes time as well and no one seems to know who does what with the information! My team might have been looking at something else, somewhere else, but that has to stop for the time being. Next week it's something different".*

Often the tactics employed amount to little more than unstructured patrolling, or directionless 'wandering', as one Constable put it:

> *"Typically these will consist of wandering a town in plain clothes looking for people committing thefts, or doing other pointless activities, not finding anyone doing anything and then considering a few random stops to justify our day or avoid a closed-door chat".*

Officers then report back about their activity with task updates such as, "Area patrolled – nothing to report". This is of no use to anyone and represents feeding back information for the sake of it, but failure to submit an acceptable number of task returns can result in harsh words along with an order from management to redouble efforts. At the end of the term of the plan, the task results submitted are not always evaluated, and as the directive for the activity was not evidence-based in the first place, it is impossible to scientifically establish if the activity has had an effect. The net result is that waste is driven into the system, and other areas suffer.

The true horror of this type of baseless directive for plans, tasks and reporting back is amplified if the next comparison made happens to indicate there has been an apparent reduction in burglaries. This is most likely to be nothing more than a symptom of normal variation but in the minds of management the decision to generate all this waste activity has been validated.

Attempting to define differentials between data by comparing them against a moving variable in this way is absolutely meaningless. (This notion is also at the root of why it is impossible to scientifically determine a numerical target, but more on that later…)

Managers! Copy out the following quote from Brian Joiner and put it on your wall:

> One necessary qualification of anyone in management is to stop asking people to explain ups and downs (day to day, month to month, year to year) that come from random variation.[12]

---

12   Joiner cited in Deming (1994) p.216

Mistake Two

Staying with the theme of burglaries, let's say that the chart below shows burglary crime patterns in another part of the same police division:

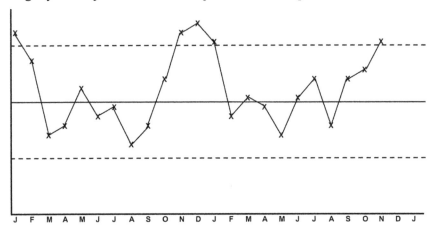

Figure 2.11: Burglary crime pattern

Looking at the above chart, it indicates that there appears to be a seasonal increase in burglaries in this part of the division. For three consecutive years, the number of burglaries has breached the upper control limit at the same time of year, and as December fast approaches it would be reasonable to interpret these signals as genuine and likely to be attributed to identifiable special causes. It is also reasonable to expect the police to take action to tackle the issue. The first stage would be to examine the narrative behind the data and establish an understanding of the problem, especially as it is entirely possible that the unusually high number of burglaries may not dissipate quickly.

In these circumstances, it would be a mistake to ignore the signals; they provide the evidence base required to formulate a response to the emerging threat. By disregarding the signals as common cause variation, the opportunity will be missed. The result of this mistake would be a potential continuation of the spike in burglaries, which may be preventable. Mistake Two is therefore not so much about knee-jerking as a result of flawed assumptions about variation, or reliance upon binary comparisons, but a case of *inaction* where action is necessary. I've used the most obvious type of signal (i.e. a breach of a control limit) to illustrate this, but any type of signal can be missed. And a missed signal is a missed opportunity.

Signals are the equivalent of a warning system – if your smoke alarm went off you wouldn't just switch it off and ignore it would you? You would want to look for the source of the smoke.

Another common SPC-related error occurs when a manager wants to act on excessively wide variation, but doesn't know how. Look at the chart below.

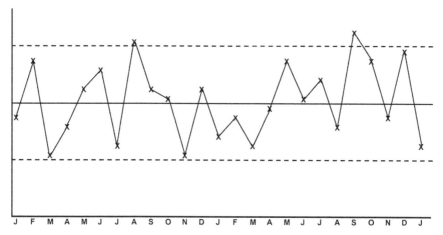

Figure 2.12: SPC chart – wide variation

The extent of variation is very wide. The chart also has a couple of data points falling outside of the control limits. But, there are no other signals; no runs of six points in one direction or the other; no runs of eight consecutive points on the same side of the centre line; no runs of 14 consecutive points alternating up and down, and no runs of three or more points closer to one of the control limits than the centre line. The chart is not in what could be considered to be a satisfactory state, due to the wide range of variation. (Technically, this degree of variation would necessitate wider control limits being calculated, but I have left these ones in the same proportion as the other charts for illustrative purposes. Stay with me.)

Whether the data is derived from crime rates, response times, or production of widgets, it is natural and desirable to want to reduce the range of variation. This is because by reducing variation, the process becomes more efficient and predictable. There is only one way to do this and that is to first accept that almost all of the variation in this chart is attributable to common cause variation (i.e. it falls within the control limits).

In other words, the variation is not down to special causes, which are by definition unusual and identifiable. This means that no matter how much managers shout at the workers or exhort them to do better, it will have little effect. The workers operate within the constraints that the system imposes on them, and *it is management's responsibility to improve the system*. If management works on improving the system then the results should manifest themselves in much narrower variation which is evident on SPC charts, such as in the chart below. This state is referred to as 'being in statistical control'.

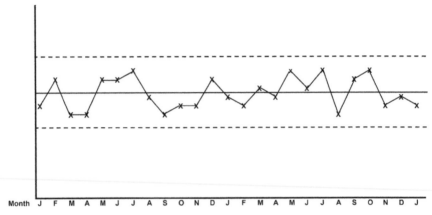

Figure 2.13: SPC chart – narrow variation

A Quick Summary

So there you have it – a taster of how traditional methods of assessing and comparing performance information (or any type of numerical data) are not as watertight as they might first appear. Hopefully, I have introduced niggling doubts about the validity of making binary comparisons and the logic behind reacting to one or two data points, moving resources around, demanding written plans, setting tasks without understanding the evidence base, or insisting on mountains of follow-up information to further populate the plans and tasks, then holding individuals to account. I hope so.

I also hope I have shown how useful SPC charts can be and why they are a superior alternative to what we have been used to. Variation is always present, and the pattern it exhibits on the SPC charts brings us knowledge about our systems. I am optimistic that the explanations about different types of signals will aid you in interpreting the data and in developing an understanding of the difference between common causes and special causes. Examples of Mistake One and Mistake Two are common so I hope they can be avoided in future.

But what now? So far we have only looked at part of the story. Binary comparisons and the awful consequences they cause have only been touched upon. What happened to those five policing teams that were compared at the start of the chapter? Team C was having a rough time if you recall – but is the team really that bad? What other information would you want to know about their performance? What sort of external factors affect performance data? SPC charts are crucial to understanding the process at hand, but how do you construct them? What was that useless-looking chart at the beginning of this chapter all about? You probably have other questions too.

We've only scratched the surface so far. Read on.

CHAPTER THREE

Binary Comparisons: Compared to What?

This chapter will follow a natural progression from our exploration of how performance is measured (both rightly and wrongly), to an examination of how managers interpret and compare the data. We will start by continuing to look at the bedrock of dodgy data interpretation – binary comparisons.

Let's look at this classic mistake in a bit more detail. It's commonplace to hear in the news that sales figures have plummeted by 9.5%, unemployment has risen by 3.1%, or share prices have fallen by whatever per cent. These stories are authoritatively presented as a matter-of-fact, with even top CEOs or Government ministers quoting the figures as though no further explanation is required. The trouble with this is that such headlines are completely meaningless.

These news reports have me screaming "Compared to what?!" in frustration at the television every time. Why should the viewer accept what is essentially a vague and meaningless statement? Worse still, my fears about the efficacy of the statement are confirmed when it is subsequently explained that it is 'compared to last year, or last Christmas, or last whenever'. This is solid confirmation that the comparison is actually worse than useless (and totally misleading).

An example from today's newspaper (I didn't have to look far) in the form of an article entitled "Road deaths reduced" illustrates this:

> Latest figures from Staffordshire Police show that 38 people were killed in road traffic accidents during 2010-11. This compares to 49 fatalities during 2009-10, a 22 per cent reduction.[1]

Should there be an implied assumption that Staffordshire Police is responsible for apparently reducing fatalities? In the article they attribute this to road safety campaigns, driver education programmes and other relevant policing activity, but what proportion of this apparent 'reduction' can really be attributed to them? We are not told anything about long-term

---

1   *Staffordshire Newsletter,* 'Road Deaths Reduced' 12th January, 2012, p.15

trends or patterns (if there are any) or what the upper and lower control limits would be if a series of data points were plotted that could assist in identifying signals. This mode of presenting data doesn't give any information about the multitude of external factors that affect the rate of road traffic fatalities, such as:

- Vehicle manufacturers' safety features

- Proximity of medical assistance following an accident

- The extremely fine line between a fatal collision and one where someone is seriously injured

- Whether passengers are wearing seatbelts or not at the moment of collision

- Bad luck

- Driver error

- Whether the vehicle happens to collide with a brick wall or a soft hedge

- Bad weather

- How many people were in the vehicle at the moment of collision.

Imagine two identical serious traffic accidents; there are four occupants in one of the vehicles and just a single person in the other. For the sake of argument, the first traffic accident may result in four road deaths; the second in none. You can re-run this scenario with any permutation of numbers of occupants plus any other variable and get different results from the same collision.

Why then should such comparisons be presented as a measurement of performance? There are so many variables and factors that cannot be controlled by the police. There are also so many unanswered questions about the circumstances of the accidents behind the annual totals that the comparisons are meaningless. Context is completely ignored, and as Donald Wheeler reminds us, "Data have no meaning apart from their context".[2]

For me, this absence of context and the infinite combination of possible external variables undermines any perceived benefit of presenting this sort

2   Wheeler (2000)

of data anyway, but to then present the figures as a 'this year versus last year' comparison is both misleading and unhelpful. No doubt had there been an 'increase' in road deaths compared to last year, the police and other relevant agencies would be blamed for it. I suspect the real answer has something to do with common cause variation and Mistake One, but no one wants to hear that.

Furthermore, apart from publicising these binary comparisons, how can it ever be considered appropriate to wave these figures at the public about road traffic deaths? Would a certain number of fatalities be acceptable? Should there be a target to reduce fatalities on the road? How would it be defined? I will delve into these sorts of questions and the astounding wrongness of numerical targets further on in this book, but for now, hold that thought. Before that, I must I apologise to you in advance, as once you have read this chapter, you will notice these sorts of meaningless comparisons all around you, and you might begin to experience the same frustration that I do, whenever I encounter them.

How Police Managers Sometimes Compare Things

The much relied-upon 'this month versus last month', 'compared to this time last year', and even 'compared to last week' comparison has been used as an indicator of police performance for as long as I can remember (I joined the police in 1995). Some managers seem to think that the robustness of making such comparisons is unassailable and will base important operational decisions on such limited data. The table below serves to illustrate this point:

Beat Number	Crimes this week	Crimes last week	% variance
1	35	33	6.1%
2	12	7	28.6%
3	67	59	13.6%
4	40	44	-9.1%
5	28	29	-3.4%
6	56	52	7.7%
7	30	32	-6.2%

Figure 3.1: This week vs last week crime figures

We have seen this type of table before. They are the ones that commonly feature at police management meetings. The only thing predictable about it is the likely reaction of managers. The team responsible for Beat Two will be asked serious questions about the 'huge' percentage increase in crime. The team responsible for Beat Three will be feeling the pressure for having the most crimes numerically, as well as an increase compared to last week. Plans will be required, and patrol strategies will be devised or amended on the basis of this limited information. Perhaps some of the others might receive a light pat on the back for their apparent reductions. (Of course when the next weekly comparison comes along, everyone's seats will have changed positions and different beat teams will be under scrutiny for 'increases'. This is especially likely following a week of particularly low crime.)

Officers who took part in the research for this book provided the following comments about this well-rehearsed practice of senior police managers:

> *"On our division the senior management hold a weekly management meeting where they get right down to the detail (this means reading individual crime reports and asking pointed questions about them rather than relating them to context) of what has happened over the last seven days. They compare the crime figures to last week, then knee-jerk over the slightest increase".*

> *"It's a lottery. One week the Superintendent is patting you on the back for having low crime on your area – the next week you feel as though you are being personally blamed for any increase. Then the week after, your crime has gone down a bit and it's someone else's turn to feel the heat. It's ridiculous. Of course these figures fluctuate from week to week. These changes in crime levels are normal, but some members of the senior management team don't seem to understand that fact".*

This method is about as short term as it gets. Binary comparisons tell us nothing about long-term trends. They do not aid us in predicting the future. They do not tell us anything about the capabilities of the system, or the narrative behind the figures. It may well be the case that the crime rate on all seven beats is under statistical control; so there is no mileage in demanding 'improvement'. It's an example of Mistake One (interpreting common cause variation as a special cause and reacting to it). Only an improvement of the system will change anything, and that is the responsibility of management.

It is entirely possible that any of the beats showing increases may actually be achieving significant long-term reductions in crime. The table is incapable of communicating this. It is also incapable of understanding that Beat Three will continue to display high numerical crime figures because its boundaries contain a busy shopping centre and leisure complex, and a very effective and proactive policing team who arrest almost all of the shoplifters who commit crime there. It is inevitable that such locations will record more crime, whilst quieter beats will continue to record less crime. The fact that hardly any of the shoplifters who commit crime on Beat Three get away with it reflects a lot of hard work and effort, yet the raw figures could be easily used as a beating stick for apparent 'failure'.

The table also highlights the dangers of inappropriate use of percentages. When dealing with very small numbers, such as those for Beat Two, any fluctuation will result in relatively large percentage changes. Although there were only five more crimes on Beat Two compared to last week (it makes my toes curl just to use the phrase), the percentage variance is 28.6%, which is likely to draw the attention of managers. It may be the case that the extra five crimes were all recorded as a result of proactive police work, such as finding people carrying weapons or drugs. It is ironic, therefore, that this good work should contribute to attracting adverse management attention. Even if the difference in recorded crime was due to nothing more than normal variation, this does not warrant an adverse interpretation of that beat team's performance. Let's face it, without looking at the long-term data and knowing what the control limits would be on an SPC chart, it is impossible to know.

This also brings into focus the utter futility of comparing work units against each other. Aside from the unhealthy competition that this causes, in the case of the seven beat areas above, it is like comparing apples and oranges. Each beat has different crime rates, different crime types, different community issues, different priorities, different socio-economic influences and so on. What makes anyone think that simply aggregating the total number of the disparate crimes recorded on each beat and presenting them as a single number in a weekly document is useful to anyone?

Why Making Binary Comparisons is Silly

The only possible interpretations of binary comparisons are either 'we are doing fine', inviting complacency when the unseen long term picture may actually indicate that urgent action is required on the system, or 'things are getting worse' (even when it isn't); both risk unnecessary organisational responses to fix the 'problem'. Binary comparisons can never tell the full story, and when percentages are introduced into the equation inappropriately, it gets *really* messy. As a rule, I would suggest that there is no advantage in using percentages if the numerical value is less than 100 in the first place, and they should never be incorporated into binary comparisons. In fact, let's make it even easier: never use binary comparisons in the first place.

For any doubters still out there, let me demonstrate the complete worthlessness of binary comparisons, using the classic 'this month vs last month' and the infamous 'compared to this time last year' approaches. I will now present each of these concepts within SPC charts:

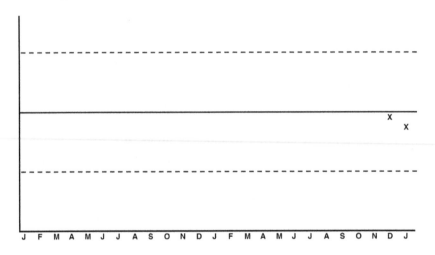

Figure 3.2: SPC chart – 'this month versus last month'

Remember this? It's the graph from the beginning of Chapter Two as an SPC chart. Depicting binary comparisons in this manner effortlessly exposes their ridiculousness. The fact that all but the last two of the data points are absent obscures the true picture; there may be runs of data points all over the place that indicate the presence of special causes. Only by plotting long-term data in SPC charts is it possible to understand what is really happening. Relying on simplistic binary comparisons is misleading, and almost always results in inappropriate operational responses and knee-jerk reactions.

For example, if the SPC chart above relates to crime rates, managers would draw false comfort from the apparent decrease compared to last month. If it relates to detected crimes they would demand answers for the apparent 'deterioration'.

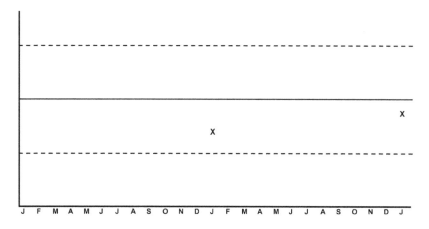

Figure 3.3: SPC chart – 'compared to this time last year'

This chart is equally unhelpful. Again, there may be important signals where the other data points should be, or perhaps only common cause variation is present. We don't know. Either way, there is insufficient data to make a judgement about what has happened. Moreover, it is impossible to anticipate what will happen in the future, or respond to it appropriately. Displaying binary comparisons in SPC charts exposes the extreme limitations of this method of interpreting data. "We have recorded more detections than at this time last year". Big deal.

> Managers! Comparing 'this week to last week', 'this month to last month' or 'this year to last year' doesn't tell you anything.

A Weighty Problem

Binary comparisons are commonplace in everyday life – for example, they apply to weight loss as much as anything else. People who are trying to lose weight often become frustrated that, despite their best efforts, they haven't lost any weight since they weighed themselves yesterday, or worse still, they have *gained* a pound or two. Some days the scales bring good news; other days frustration, based on whether the numbers are slightly higher or slightly lower than the previous day. This also applies when comparing one's weight to this time last week, or any other single point in time.

Apart from being useless, the method can end up making people feel really unhappy about themselves. They wonder what they are doing wrong, but the answer is probably nothing – the fluctuations are just normal variation. In the same way, it can be tempting to feel elated when the scales show an apparent decrease compared to the previous day. Don't be fooled however – as with the complacency of a police manager who relaxes because crime is down compared to this time last year, the 'decrease' is just probably normal variation again.

If you or anyone you know has ever tried to lose weight, then I hope you take some comfort from my observations on the subject. The best way to assess weight loss is to plot the readings on a chart and look for any downward trends, rather than compare today's moving variable against yesterday's. Good luck!

Binary Comparisons in Sheep's Clothing

There are a couple of common variations on the binary comparisons theme to be aware of. The first is the misguided notion that adding a 'year-to-date' column to a binary comparison table is useful to anyone. The year-to-date figure is merely the cumulative total to that point in the year divided by the number of months that have passed, so as the year progresses the overall difference between the year-to-date figure and individual monthly totals will tend to lessen. This is not surprising really – all it demonstrates is that natural variation has been occurring. Cumulative year-to-date figures do not show any patterns (or any useful signals that may be present), so there is no way to interpret the data. Furthermore, the approach does not demonstrate the capabilities of the process or indicate how it will behave in the future. (I've also seen 'month-to-date' comparisons – these are even worse.)

The second one to watch out for is the performance measurement barometer much relied-upon by the uninitiated, known as the 'comparison to the average' technique. It is used within the police, in education and healthcare, and is a favourite amongst politicians and anyone looking for a sound bite. At school I was above average in some classes and below average in others. Oddly enough, about half of my classmates were also in one of the two categories. Guess what – about half of the people/teams/things being compared at any given moment will be above average and the other half below average! That's what averages do. It is surprising that comparisons to the average seem to have so much currency.

Comparison to the average is just another type of binary comparison. When management action ensues following the discovery that something is either good or bad compared to the average, this skews operational activity and consequently drives waste into the system, just as with any inappropriate response to a binary comparison. Even when looking at data plotted on an SPC chart you will notice that usually about half of the data points are above the centre line and about half are below. This is especially true where the process is under statistical control. Trust me – let averages go.

You Can't Subtract People

One consequence of relying on binary comparisons that I am particularly uncomfortable with is when police forces trumpet apparent crime reduction successes using phrases like these:

> Almost 14,000 less victims of crime in South Wales.[3]
> Walsall sees a dramatic fall in crime with more than 1,600 fewer victims.[4]
> Throughout the Wakefield District there have been 493 less victims of crime.[5]

The first point I want to make is that if proper analysis indicates there has indeed been a genuine reduction as a result of police intervention, then it is right and proper that this should be celebrated. The second point is that those who furnish the media with these headlines genuinely believe

---

3   South Wales Police (2010)
4   West Midlands Police (2012a)
5   West Yorkshire Police (2012)

them, largely because they don't understand the hollow nature of making year versus year comparisons. The third point is that, in all these cases, the words you read are almost always suffixed by 'compared to last year', rendering them meaningless.

It is unintentionally misleading, and a little dismissive of this year's crime victims. Although senior managers are genuinely pleased that crime appears to have fallen and therefore want to share the good news, there are a couple of rather large holes in the message. The first is due to the shaky nature of the 'mathematics' used to generate the headline; the second is the fact that although there might have been 14,000 fewer victims compared to last year, there still were 70,000 victims or whatever this year. That's *an additional* 70,000 victims of crime, not 14,000 fewer! The figures go *up* every time there's a new crime. You can't subtract victims of crime. It's like going to the sales and telling people how much you've saved. No – you *spent* money![6]

Measures That Don't Measure Anything

I want to briefly consider one more horror of badly done performance measurement. Once you know it exists, you can spot it and avoid it. I call it the 'totally made up performance measure that attempts to count the impossible'. The way it is used adds insult to injury, as we shall see.

A good example that I can show you from my own experience is what is erroneously entitled the 'conversion rate' measure on some police performance documents. The conversion rate is supposed to be the proportion of arrests that ultimately result in a crime being detected. For example, if a team records 50 arrests in a month and, of these, 25 cases result in an offender being charged, the team would record 25 detections. This would result in a 'conversion rate' of 25/50 = 50% (except it isn't really a conversion rate, which is why I have put inverted commas around it. This will be explained very soon.)

The 'conversion rate' measure is presented as an antidote to the evils of just chasing either arrest or detection figures. Unfortunately, the measure is nothing more than a classic example of what Russ Ackoff calls "Doing the wrong thing righter".[7] It also has the major drawback of being a measure that counts something that doesn't actually exist. Let me explain.

---

6   I 'borrowed' the sales story from John Seddon, after hearing him make this point during his 2012 Evidence Tour.

7   Ackoff (2004)

	Arrests	Detected Offences	Conversion Rate
Team A	75	45	59.2%
Team B	55	38	69.1%
Team C	79	39	49.4%
Team D	81	46	56.8%
Team E	83	48	57.9%

Figure 3.4: Conversion rates table

This table represents the arrests, detections and 'conversion rate' figures for each of five policing teams. It is intended to discourage hasty arrests that are unlikely to ever achieve a detection (i.e. in an attempt to record a high number of arrest figures), as well as to promote the value of finalising cases successfully. This is another example of well-meaning managers interfering with the system without knowledge. As the proverb goes, "The road to Hell is paved with good intentions". Deming's version is, "We are being ruined by best efforts".[8]

The problems with the 'conversion rate' measure are numerous:

- Not all offences result in a crime number being generated because under Home Office Counting Rules (HOCR)[9] not every type of incident that results in an arrest is classed as a 'recordable crime'. This means that arrests for things such as drink driving, being wanted on warrant or committing a breach of the peace can never generate a detection, even if the offender is charged. Consequently, if a particular team has several of these types of offences amongst its arrests, this will reduce the achievable 'conversion rate' between arrests and detections. Even if every single arrest resulted in a charge and conviction, it would be impossible to achieve 100% conversion rate from those arrests. (This is perhaps what has happened to Team C, which has a high number of arrests, but a relatively low number of detections.)

- Often, an arrested person will be dealt with by officers from a different team to that of the arresting officer. This could happen if a person is drunk at the time of arrest and cannot be interviewed or charged until after the arresting officer has gone off duty. Alternatively, it could occur because he or she has committed a

8   Neave (1990) p.89
9   Home Office (2011b)

serious offence that has to be handed over to CID to deal with. The officers who eventually deal with the prisoner will record the detection against their own team's total, resulting in an artificially high number of detections and enhancing that team's 'conversion rate'. (Maybe this has happened to Team B, which has a relatively low number of arrests but a high proportion of detections.)

- Another factor that affects 'conversion rates' is the simple fact that there is often no relationship between the individual arrests and detections that are recorded in any given month. If an arrested person has to be bailed for further enquiries to be conducted, it may well be a month before the suspect is eventually charged and the detection registered. The detections in the above table could have resulted from arrests several weeks ago. It follows that if a lot of prisoners are bailed from this month's arrests, the 'conversion rate' suffers; it is impossible to register pending detections. Conversely, if an old investigation reaches its conclusion and a suspect is charged, this artificially boosts that month's 'conversion rate'. It is not unheard of for teams to record 'conversion rates' in excess of 100% in any given month. That should tell you something.

- If there are multiple offenders for the same crime (e.g. six people beat up one victim and they are all charged with assault), this can still only ever result in one detected crime. This means that for six arrests, only one detection is possible, thereby adversely affecting the 'conversion rate'.

- If one offender is charged with several crimes at the same time, then for just one arrest the officer is able to record multiple detections. This helps to artificially boost the 'conversion rate' and can also be responsible for teams recording in excess of 100% 'conversion rate' in a single month.

There are many other factors that affect the 'conversion rate' measure, but these are the main ones. I hope they demonstrate why the measure does not actually measure anything at all. Indeed, it is not even a conversion rate.

When management scrutiny and operational adjustments occur as a result of binary comparisons and the 'conversion rate' measure, it is easy to see how complete chaos can ensue. In effect what managers are doing is using a measure of something that doesn't exist to make ill-informed comparisons about things that can't be compared, using methods that are completely unsound. For anyone who still thinks this approach is acceptable, I can save you time and effort – a much quicker, equally effective and more transparent way to judge performance is to blindfold oneself and stick a pin in a board, or choose from a bucket containing random numbers.

Putting Things into Perspective

The performance table towards the start of Chapter Two (*Figure 2.3*) compared five individual policing teams in respect of total detected offences recorded this month as compared to last month. I have reproduced it below, as we will now use the lessons and techniques covered in this and the previous chapter to challenge the assumptions generated by that table of numbers.

	Detected Crimes (This Month)	**Detected Crimes (Last Month)**	**Percentage Variance**
Team A	75	73	2.7%
Team B	83	75	10.7%
Team C	54	71	-24.0%
Team D	77	51	51.0%
Team E	74	79	-6.4%

Figure 3.5: Table of detected offences (this month versus last month)

You will recall the teams that attracted the most attention from management were Team B for consistent good performance, Team D for significant improvement, and Team C for ongoing poor performance and deterioration. You will (hopefully) now be uncomfortable about managers labelling these teams in this way based on the limited information on which the judgement was made. You will understand that the binary comparisons employed mean nothing, and that the use of percentages in these circumstances is likely to produce misleading results. I hope that you would want to know what the true picture of performance looks like, using SPC charts. So let's do it.

First of all, this is the SPC chart that plots the long-term picture for those 'high performers', Team B:

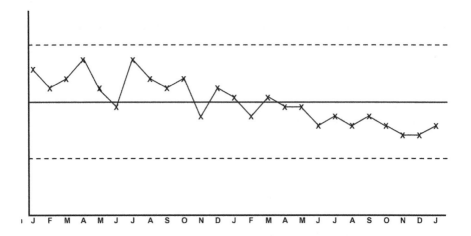

Figure 3.6: SPC chart – Team B: detected offences

This SPC chart clearly indicates long-term deterioration in the number of detected offences recorded by Team B. Most significantly, there is a run of more than eight data points on the same side of the centre line, beginning last April and continuing until the current month. This suggests that something has changed within the process from about this point onwards and stayed that way. It is certainly enough to warrant taking a look to see if there is a special cause affecting the data.

The irony is that this team was recognised as being high performing, based on the marginal increase between the last two data points. Managers will have missed the opportunity to understand the true picture of Team B's performance by relying on a table of numbers that makes an isolated binary comparison, rather than aiming to attain a comprehensive appreciation of trends by using SPC.

Next, let's look at the SPC chart for 'most improved' work unit, Team D. Remember, it achieved a dramatic increase of 51% this month, as compared to last month.

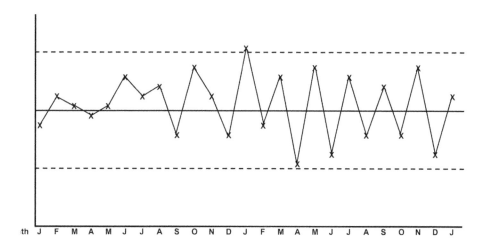

Figure 3.7: SPC chart – Team D: detected offences

By looking at this chart it becomes immediately apparent that the sudden 'improvement' on last month's total is part of a wildly fluctuating series of data points. Indeed, there are 14 data points alternating up and down, beginning two Novembers ago. (This signal may even have its roots beginning to emerge as far back as September before that.) There is also another signal in the form of a breach of the upper control limit that occurred last January.

In any case, the process is not in a desirable state of statistical control; it exhibits extreme oscillation and instability. It is, therefore, foolish to presume that the marked increase compared to last month represents improvement. Work needs to occur on this process to identify the cause of the loss of statistical control and address it. This is another example of a signal that would never have been picked up using the traditional method of presenting rows of numbers in a table.

Next we move on to look at the SPC chart that records the long-term performance of Team C, which has endured pointed management scrutiny as a result of apparent continued poor performance and deterioration from last month's figure. Poor Team C has been forced to produce lengthy plans detailing what action it will take to improve future performance. No doubt the management intervention will also have involved harsh words and exhortations for staff to work harder from now on.

Team C's SPC chart is displayed below:

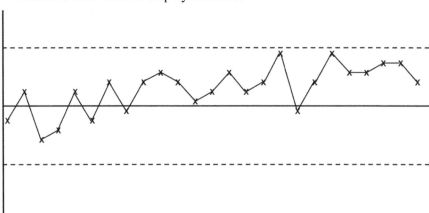

Figure 3.8: SPC chart – Team C: detected offences

In this case it would appear that Team C has suffered a monstrous injustice at the hands of managers who put their complete trust in the 'this month versus last month' comparison. It is evident that Team C's performance has been on a sustained upwards trajectory for some time, with the difference between this month and last month being nothing more than the result of common cause variation, well within the control limits. There is even a signal comprising a run of nine data points above the centre line starting from Septembers ago.

I will leave the SPC charts for Teams A and E to your imagination. You may recall that they tended to escape management notice as they appeared to drift along somewhere in the middle. It is entirely feasible that either of their SPC charts could be littered with dramatic signals that should have drawn management attention to something very good or very worrying about their performance. Genuine signals, which might have aided managers in predicting the future or to make systemic adjustments to ensure that good performance was consistently achieved, will have been missed.

By focusing on differences between teams and only paying attention to those values that appear at the extreme ends of the spectrum, management neglected Teams A and E. Only SPC charts act as an effective method of increasing understanding of actual performance and the capabilities of the system, whilst simultaneously preventing vital signals from being lost under the radar.

SPC Charts versus Rows of Numbers

I think I have put forward a pretty cogent case for the use of SPC charts instead of tables of numerical data, but I know there will be some managers out there who still obstinately oppose this approach. I guess their argument may run along the lines of denying that their performance assessments are made on a month-by-month comparison and that they somehow 'know' what the long-term trends are. Perhaps they employ super detailed tables that include more than one or two month's data. As a final plea to consider using SPC charts, let's look at such a table to gauge its usefulness.

J	F	M	A	M	J	J	A	S	O	N	D
38	51	31	36	51	40	55	46	54	63	55	47

J	F	M	A	M	J	J	A	S	O	N	D	J
52	70	50	54	85	46	53	84	65	65	71	71	54

Figure 3.9: Data table – Team C: detected offences

This table represents the monthly totals of detected offences recorded by Team C for the same period as for the SPC chart at *Figure 3.8*. Ask yourself:

1. Is it easy to see patterns by adopting this approach?

2. Are there any signals?

3. What are the upper and lower control limits that define the parameters for normal variation?

4. Which is the better way of interpreting data – SPC charts or numerical tables?

Figure 3.9 represents the data for just one team. Imagine how complicated it becomes when several teams are compared against each other using this method. Next, consider how much messier it gets when trying to insert percentage variances into the rows of data. It is absolutely impossible to interpret any of the data meaningfully due to all the noise of common cause variation. The cognitive limitations of the human brain prevent information from being absorbed effectively when looking at large amounts of data in this format.[10]

The table method also does not tell us anything about the capabilities of the process. It is completely retrospective and incapable of predicting

---

10   Wheeler (2000) pp.5-6

how the process will operate into the future. Moreover, attempting to use data in this format is doomed to failure: it is impossible to interpret the data effectively, plus the use of tables encourages the application of binary comparisons. Absolutely none of this aids understanding of the process or achieves anything useful.

How to Do It

Now the science bit. There are some excellent books that explain Statistical Process Control in much more detail than I intend to go into here. I would particularly recommend *Understanding Variation – The Key to Managing Chaos* and *Avoiding Man-Made Chaos*; both by Donald Wheeler. (I like the repeated references to 'chaos'. Wheeler is absolutely right.) Up until now, all the SPC charts in this book have deliberately omitted the numerical values on the vertical axis, as I wanted to focus attention on the patterns, rather than the numbers. 'Real' SPC charts include numbers of course, so we will now construct an SPC chart properly to demonstrate how the numbers fit into the picture.

By learning how to construct SPC charts (and practising doing so), we can gain a wider understanding of how they work. Some organisations (including my own) have excellent computer programs that build SPC charts automatically by extracting data from other computer systems or 'data warehouses', such as electronic crime records. This enables almost instantaneous creation of SPC charts and requires no actual knowledge about how to build them from scratch. It also means there is no excuse for not using SPC charts in performance measurement and data interpretation.

This is the reason that the bulk of this and the previous chapter concentrate on interpreting the charts, rather than constructing them. Nevertheless, it is useful to know how SPC charts are put together. So as not to overburden you with (what is to me) impenetrable algebraic formulae and complex mathematical theory, I will demonstrate how to construct an SPC chart quickly and simply, using a straightforward approach based on a method outlined by Brian Joiner.[11]

The first step is to assemble the data. For this, we will use 25 months' worth of detection figures for a policing team because this is a comparable period to the SPC charts we have looked at so far. These figures will be placed in chronological order by month in the first column of a table.

---

11   Joiner (1994) pp.148-149

The next step is to calculate the differences between each pair of figures to determine the *range*. To do this, simply look at each month's figure and note down the difference between it and the next month's figure. For example, if January's value is 45 detections and February's value is 50 detections, then the range is five for that pairing. The next range would be the difference between February and March, then between March and April, and so on. Do this for each pair of months and you will end up with a column populated with ranges, as in the table below.

The next stage in preparing the data is to determine the *median* range. One simple way to do this is to list the ranges in order from the highest range to the lowest range and find the middle of the list. The ordered list of ranges can be placed in a third column, as in the table below.

Month	Detections	Range		Ordered Range
J	45			
F	50	5		18
M	33	17		18
A	46	13		18
M	61	15		17
J	55	6		17
J	59	4		15
A	67	8		13
S	58	9		12
O	46	12		11
N	44	2		11
D	53	9		11
J	62	9		9
F	80	18		9
M	69	11		9
A	58	11		8
M	64	6		8
J	46	18		7
J	28	18		6
A	39	11		6
S	46	7		6
O	52	6		5
N	44	8		4
D	61	17		2
J	59	2		2

Figure 3.10: SPC chart data table – detected offences

As you can see, by putting the ranges in order, then counting from each end of the column to the middle, the *median range* is found to be nine. (In this case, there are two middle values; both nine.)

Next, multiply the median range by 3.14 (this figure is determined by minds much greater than mine). This gives us the value that will become the distance between the centre line of the SPC chart and each of the control limits: **9 x 3.14 = 28.26**

Put that figure to one side for a minute and calculate the average number of detections per month throughout the entire period by adding together all of the monthly detection totals, then dividing the total by the number of months. In this case, the total number of detections recorded during the 25 months is 1325.

1325/25 = 53

This average monthly value of 53 then determines where the centre line of the SPC chart is set. To calculate the control limits, we simply add or subtract the figure derived from multiplying the median range by 3.14. In this case it was 28.26. So, to calculate the upper control limit, just add 28.26 to 53, and to calculate the lower control limit, subtract 28.26 from 53.

Upper control limit: **53 + 28.26 = 81.26**
Lower control limit: **53 – 28.26 = 24.74**

Now we have all the figures necessary to create the SPC chart. Draw a solid horizontal line at 53 on the vertical axis to create the centre line, and add dashed horizontal lines at 81.26 and 24.74 respectively on the vertical axis for the upper and lower control limits. Next, plot the monthly data from left to right, and you will have your SPC chart.

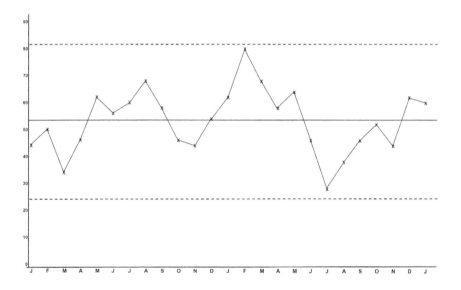

Figure 3.11: SPC chart – detected offences

Interpret the Data: Understand the Context

Let's look at what it tells us. Firstly, all the data points fall within the control limits. This tells us that the process is stable and that the control limits represent the parameters within which the process will continue to operate. If the team that recorded these detections remains the same in size and continues to operate in the same way, in the same area, then future monthly detection figures will continue to appear between these control limits.

The chart also tells us that there are no signals. Last February 80 detections were recorded, which was just under the upper control limit of 81.26, and last July 28 detections were recorded, which was close to the lower control limit of 24.74. Despite this, there is no need to react, as both values fall within the parameters. Imagine the traditional management response to these figures after making a binary comparison using the previous month's figure. February's reaction would be along the lines of, "80 detections compared to 62 last month! Well done. Have a gold star for such a fantastic improvement!" Management would want this team to share their 'good practice' with the other teams. The shine would come straight off the gold star the very next month as detections 'plummet' to just 69.

Now consider the traditional management response to the 28 detections recorded last July. "You had 46 detections last month and 64 the month before – what has gone wrong? Plans are required! Management expect to see an improvement next month!" As luck would have it, the next month's figure is higher, which has the unfortunate effect of cementing management's view that July's telling-off must have worked.

Of course, these fluctuations are down to common cause variation, and therefore no one should be reacting to anything. Look at the chart again. There are no breaches of either control limit; no runs of six points in any single direction, no runs of eight points on the same side of the centre line; no runs of 14 points alternating up and down, and no runs of three points closer to either control limit than the centre line. In other words, there are no signals and every fluctuation you see is normal.

Management! Stop reacting!

Ask Yourself 'Why?'

Common cause variation in respect of detection figures occurs because of a multitude of factors outside the direct control of the team being measured. We looked at some earlier. Here is a more comprehensive list:

Reasons why detection figures might be at the lower end of the scale:

- Suspects might be on bail, so potential detections are pending.

- The team's best arrests may have been handed over to other teams.

- The proportion of offences charged that do not result in a crime report or a detection being generated (e.g. drink driving) is relatively high.

- The Crown Prosecution Service (CPS) might have advised there was insufficient evidence to charge a suspect.

- Witnesses may have refused to provide statements.

- An investigation may be lengthy, complex and involve several offenders being charged. This is work-intensive, yet will still only generate one detection. Note that a detection for murder and a detection for stealing a Mars Bar each count as 'one' in this system.

- Some crimes will never be solved – let's be realistic. If someone steals your garden gnome whilst you're on holiday, but no one sees them do it and there's no forensic evidence or CCTV, then the gnome thief is never likely to be caught. This will affect detection rates, but it's not the fault of the officer who took the report, or anyone else.

- Police officers deal with a whole range of incidents that do not generate detections, no matter how good a job is done or how satisfied the member of the public is. Examples include dealing with missing children, traffic accidents, neighbour disputes, or sudden deaths. A month where the team dealt with a large proportion of these types of incidents will be reflected in common cause variation that is manifested in a lower number of detections.

Reasons why detection figures might be at the higher end of the scale:

- A lot of suspects who were on bail for old offences may have returned for case finalisation this month.

- One suspect may have admitted multiple offences.

- The team may have picked up a number of fruitful handovers from other teams.

- The team may have dealt with a higher proportion of straightforward crime incidents, resulting in more detection opportunities.

All these factors will affect the volume of detections recorded, without anyone doing anything differently. The officers on this team may have worked just as hard last July as they did last February. Just because the monthly detection figure was at opposite ends of the scale during these two months doesn't mean that management's typical responses of exhorting the workers to work harder, demanding explanations for 'poor' performance or insisting on written plans is appropriate. It certainly won't make a jot of difference, as none of these reactions improve the system or affect the external factors responsible for normal variation. Those being shouted at are doing their best to work on the relatively small proportion of the process that they influence.

The Greatest Opportunities for Improvement are in The System, but…

I've talked a lot about how the system is mainly responsible for performance, as opposed to the people who work within it. Indeed, Deming estimated that 94% of performance is down to system conditions, with just 6% being attributable to the individual. He also asserts that management bears the brunt of responsibility for improving the system. Now, I am going to be careful about how I word the next bit, as I don't want to provoke any systems purists out there, but I am specifically applying systems thinking to policing here and I think I know a bit about both, so here goes.

In all public services, and particularly in policing, there is a greater variety of demand to absorb than in much of the manufacturing industry where systems thinking began. It is more difficult to quantify activity and devise effective performance indicators for policing than it is for the production of a single type of steel component produced by a particular machine in a factory. It also follows that a worker who operates a repetitive action on such a machine has less influence over variation in respect of the characteristics of the component it produces. This is in direct contrast with a police officer who deals with a wide range of incidents, with varying degrees of influence.

It is, therefore, my view that despite sometimes-clunky systems, management interference and restrictive policies, frontline police officers still generally retain a degree of autonomy. This extends to deciding which vehicle to stop, knowing who your local burglars are, or having an eye for something that looks out of place. Responding to incoming intelligence and knowing your local crime hotspots determines whether an officer turns left or right as he or she leaves the station. Understanding powers and procedures aids officers in making lawful arrests, conducting searches and making split-second decisions that affect people's lives. To sit back and say, "I can only make a negligible difference to the system because I'm not a manager" is defeatist and just plain wrong.

Deming's estimation that 94% of factors affecting variation belong to the system is not a mantra that absolves workers of responsibility, especially in a policing context. (Neither was it intended to be. Deming himself said this percentage was an *estimation* based on his own experience, much of which was in the manufacturing industry.) It may be the case that management has the power to act on systemic causes, but frontline staff will often become aware of a systems issue before management notice it (if they notice it at all). In policing it would be ridiculous to imagine that police officers are totally powerless to act when they see an opportunity to take the initiative. The local organisational culture will dictate how receptive managers are to new ideas, but that doesn't stop people trying. The alternative is to remain passive and allow the system to break. To me, that would be morally wrong.

What I am saying is that the public put a lot of trust in the police and the message I don't want to give is that no one can do anything about the system because 'that's management's problem'. Yes, workers are constrained by the parameters of the system as defined by management, but the degree to which this applies varies considerably according to the context; it is therefore not an excuse for individual workers to choose not to contribute towards organisational purpose. Even limited influence is still influence, and true leadership needs to thrive at all levels. Indeed, unlike the variation evident within the characteristics of components produced by a single metal pressing machine, variation in public services is derived from multiple interlinked systems at numerous levels.

As an example, at the time of writing I am posted as a Sector Inspector. This means I have geographical responsibility for a large policing area and approximately seventy members of staff. At the same time I am part of a bigger divisional structure, alongside other Sector Inspectors, and I report to more senior officers. This means that I am afforded a degree of autonomy, allowing me to improve local systems and to try to influence my peers and senior management, but I am not always able to significantly affect systems that sit above or around my own.

In other words, I can introduce significant local changes but am still subject to (sometimes incompatible) force-level mandates and policies that affect the boundaries of local processes. In one dynamic I am the manager who has the greater opportunity to affect systems, whilst simultaneously I am the worker who has a much reduced influence on other systems that are controlled by my bosses. It doesn't stop me from trying though.

In short, let's not get hung up on 94% and 6% being set in stone. They aren't. I believe that the exact proportions vary depending on the context, but the fact remains that management holds the key to improving the lion's share of any given system or process. Everyone has a responsibility to work together to improve the system, but the workers can only influence a relatively small proportion of it. The notion can be illustrated by imagining a fried egg, as in the diagram below. The yolk represents the proportion of the system's performance that can be influenced by the workforce. It is always surrounded by the much larger albumen.

Figure 3.12: The Fried Egg Model of System Performance

Even if every worker performed to full capacity at all times, always did their very best, and never made any mistakes, they could still only affect a relatively small proportion of organisational performance. In other words, the weight of responsibility lies with management; but with everyone working to improve the system the possibilities are limitless.

The Ostrich Technique

I recently had a discussion with a colleague about performance. Part of it went like this:

> *Me:* "The greatest opportunity for enhancing performance lies in improving the system".
>
> *Colleague:* "No it doesn't! It's the people!"
>
> *Me:* "It's definitely the system. The people have an important role to play, but they can only operate within the parameters that the system imposes on them".
>
> *Colleague:* "No, you're wrong! People need to be held to account! They need intrusive supervision and clear targets to be measured against".

I then ran through Deming's 94:6 concept, along with some real life examples, and explained how despite everyone doing their best, delays, waste and lengthy end-to-end times occur because of the system design, rather than as a result of a 'people problem'. My colleague's response? Pretty much, "La la la. I'm not listening".

As Aldous Huxley puts it:

> Facts do not cease to exist because they are ignored.[12]

Final Thoughts

Hopefully this chapter and the previous one have exposed some of the plausible, yet counterproductive practices that are commonplace within traditional performance measurement systems. Using binary comparisons and limited data does not provide an accurate picture of performance and is akin to flying in the dark, with a blindfold on, and upside down. The natural antidotes to this are the far superior methods associated with SPC that allow managers to intelligently interpret data so as to respond (or not respond) proportionately to existing patterns. These methods are much more efficient and cost effective because they reduce waste activity, such as knee-jerk operational responses. They also prevent unfair and inaccurate assumptions about officers who are genuinely doing everything they can within the limits imposed upon them.

The apparent objectivity of numbers is not as objective as it first appears. Reliance on averages will always result in about half of the data

---

12   Baker and Sexton (2000)

(or teams, or individuals) being ranked as 'below average'; an unpleasant and meaningless stigma when you are only 'below average' because of common cause variation that you cannot control. The misuse of year-to-date figures, percentages and data tables causes operational chaos and adversely affects service delivery. Comparison between teams is destructive and causes unhealthy competition that generates short-term individual winners at the expense of the long-term aim. Ultimately, this lack of cooperation will destroy the system.

Variation is everywhere and is impossible to avoid, yet by understanding it managers can unlock powerful knowledge that fosters true appreciation of data. SPC charts enable noise to be filtered from data and expose signals that we can respond to meaningfully. They are one of the best tools available for displaying and interpreting data and, in my opinion, no method exists that surpasses them. Their proper application allows police managers to deploy resources in the right places at the right time. Only SPC charts can instantaneously highlight patterns that would be otherwise invisible; indeed they may expose trends that actually run in the opposite direction to the one determined as a result of making a binary comparison. Relying on binary comparisons to decide operational priorities is like sticking one's finger in the air or drawing straws.

It is important to remember that the majority of variation exists because of common causes that can never be traced to an identifiable source. Managers waste time, effort and money searching for sources of common cause variation when none exist. Officers' time should not be wasted. Taxpayers' money should not be wasted. After all, this waste has been forced into the system by diverting resources to address a non-existent 'problem'. Unfortunately, if the next data point shows an 'improvement', managers will continue to believe that their actions have been effective and the vicious circle intensifies. Blindness to external influences and common cause variation results in performance indicators that attempt to measure things that don't exist (such as the arrest versus detections 'conversion rate' measure we looked at earlier). This makes things even messier and mires management thinking further.

The only way to reduce variation and improve systems and processes is through understanding what the data are telling us and then acting upon the evidence base. Simply redrawing the lines because you don't like them or setting arbitrary specifications, at best, achieves nothing and, at worst, destroys the system. If prevailing organisational culture makes it difficult to challenge management norms then yes, this can be uncomfortable but it still must be done. Everyone has a responsibility to improve the system, but especially management. The public deserve it. Our officers deserve it. If you are not a manager – challenge it. If you are a manager – just do it.

I hope that I have generated curiosity about SPC and demonstrated how easy it is to do performance measurement properly. Below, I have added bullet points to recap some of the main themes.

Some things to avoid at all costs:

- All binary comparisons

- Comparing work units with each other

- Applying percentages to small numerical amounts

- Isolated year-to-date figures

- Comparisons to the average

- Measures that try to count the impossible

- Expecting staff to account for normal variation

- Determining operational responses based on limited data

- Demanding plans without evidence

- Setting arbitrary specifications

- Measures that do not benefit the service user.

Some things to do at all costs:

- Ask, "*Why* are we measuring this thing as a performance indicator?"

- Select only measures that are derived from purpose

- Appreciate that data have no meaning without context

- Use SPC charts

- Understand the difference between signals and noise

- Avoid Mistake One and Mistake Two. (See Chapter Two)

- Remember that management are responsible for improving the system.

One final thought, and it brings us back to the fundamental question about why performance measurement exists in the first place (or at least why it *should* exist). Public management experts Geert Bouckaert and Wouter van Dooren assert;

Performance measurement is only useful if it improves policy or management.[13]

If we are doing performance measurement wrong in the first place, how can we ever expect to see any benefit?

13　Bouckaert and van Dooren (2003) p.135

CHAPTER FOUR

Tamper Tantrums

So far we have looked at the limitations of traditional performance measurement practices and the dangers associated with binary comparisons, as well as the importance of intelligent data interpretation and understanding variation through the superior alternative of SPC charts. Next, I want to spend some time looking at what happens when management interferes with the system. Whether this is by knee-jerking from one priority to another, setting targets, pressuring staff to work harder or even well-intentioned meddling, the results are often the same. In systems terms this is known as 'tampering', and one of the best ways of illustrating what happens is through an experiment that Deming performed at his seminars – The Funnel Experiment.[1]

The Funnel Experiment

For the purposes of demonstrating how its lessons apply to the policing environment, I will just briefly outline the main principles here.

The experiment involves repeatedly dropping a marble through a funnel onto a tablecloth marked with an 'X', and using a felt-tip pen to mark where the marble comes to rest after each drop. There are four stages to the experiment; at each stage the marble is dropped fifty times, then the resulting pattern is analysed to determine how accurate each method is at clustering the marks as close to the 'X' as possible.

The purpose of the experiment is to demonstrate how management (i.e. the person dropping the marble) can inadvertently adversely affect the desired outcome (clustering the felt-tip pen marks near to the 'X') by blindly adjusting aspects of the system.

The first stage of the experiment simply involves dropping the marble through the funnel from a static position directly above the 'X'. This

---

1   See: Deming (1986); Deming (1994); Neave (1990); Latzko and Saunders (1995)
     For an animated version of this experiment, see *www.symphonytech.com/dfunnel.htm*

method is called Rule One. It results in a relatively tight cluster of marks around the 'X', which if plotted on an SPC chart would produce a stable pattern of common cause variation. As the marble will tend to roll a short distance in one direction or the other after hits the tablecloth, there will always be some degree of drift; nevertheless, the Rule One method will produce a predictable pattern that remains quite closely clustered around the 'X', no matter how many times it is repeated.

If we were to measure the distance of each dot from the centre of the cross and plot the data on an SPC chart, it would look something like this:

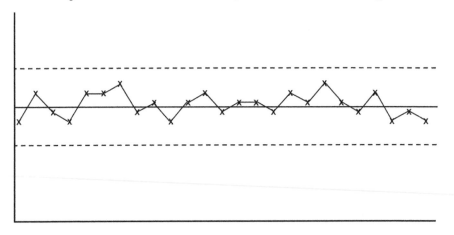

Figure 4.1: SPC chart – Funnel experiment (Rule One)

To apply Rule One to the policing environment, it could be that the pattern of tablecloth marks when transferred to an SPC chart relates to the crime rate, whilst the action of dropping the marble under Rule One conditions is the chosen police tactic designed to tackle it. A common tactic for reducing crime in a given location is to deploy high visibility patrols. (This may not be the most sophisticated tactic in the world but it is likely to have some effect.)

Now, let's assume the manager performing the experiment decides that the degree of variation produced by the Rule One method is still too much – in other words, he or she wants to reduce the crime rate even further and see this reflected in a downwards step change. The proper way to achieve this would be to gain an understanding of what the crime data are telling us, identify any patterns and devise a response that is based on the evidence presented. What sometimes happens, however, is that well-meaning managers respond to a perceived issue and implement an alternative method that ends up actually being worse than the original tactic.

This takes us to Rule Two. Our police manager has identified a crime issue that needs addressing and isn't satisfied with the effectiveness of tactics to date. He or she then decides to move resources around without first gaining a proper understanding of the crime data. In funnel experiment terms this equates to adjusting the position of the funnel after every drop, in the hope that this recalibration will compensate for errors and cause the marble to land closer to the 'X'. Under Rule Two therefore, the funnel is moved after each drop *relative to its current position*; i.e. if the marble ends up two inches to the left of the 'X', the funnel is positioned two inches to the right of this position for the next drop.

Whilst the Rule Two method might seem like a good idea at first, it is guaranteed to produce a wider range of variation than the previous method, with the marks on the tablecloth being clustered around the 'X' in a circle roughly twice the size of that produced under Rule One conditions. This is also a classic example of Mistake One (see Chapter Two) – reacting to common cause variation as though it were a signal.

If the distance from the centre of the cross to the location of each dot on the tablecloth were plotted on an SPC chart, it would look something like this.

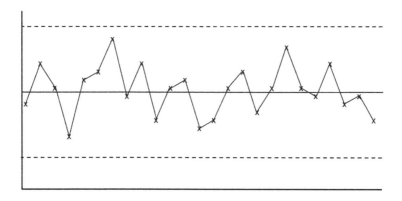

Figure 4.2: SPC chart – Funnel experiment (Rule Two)

Real life examples of Rule Two include recalibrating machinery on the basis of *only one* output, or the following story from a delegate at one of Deming's seminars:

"My son is on a submarine. It is the practice there to take a shot at a target first thing in the morning, then adjust the sights to compensate for the error. This adjustment, I now understand, is almost a sure guarantee of worse performance for the rest of the day than if they had left the sights alone."[2]

So, our police manager has implemented a change in tactics in response to the crime rate, and unwittingly lost the little control that existed when deploying resources under Rule One conditions. The crime rate has become more unstable. A quick assessment of tactics may result in the desire to try something different – this brings us to *Rule Three.*

Rule Three is an even cruder attempt at error compensation, which is similar to Rule Two, but which involves moving the funnel *in relation to the position of the 'X'*, rather than where the previous marble drop landed. Therefore, if the marble ends up two inches to the left of the 'X', the funnel is positioned two inches to the right of the 'X' for the next drop.[3] The result is widely-fluctuating variation, which if plotted on an SPC chart, would produce an ever more extreme zigzag pattern. (Remember the '14 points up and down' signal from Chapter Two?)

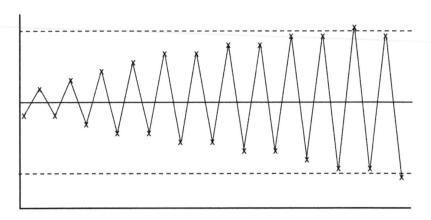

Figure 4.3: SPC chart – Funnel experiment (Rule Three)

Again, this is another example of Mistake One, where tactics are hurriedly implemented in response to mistaken assumptions about a perceived problem, without resorting to understanding the data or designing an evidence-based solution. In many ways, it can be considered to be

2   Deming (1986) p.330
3   For clarity, an animated version of this experiment is available at www.symphonytech.com/dfunnel.htm

the ultimate binary comparison foul-up, with each knee-jerk being more extreme than the last, as managers desperately over-compensate for the last data point.[4] In policing, Rules Two and Three can manifest themselves when managers repeatedly deviate from tried and tested crime reduction tactics in flawed attempts at bringing crime rates under control.

Finally, we come to *Rule Four*. This method simply involves positioning the funnel over where the previous marble drop ended up. Apart from the first drop, there is no reference to the 'X'. This produces a pattern that moves further away from the 'X' in one direction. If transferred to an SPC chart, the data points would break through one or the other of the control limits pretty quickly and keep on going The system has totally collapsed.

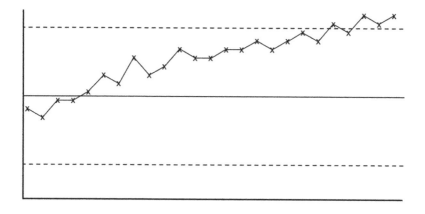

Figure 4.4: SPC chart – Funnel experiment (Rule Four)

Examples of Rule Four include the classic practice of 'worker training worker'; i.e. someone on the job trains a new recruit, who subsequently trains another new worker, who then goes on to train a further new recruit, and so on. As time progresses, this results in a drift from the original purpose due to slight differences in each worker's style and ability. The cumulative effect is that the further down the line we go, the further away from the theoretical 'X' we wander. This is similar to the game of 'Chinese Whispers' where a phrase is whispered from one player to the next, usually resulting in a wildly inaccurate version of the phrase emerging when the last player tries to repeat it. It's like taking a photocopy of a photocopy of

---

4   Note: In *Figures 4.3* and *4.4* the control limits would normally be recalculated to take into account the extreme values towards the right of these charts. I have left the original control limits in place to illustrate the significance of the increasing variation.

a photocopy of a photocopy, and so on. With no reference to the original aim, or phrase, or picture, we see a progressive degradation of quality and deviation from purpose.

In policing, we see examples of Rule Four occurring where operational practice is simply based on 'what we did last time', without taking into account any new learning, or adapting to context. This can happen where a force objective is interpreted differently in different areas, and one police division will look to another for 'best practice'. The result is that one area will copy what another area is doing without taking into account local nuances or considerations. Yet another division may take notice of what that area has been doing and copy them, resulting in a third generation version of the original process that is riddled with successive distortions.

In all cases, the experiment demonstrates why it is dangerous to meddle with a system or process without understanding it. Rule One may be imperfect, but it is still a better option than the others. Managers must understand that the variation present from the outset occurs naturally, and any attempt to interfere without knowledge is simply blind tampering.

Reducing Variation

We have seen how tampering with the system guarantees worse performance and extreme instability in some cases, but what steps can be taken to reduce variation (equating to improved performance)? The starting point would be to never adopt Rules Two, Three or Four. The next step is to understand when *not* to react (i.e. Mistake One) but to delve into the data to understand what is occurring within the system. This should clarify whether there are any evidence-based opportunities for changing tactics.

Clearly, the type of repetitive activity conducted during the funnel experiment has more similarities with machine production of identical components than the range of activities undertaken by the police. Factors that affect crime rates are complex and often difficult to influence. Whilst policing activity, such as arresting active criminals, will have some effect on crime in that area, other influencing factors (for example, poor personal security) cannot be directly controlled by the police.[5] A classic example of this is that despite yearly media campaigns, people still leave their cars unattended with engines running whilst waiting for the frost to clear from their windscreens, and opportunist thieves steal them. Nothing about the

---

5   Loveday (2000) pp.215-237

veracity of police efforts or constant crime prevention messages stops this from occurring, so is it appropriate to apportion blame to local police commanders for vehicle crime rates?

There will be circumstances where exogenous factors account for much of the variation evident within a given process, so opportunities to reduce the variation are limited. A good example is provided by Bird *et al,* who cite the inevitability of variation within the outcomes of surgical operations:

> Even if a surgeon's ability is constant and the number and case mix of patients on whom she or he operates are identical this year and next, her or his actual number of operative successes need not be the same this year and next – owing to inherent variability and despite constant ability.[6]

There is no point telling the surgeon to try harder. There is no point setting a target for the number of successful operations. There is no point insisting on a written plan. In these circumstances, despite the best efforts of a skilled surgeon, there is always going to be a degree of variation. Stick to Rule One.

However, some processes can be influenced. Take waiting times in police station front offices, for example. Whilst it is always going to be impossible to precisely predict the demand at any given time, by understanding the current demand profile (i.e. main types of demand, peak times, peak days, etc), it is possible to estimate what type of resources are going to be required most, and when.

Straightforward actions could include ensuring that sufficient front office staff are available at peak times, including staff who are able to resolve as much of the predictable demand[7] as possible at that first point of contact. By plotting demand data before and after a change such as this, the degree by which variation is affected will be apparent.

Police managers have a general duty to understand the variation in all processes within the system. This provides managers with the evidence required to make decisions about which processes can be most improved, and which are most affected by factors directly outside their sphere of influence. Exercising knowledge-based judgement about when *not* to interfere with a process is just as important as being able to identify and act upon a process that requires adjustment. Therefore I argue that the funnel

---

6   Bird, *et al.* (2005) pp.24-25
7   Seddon (2003), p.149

experiment reveals important lessons about the dangers of tampering, which are as relevant to the policing environment as any other.

Anti-Tampering Devices

Those willing to adopt a systems-based alternative to traditional methods of management need to be aware of the likely reactions of those managers who don't understand it. As so much of the systems approach is counterintuitive, it is easy for doubters to believe that it simply doesn't make any sense. Confronting accepted management practices or questioning whether you, as a manager, have inadvertently made things worse for years takes courage and may well be a little frightening. This is normal. Stay with it and emerge stronger at the other side! Do you remember the playground adage that if you accidentally swallowed chewing gum it would wrap around your lungs? When it happened to me I was worried at first, but then the fact that I didn't die reassured me that it was a myth.

One predictable response of critics is that by not instantly changing aspects of the system (as in Rule One), the police are passively accepting something that is unacceptable and must be addressed. Take, house burglary for example. It is a serious crime and one that every police officer wants to tackle. There's nothing better than catching a burglar. If, however, the rate of burglaries across a large police division is relatively stable and there are no patterns, then for the sake of the whole system it is better to adopt a dispassionate, objective stance and maintain the 'keep calm and carry on' approach of Rule One.

There are, however, two important caveats to this. The first is that Rule One is not the solution, merely a starting point. Just because the burglary rate is in statistical control, this does not mean that burglaries are acceptable. The optimum burglary rate is always going to be zero. Whether or not this can ever be achieved, especially in a large area, is debatable, but the magnitude of the challenge should not prevent us from trying. 'Aim for the stars and you might hit the moon', as they say. In any case, striving for perfection is far better than aiming for any arbitrary man-made target.

It will be counterintuitive and unsettling for traditional police managers not to react when two or three burglaries are reported in the same locality. The natural reaction is to want to do something but it is better to stick with Rule One whilst devising a 'whole system solution' based on evidence, rather than to react without considering the data. We know now that opting for any of the other three rules makes the situation worse. Once the data have been evaluated and the facts are understood, only then is it time to do something differently. Such a measured and considered response far outstrips the short term benefits of the standard reaction of moving resources around or demanding written plans.

By moving resources without understanding the problem, management will at *best* be 'flattening a bump in the carpet', only for another bump to appear somewhere else. The new bump may be larger as a previously well-contained crime problem on another part of the division erupts there instead. Suddenly, as a result of reacting to two or three unrelated burglaries (different times of day, different days of the week, different property stolen, different everything), management opens a can of worms resulting in a crime spree of fifteen offences elsewhere. This is a good example of sub-optimisation; i.e. optimising one part of the system at the expense of other parts of the system, and ultimately at the expense of the overall system. The net result here is that good (and necessary) work in another part of the division is undone, in return for negligible benefits (if any) at the new location, plus an overall increase in the burglary rate across the whole division. Nice work, management!

The second caveat to raise in response to any accusation that Rule One is a defeatist, passive option is that nothing about it precludes any of the usual investigative activities that occur following a report of a burglary. The crime will still be recorded as such, officers will still attend the scene, CCTV will be viewed, fingerprints will be dusted for, witnesses will be spoken to, and any information about the identity of the suspects will still be acted upon. Likewise, where proper analysis unearths patterns of offending behaviour or a genuine 'hotspot' of offending in a small area, then these avenues can still be explored. Rule One does not stop any of this from happening, nor should it.

The decision about how best to respond to burglaries (or any other crime) must be based on an understanding of *all* relevant factors. If viable lines of enquiry exist, these will be pursued anyway and quite rightly so. If no immediate lines of enquiry exist but there is information suggesting that evidence-based deployments may be fruitful (for example, houses in a particular street are being targeted on a nightly basis between 10pm and 11pm) then it is clearly appropriate to devise a policing response to this. If however, there is no evidence base for action and nothing more than raw data that tells us that there have been a certain number of burglaries, then it is wrong and counterproductive to react. In the absence of actionable lines of enquiry, check for signals on SPC charts; these should be the final, objective arbiter.

The Benefits of an Evidence-Based Response

It is critical that managers avoid the temptation to do something – anything – just for the sake of it. Organisational responses should only ever be evidence-based and proportionate. If in doubt, stay cool and revert to Rule One – understand what the data are telling you, then work to reduce variation if it is achievable and proportionate to do so. That is all. Interfering with the system or attempting to adjust it without knowledge generates adverse consequences in every case, regardless of the setting. These consequences range from not achieving the desired outcome to a perceived problem to apocalyptic destabilisation of the entire system, as in Rules Three and Four. Oddly enough, doing nothing is actually better.

Having said this, I certainly don't advocate resting on one's laurels just because a system or process is ticking along nicely. There is almost always scope for further improvement, but there are also considerations to be made about how much improvement is possible. These include cost implications, the extent of benefit that can be achieved by adjusting a particular process, the potential effects on other parts of the overall system, and how much of a priority it is at that time. Managers seeking organisational improvement should focus effort on those processes that have greatest impact on the system, paying particular attention to how they affect service delivery and organisational purpose. Processes that exhibit wide variation or are not in a state of statistical control should also be prioritised. This will achieve maximum benefit for the organisation and, more importantly, the service user.

In applying the lessons of the funnel experiment to policing, the most important consideration is to ensure that responses are proportionate and only ever occur following an assessment of the evidence base. I have devised the following diagram to illustrate this:

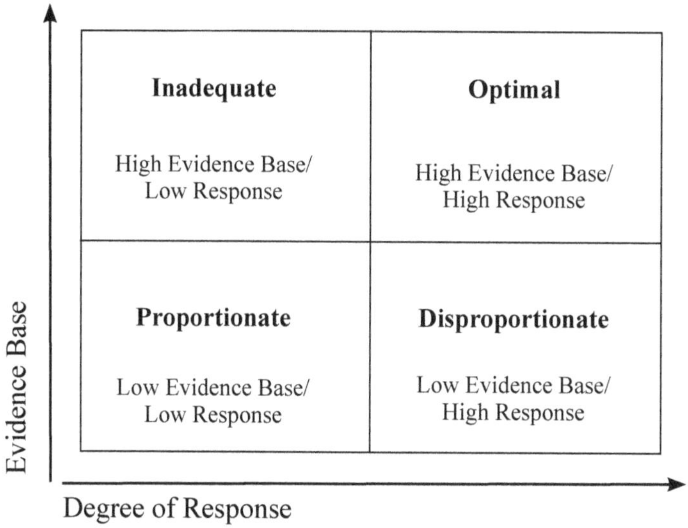

Figure 4.5: Evidence-Based Response Model

This model comprises a simple typology which demonstrates the importance of balancing the evidence base with the degree of response. As the evidence base grows, the justification for initiating an operational response grows proportionately with it. For example, the lower left quadrant (Low Evidence Base/Low Response) represents a situation where there is limited information about a perceived problem. The most appropriate and proportionate response would, therefore, be relatively restrained, only growing as the evidence base grows. If the evidence base remains limited, this should restrict the degree of response.

The upper left quadrant (High Evidence Base/Low Response) shows a situation where despite a high evidence base (perhaps the existence of actionable lines of enquiry, coupled with clear signals on SPC charts), the response is unduly limited. (It may well be that this situation has occurred because resources are inappropriately deployed elsewhere.) This quadrant represents an inadequate response to a genuine issue.

The upper right quadrant (High Evidence Base/High Response) reflects a situation where an appropriate response is initiated as a solution to a problem, based on sound evidence. This is the optimal response, focusing resources correctly towards a genuine issue that is validated by evidence (typically 'hard' information, SPC data analysis, or better still, both). This position is the most effective in actually solving the problem, plus it ensures resources and effort are only deployed to this degree when it is appropriate.

The lower right quadrant (Low Evidence Base/High Response) is the one that is fatal to the system. This is where Rules Two, Three, and Four live, along with numerical targets, knee-jerk reactions and all manner of other unspeakable horrors. Here we see the spectre of disproportionate reactions to perceived problems that are either not there or do not come with an evidence-base that we can use as a foundation to formulate an appropriate response. As outlined above, these baseless reactions drive waste into the system, prevent tractable issues elsewhere from being addressed, and cause inefficiency and instability to thrive. The activity in this square is, therefore, classed as disproportionate.

The Evidence-Based Response Model in Action

Below, we see the Evidence-Based Response Model in operation:

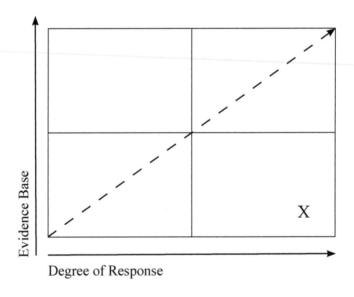

Figure 4.6: Evidence-Based Response Model – optimal balance

Here, the titles of each quadrant have been removed for ease of viewing, although they remain the same as before. The diagonal dashed arrow represents the optimal balance between the extent of the evidence base and the appropriate degree of response. (Note that this is not intended to be a mathematically accurate depiction: the angle of the arrow is representative only – the relationship between evidence base and response will depend on the type of problem encountered. Even within each quadrant there will be variables. Also, the dashed arrow may not be linear in every case, and the proportions between the factors may vary.)

The arrow in this model expounds the simple notion that as the evidence base increases, so does the justification for a greater response. Deviation from the path plotted by the dashed arrows represents increased waste and failure to address the problem. The 'X' in the lower right quadrant (Low Evidence Base/High Response) represents a disproportionate operational response to a problem that is not supported by evidence. This corner of this quadrant is the area that robs deserving evidence-based priorities of their rightful levels of resourcing. It is responsible for drawing resources away from genuine actionable issues in other areas, and is often the reason for inadequate responses in the top left corner of the High Evidence Base/Low Response quadrant. As the reaction at 'X' is not evidence-based it is unlikely to achieve anything, plus it is guaranteed to adversely affect other parts of the system.

From a Model to a Flowchart

In order to demonstrate how managers can formulate an evidence-based response to an apparent crime series, I have devised a simple flowchart. It operates by using a series of tiered filters that identify key areas for consideration when making an objective assessment of the opportunities that exist to tackle an issue. It provides guidance not only on what is actionable but also on the degree of response that is appropriate, given the nature and weight of the evidence base. The flowchart also starkly highlights occasions when there is insufficient evidence to justify a reaction at all. Used in conjunction with the Evidence-Based Response Model, the flowchart will prevent inappropriate knee-jerk reactions to perceived crime problems.

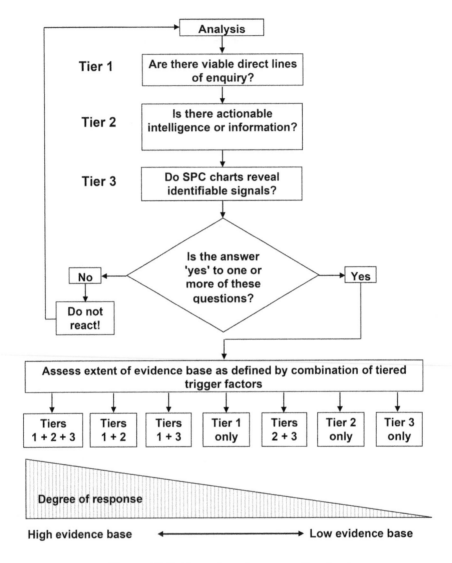

Figure 4.7 Evidence-based response flowchart

Using the flowchart is straightforward – simply start at the top and work your way through the three hierarchical tiers, which portray the greatest opportunities for addressing a crime problem. The first tier question, "Are there viable direct lines of enquiry?", relates to the most obvious opportunities to solve a reported crime or crimes; for example, is there any CCTV or forensic evidence, or can a witness name the offender? Direct lines of enquiry are both the most straightforward and effective actions that can be undertaken to identify and arrest offenders. It follows that the evidence base for formulating a response to the event(s) is likely to be solid, thereby providing a mandate for action with a realistic prospect of success.

It must be noted, however, that it is relatively uncommon for such actionable evidence to be available for a number of offences in the same area, at the same time (or for an identified series). It is more common that such evidence will only be present in isolated offences. For example, of 20 burglary offences in an area, only one or two may produce an identifiable fingerprint or CCTV footage. Nevertheless, if additional supporting information is available and considered in conjunction with this, (such as analysis that identifies common factors amongst the 20 offences) the evidence identified at Tier One is the most logical and productive starting point for an investigation into other potentially linked offences.

The second tier question (regardless of whether or not there are direct lines of enquiry) is, "Is there actionable intelligence or information?" This refers to any intelligence that could trigger a productive police response, such as an anonymous call stating, 'Joe Bloggs is committing burglaries in the town centre and hiding the stolen property in his shed'. This type of intelligence (despite not being 'direct' evidence) is still a good first step, especially if it is corroborated by similar intelligence reports from other sources. It may lead to the execution of a search warrant or provide an evidence base that justifies extra patrols in the area concerned. This tier also incorporates officers' local knowledge and other information gleaned from police data systems; for example, maps that plot where crime is most frequent, or data that identifies peak days or times that offences have been committed. The second tier, therefore, involves consideration of information that may not provide a direct opportunity for making an arrest, but which often generates actionable opportunities.

After considering the questions posed at the first two tiers, regardless of whether the answers are positive or negative, we move onto the third tier. This involves looking at SPC charts and asking, "Do SPC charts reveal identifiable signals?" For the sake of argument, relevant SPC charts in a crime analysis context could be those that plot data relating to the number of recent burglaries in a particular area. As discussed previously in this book, the idea would be to understand the data and to look for any of the recognised signals. If there are signals, or if either (or both) of the first two questions produce a positive answer, then the next stage is to assess the extent of evidence available on which to base a response.

If the answer to all three questions is 'no' then there is insufficient evidence on which to justify taking action. Such a move would be pure tampering and would be an example of the 'Disproportionate' quadrant of the Evidence-Based Response Model. Any activity will be based on nothing more than guesswork and will ensure that waste is driven into the system. In these circumstances managers should not react but constantly review the situation and reassess the possibility of initiating an appropriate response if the potential evidence base improves (e.g. fresh information suggests who may be responsible for the burglaries).

Assessing the Extent of Available Evidence

After working along the flowchart through the three tiers, we come to the final stage where the extent of evidence is assessed to ensure that any response is proportionate. If one or more of the questions posed within the three tiers is answered with a 'yes', then we will have progressed to this lower portion of the flowchart that shows the various permutations of possible outcomes.

Of the possible combinations, the strongest combination is where there are viable direct lines of enquiry (Tier One), in conjunction with actionable intelligence or information (Tier Two) and where SPC charts reveal identifiable signals (Tier Three). The combination of three 'yes' answers indicates a high evidence base that justifies a response. (This is equivalent to the 'Optimal' quadrant of the Evidence-Based Response Model).

Conversely, if there were no obvious lines of enquiry, no actionable information, and just a signal on an SPC chart, this might warrant a much-reduced response, if any. (This is equivalent to the 'Proportionate' quadrant of the Evidence-Based Response Model.) In the event that the cause of such a signal could not be traced, then the appropriate police response should simply be to stay alert.

The various permutations are arranged at the bottom of the flowchart, in an order based on the extent of the evidence base they generate. The further to the left a particular combination is situated, the greater the mandate for a response, and *vice versa*. In reality, the various combinations may exhibit a degree of overlap, but any combination that includes a positive response to the question at Tier One will tend to increase the evidence base and therefore position that combination towards the left. At the opposite end of the scale (to the right of the 'Tier Three only' box) there exists the barren wilderness where there is no evidence base to react to at all. If the user answers 'no' to the questions at all three tiers then there is no evidence base to justify a response. In these circumstances, stick to Rule One.

Although the tiers are positioned sequentially, it is entirely feasible for the actual analysis to start at any level. Indeed, it may be the discovery of signals on an SPC chart (Tier Three) that triggers the requirement to look deeper into crime patterns (Tier Two), leading to the discovery of a direct line of enquiry (Tier One). The important thing to remember is that all three tiers must be examined to reach a comprehensive assessment of the evidence base.

The flowchart acts as an independent arbiter of the evidence available in a given set of circumstances. It enables managers to conduct an objective assessment of the facts and devise appropriate operational responses. By looking at the facts in this way and applying the typology of the Evidence-Based Response Model, it should become clear when and to what degree it is appropriate to act.

After the Theory Comes the Application

To contextualise the application of the Evidence-Based Response Model and the accompanying flowchart, have a look at this example:

A vehicle crime review identifies that six cars have been broken into on a large housing estate during the course of a month. Each individual offence would be investigated as a matter of course, which may unearth viable direct lines of enquiry to build an evidence base. The next step is to see if any additional information reveals a pattern, such as the method used to break into the cars, whether certain types of cars were targeted, whether the offences have occurred at a similar time of day, whether anyone has been recently arrested for vehicle crime in the area, and so on.

These considerations are entirely proportionate, and may identify actionable information such as the discovery that all the offences occurred between 8pm and 8.30pm on two unlit pub car parks in one part of the estate. This would provide the evidence base to consider a targeted policing operation between these specified times at the locations deemed likely to be targeted. Likewise, a recognised signal on an SPC chart that plots vehicle crime on the estate would indicate something had changed about the crime rate that warrants closer attention. This combination of factors would position the response in the Ideal quadrant of the Evidence-Based Response Model. (Using the flowchart would produce the strongest combination of factors; i.e. positive responses to the questions at Tiers One, Two and Three, thereby justifying a response predicated on a high evidence base.)

Conversely, if all investigative routes had been fruitless, there were no similarities between the offences, and SPC chart analysis revealed only common cause variation, then it is absolutely wrong to tamper with the system. Any subsequent demands for written plans (how can you plan when you have nothing on which to base your plan?), routine reporting of activity (more writing) or holding people to account, are not evidence-based, nor proportionate. Without the evidence base to justify deviation from Rule One, all other forms of blindly adjusting the system are examples of Rules Two, Three or Four. This is guaranteed to harm the system, whilst spectacularly failing to address the perceived problem. Such reactions are squarely sited in the Disproportionate quadrant.

More Examples That Will Make You Weep

Other examples of management-initiated activity that sit around the 'X' in the Disproportionate quadrant at *Figure 4.6* are:

Mobile Phone Theft

Senior managers instructing officers to visit every school in a huge area to deliver a centrally-produced one-size-fits-all presentation about mobile phone robbery prevention within the next three days. No one has considered:

- o Whether the local crime profile includes a significant number of mobile phone robberies
- o Whether a significant proportion of locally-reported mobile phone robberies involve school-age victims
- o How many schools need to be visited
- o Whether local officers have capacity to achieve the task within the time scales
- o Whether the schools actually want the input, or have capacity to fit external presentations into their schedule at such short notice

o   Any alternative method of getting the message across; for example, circulating the presentation electronically to the schools for teachers to deliver it to students (if they wish to)

o   What the effect will be on the other priorities that local officers are expected to manage.

Theft of Lead Flashing

During a daily management meeting, where the last 24 hours' crime reports are reviewed, a theft of £35 worth of lead flashing from a roof is discussed. There are no witnesses, no CCTV and no forensic opportunities. If anyone had thought of looking at this offence type on an SPC chart it would also be apparent there are no signals. Despite this, there is a resolve that 'we must do something!' (This resolve is good, as the police are supposed to tackle crime, but resolve that is devoid of method does more harm than good. Stay cool and stick with Rule One.) During the discussion, someone mentions that there have been other thefts of lead recently within the borough. This results in an instruction from senior management that:

o   The divisional crime analyst must produce a detailed profile of lead thefts

o   Each sector must produce a written plan explaining what action local officers will take to address lead thefts

o   An internal electronic task system requires officers to regularly enter information that records what they are doing about lead thefts

o   An instruction is issued to visit similar buildings that have lead on their roofs and issue crime prevention advice (you've guessed it – there are hundreds!)

o   An instruction is issued for officers to visit scrapyards to inspect them for stolen lead (stolen lead looks the same as legitimate lead);

o   Management demand results and an update within a specified time period, with individuals being warned that they will be held to account, of course.

Report Writing

Management develop the impression that some crime reports for burglaries are completed to a poor standard by attending officers and introduce an overnight policy that no frontline office can record a burglary offence without their work first being scrutinised by a CID officer. Management's intention is to drive up standards, but no one knows what the extent of the perceived quality problem is – there is no data. No one has looked to see if there is an evidence base for this move, or whether it is a classic 'finger in the air' moment. If there really is a problem, is it associated with particular officers, teams or supervisors? Does the same problem extend to crime recording for other types of crime, such as criminal damage or theft? No one knows, yet management forge ahead with the policy, which has the following effects:

- o   Frontline officers feel disempowered, particularly those who are confidently able to identify what constitutes an offence of burglary
- o   Supervisors feel undermined, as the policy removes their authority to supervise their own officers when dealing with burglaries
- o   Victims of burglary are subjected to delays, as the frontline officer who attends their burglary is unable to finish off the paperwork and give them a crime number to pass to their insurance. This also perplexes these victims and can cause them to suspect that the attending officers may not be competent at their job
- o   The whole recording and investigation process slows down; the CID officer will often have to ask the attending officer (and/or the victim) the same questions that have already been asked. This causes delays and unnecessary duplication
- o   As the crime papers cannot be entered onto the electronic crime system until a CID officer has endorsed them, this causes further delays. CID officers are not always around at 3am so these burglary offences will not appear on crime data records for one, two or possibly even three days after the offence. This makes it difficult to identify emerging trends and plan accordingly. Guess what – sometimes the papers are accidentally misplaced, so the victim will have to be revisited, and further delays ensue. I've known it happen – it's embarrassing.

The standing joke is that officers and supervisors, who have many years of experience and who may even have spent part of their career in CID, cannot record a burglary offence, yet a relatively inexperienced officer who is on a short term attachment to CID can. It is ridiculous.

The Policy Roulette Wheel

A slight variation (no pun intended) on tampering is what I call the 'policy roulette wheel' approach. This is where priorities are decided and resources moved around to concentrate on particular aspects of policing, based not on geography or perceived crime rises, but themes. Thematic tampering occurs when management decides to prioritise whatever type of issue is in vogue at the time; either as the result of a high profile incident, or simply because it seems like a nice idea.

Thematic tampering can also occur simply because management decides that a particular issue should become a priority for the next few weeks. It can manifest itself in seasonal campaigns, such as anti-drink-drive campaigns at Christmas, or operations to tackle off-road motorbikes during the summer. There is nothing wrong with such campaigns, but management needs to appreciate that resources are finite and whilst one worthwhile cause is being targeted, others may become neglected. It is also important to consider that drink-driving occurs all year round so there is a risk that the focus may be lost if it is only prioritised at particular times of year.

Other examples are highly publicised force operations that choose one offence type, such as robbery, then plough resources and attention into exclusively tackling that for a few weeks at a time. These monthly, weekly, seasonal or unpredictable changes in priorities are symptomatic of the policy roulette wheel approach. The point here is that if prioritisation is not evidence-based, then priorities may as well be decided by spinning the wheel.

Figure 4.8 Policy roulette wheel

All the themes in *Figure 4.8* are deserving of police attention, but the roulette wheel approach is fatally flawed. It does not take into account any evidence base that would justify a change in tactics and is incapable of striking the right balance between multiple priorities; indeed it fosters an adversarial culture amongst advocates of individual policing issues, where one theme 'wins' at the expense of others. This reduces the flexibility and effectiveness of the policing response, as well as cooperation between individuals and departments. This is a classic example of sub-optimisation that always damages the overall system.

There is a further side effect when offences are considered in isolation. Robbers, for example, can commit other types of offences, such as car thefts and assaults, but this will not receive the same attention whilst the pressure is on to concentrate on just one type of offence. In my experience, criminals do not tend to recognise boundaries, thematic *or* geographic.

Another drawback is that switching focus from one priority to another on a regular basis causes confusion at ground level. This situation is described by one Constable who participated in the research for this book:

> "Knee jerk priorities are common-place. This week it's ASB, next week its metal theft, then dwelling burglaries and so on. We will receive highly focused patrol plans and default areas to spend our time in dependent on what has happened in the last seven days".

A Sector Inspector, who also took part in the research, described the effect of management interference as follows:

> "I consider myself to be a pretty competent individual and good at my job. I know my area and its crime patterns. I'd like to think I'd be trusted to deploy my officers accordingly, but usually the senior management bombard us with priorities and dictate where and how to post officers. Often these 'priorities' bear no resemblance to what is actually required on the ground. It's frustrating for my officers, especially as they know what the issues really are, plus, as an experienced manager, I find it incredibly disempowering".

There is sometimes very little scope for local interpretation, adaptability or the application of professional judgement; this results in a one-size-fits-all approach that guarantees sub-optimisation. It is the thematic equivalent of departments operating as individual units, i.e. in silos.

Management would do well to remember that priorities should only ever be founded on a verified evidence base. If analysis indicates the likelihood of a seasonal increase in burglaries during the run-up to Christmas, it makes absolute sense to devise a policing response to this. The caveat is that management also needs to appreciate that focusing effort on one particular area (thematic or geographic) will result in diminished attention elsewhere. If this decision is evidence-based then it is the right thing to focus attention on the new priority. Whilst the decision will need to remain under constant review, this type of evidence-based decision-making reflects a mature and realistic attitude to resourcing.

As we have discussed, not everything can be a priority and it is just as important to carefully review existing priorities as it is to properly select new ones. Managers need to be rigorous in deselecting former priorities (subject to the evidence base) in order to create the space for appropriate fresh priorities. Unfortunately, what often happens is that priorities are constantly loaded on top of each other – 'everything that was a priority stays a priority forever' – and it becomes impossible to effectively tackle *any* of them.

Operational officers bear the brunt of this indecisiveness, and the frustration caused by multiple competing priorities is evident across police forces. One Constable made the following observation in the David Copperfield book, *Wasting More Police Time*:

> *"Everything is a priority nowadays... out come the emails with graphs, charts and spreadsheets seeking to identify how the priority is being 'addressed', constantly troubling us for results and action. How do I prioritise which priority takes priority over which other priority?"*[8]

Outdated priorities that are never removed generate waste (they still require reports for management about what action is being taken) and adversely impact on capacity. This is where the policy roulette wheel gets stuck and the system explodes.

Summary

This chapter has taken you through an adventure featuring funnels, theoretical models, a flowchart and a wheel. Building on the earlier chapters that emphasise the importance of understanding variation and interpreting data through the use of SPC charts, we have seen what happens when managers tamper with the system. Even if actual system design improvements are beyond the understanding or capability of managers,

---

8   Copperfield (2012) pp.177-178

just think how much better things would be if they could just resist the urge to interfere. Not imposing ill-conceived adjustments or baseless priority changes would be a significant improvement in itself.

As we have seen, well-intentioned meddling is just as destructive as other types of meddling. But, when adjustments are made on the basis of evidence, the system will improve, as if by magic. By understanding when to intervene and to what degree, managers will discover that instant opportunities for systemic improvements are pretty obvious. They will also understand the damage that is caused when action precedes understanding. Not tampering with the system is a simple and free option that can massively improve it. Think about that.

> Managers! If you don't understand the system or how to improve it, please just leave it alone until you do. You will make it worse.

CHAPTER FIVE

From Measurement to Management

So far we have looked at how police performance is traditionally measured. For the next couple of chapters we are going to stay with performance, but move from performance measurement to performance management. These terms are often used interchangeably, but performance measurement is about understanding and interpreting data whereas performance management is about managerial influence and direction. When performance management is proportionate and founded on purpose-derived priorities and measures, the knowledge gleaned from effective performance measurement can be used to enhance actual performance. This then fosters continuous improvement to the system and focuses attention on organisational purpose.

Sounds great, and it would be if it were always done properly. It's bad enough when performance measurement is done badly, but when performance management goes bad it can be little short of Armageddon. However, unlike the biblical prophecy, 'Performance Management Armageddon' is quiet, sneaky and insidious. It silently destroys organisational effectiveness and morale, and stifles any cohesive and meaningful learning. It replaces intelligent and evidence-based improvement with aggressive and caustic institutional self-destruction. You can tell I like it.

Performance management represents a seismic shift from the passive realms of just measuring performance to active intervention that is designed and intended to change behaviour. Common practices used by managers to 'improve' performance include management by objectives (MBO), SMART plans, management by results (MBR), audit and inspection regimes, annual performance appraisals, performance-related pay and numerical targets.[1]

These management practices are all perfectly capable of achieving exactly the opposite of what management intends. This is particularly true when numerical targets form part of the performance management

---

1   Deming (1994) pp.24-33

armoury; indeed targets pervade nearly all of these techniques in various guises, creating a culture of unhealthy competition and fear. For this reason, I am going to briefly examine some common performance management techniques individually before turning my attention to specifically explore targets in more depth.

Common Performance Management Techniques

In command and control organisations, the performance management techniques listed above are widely applied. Elements of some of them *can* be beneficial (e.g. inspection) as long as they are implemented proportionately, whereas the detrimental effects of other techniques (e.g. numerical targets) outweigh any perceived usefulness. We will now conduct a whistle-stop tour of some of these main approaches.

Management By Objectives

Management by objectives (MBO) pretty much does what it says on the tin. The approach involves setting clear goals for workers so that they can align their efforts with organisational objectives. Ideally these should be decided participatively rather than imposed on the workers, although it could be argued that the workers are at the mercy of an imbalance of power when it comes to negotiating with management about what their goals are going to be. Progress against the set objectives is then measured, with workers' performance being compared to the agreed goals[2] This method does provide clarity about management's expectations but is prone to many of the same deficiencies and risks that are associated with numerical targets.

MBO can also be applied departmentally and the performance of each is then judged against the goals. The intention is to create clear areas of responsibility and increase departmental or local managerial autonomy.[3] In principle, devolved responsibility and localised autonomy are consistent with systems theory but this is nullified by holding people to account and making comparisons between departments. MBO in this context causes sub-optimisation and interdepartmental competition, which increases silo working, reduces cooperation and damages the overall system.

---

2   Drucker (1954)
3   Odiorne (1965)

Don't Try to Be SMART

One common tool of MBO is the much-vaunted SMART method (Specific, Measurable, Achievable, Realistic, Timed). The SMART approach can, at first, seem like an attractive and structured option for encouraging progressive development but it is hamstrung by its dependency on targets, an inevitable by-product. SMART plans that I have seen tend to focus on numerical goals, such as to produce 'X' amount of outputs by 'Y' date, or reduce 'A' by 'B' quantity during 'C' number of weeks, and so on. The method is reliant on many assumptions and conditions that may be irrelevant or totally impractical in the circumstances.

For example, SMART assumes that:

- There will always be a precise definition of 'specific'.

In reality it is not always possible to nail down a precise definition that is understood by all parties and appropriate to the situation. (Deming's work on operational definitions[4] expounds the problematic nature of attempting to define 'specific' and I recommend reading his authoritative text.)

- It will be possible to accurately measure the thing being addressed.

Einstein had a sign hanging in his office that read, "Not everything that counts can be counted, and not everything that can be counted counts".[5] Enough said.

- The thing being measured has an aspirational future state that is not only desirable but also achievable; furthermore its attainment is realistic.

'Achievable' and 'Realistic' seem to be more or less the same thing in this context, although the 'A' in SMART is sometimes taken to stand for 'Agreed'. In any case, to decide in advance that something is 'achievable' or 'realistic' is to assume knowledge.[6] It also lends itself to creating an arbitrary target.

- Progress is capable of being measured through time.

---

4   Deming (1986) pp. 276-296
5   For this and other Einstein quotes see: http://rescomp.stanford.edu/~cheshire/EinsteinQuotes. html
6   Seddon (2008) p.105

Progress may not be measurable through time, plus the 'timed' element of SMART inevitably builds in time-based targets. These cause just as many adverse consequences as other types of numerical targets and should be avoided.

In SMART's defence, it encourages effort towards a clearly-articulated aim. The problem is that the approach is prone to the creation of arbitrary measures and sub-optimisation, and the strict target-based framework undermines the whole purpose of what it seeks to achieve.

Management By Results

Management by results (MBR) is a performance management method that is closely related to MBO. As with MBO, it is heavily reliant on objectives and measurement against predetermined standards, but has a greater focus on results and value for money. Performance indicators, monitoring regimes, comparisons against targets and accountability for results are central features of MBR methodology. The approach is particularly favoured in financial management and budgeting, where "The ultimate objective is ensuring that resources are allocated to those programs that achieve the best results at least cost and away from poor performing activities".[7]

This approach is widely considered to be an acceptable (and desirable) practice within many organisations in both the public and private sectors, and may at first appear to be very sensible. However, there are inherent drawbacks. A system of reward and punishment that allocates or removes resources from departments, depending on whether they 'achieve' results, once again encourages sub-optimisation and harms the overall system. Those departments which *most need* additional resources to meet their objectives may have them removed. MBR increases the risk of the sorts of unpalatable behaviours associated with target-driven performance management; furthermore, nothing about the approach fosters organisational learning or continuous improvement to the system.

In addition to this, the focus on measurement and outputs that is inherent within MBR can encourage managers to react to any apparent change in performance data, however inappropriate this might be ("There's more crime in your area this week than there was last week"). When managers react to everything as if it were a special cause (Mistake One – see Chapter Two) we are reminded of the problems associated with binary comparisons and tampering..

---

7   DAC Working Party on Aid Evaluation (2001))

Objectives, standards, results, performance data, budgets or any other figures never tell us the full story, especially if considered in isolation. Lloyd S. Nelson tells us, "The most important figures needed for management of any organisation are unknown and unknowable".[8]

For example, how do you measure morale or time saved, especially in a complex public services environment? Both of these are critical to an effective organisation, yet they are impossible to quantify. What about the victim of crime who, having received a prompt and sympathetic service from officers, tells five of his or her friends about how good the police were? (This is just as applicable to private industry – think of the happy customer who generates business through word of mouth and also becomes a repeat customer.) Conversely, what about the member of the public who thought the police were rude and unhelpful when they were trying to report an incident? Trust me, they won't just tell five people – it will be more like hundreds, for years to come!

Traditional performance measurement and management methods cannot capture or quantify any of these figures, yet they are crucial to understanding and improving service delivery and organisational effectiveness.

Audit and Inspection

Management hopes that defects and mistakes can be retrospectively identified and corrected through audit and inspection. As with other established management practices, audit and inspection are rarely given a second thought because they seem to be an absolute necessity. But is it better to have 'safety net' inspection procedures that find defects after the event, or is it better to ensure quality is present from the outset?

Audit and inspection regimes provide false security for management. For a start, there is no guarantee that they will be successful in catching defects or errors before they reach the next stage of the process or, worse, the last stage of the process when the customer or service user could suffer as a result. In policing, the interaction between officer and service user has often already taken place before any aspect of it can be inspected. Furthermore, the inspection process is not free. Auditors come at a cost and management should consider whether this is the best use of finite resources. For example if a common error is identified then it makes sense to address the *cause* of the error to reduce further incidences rather than

---

8   Deming (1986) p.20

simply continue to find them. Addressing the cause ensures that the product or service is of requisite quality from the outset.

If an inspection simply identifies problems and then sends them back through the same process for correction this does not actually improve the process – rework by definition is inefficient and does not contribute any value towards the purpose of the process. Maybe defects occurred *because* of the process in the first place. Unless the data from the inspection are used to understand *why* the errors occurred, then any opportunity for learning is missed and there will be no improvement of the process. Errors will continue at the same rate as before, and the inspection process will continue to find them at the same rate as before. Once the process is brought under statistical control, inspection can then be either significantly reduced or even dispensed with.

In systems terms, audit and inspection regimes do not generate any benefit for the service user or customer. An example of this is the amount of effort that goes into ensuring that police incident logs are classified correctly, under the terms of the National Standard for Incident Recording (NSIR).[9] NSIR dictates the exact closure fields required for different types of incidents so that the Home Office can monitor them. The benefit of accurately classified records is that a true picture of, say, anti-social behaviour can be recorded for analytical purposes. The downside is that the auditing that takes place to ensure compliance can be disproportionately burdensome and punitive.

Auditing occurs both externally (i.e. by the Home Office) and within police forces. Headquarters will audit local policing divisions on their NSIR compliance and then the results will often be compared with other divisions. This leads to comparative league tables, and people being held to account. Sometimes there are also compliance targets attached. The intrusive and coercive nature of such audits has led some local divisions to install someone to specifically review closed incident logs and to reclassify the incidents if there is a possibility of failing the audit.[10] Whether this becomes a full time job, or an add-on to someone's existing workload, it still represents unnecessary waste and adds absolutely no value to the experience of the service user.

---

9   Home Office (2011a)

10   West Midlands Police (2008)

In some circumstances, incident logs can fail the internal audit on a technicality, despite the police delivering an excellent service and achieving purpose from the perspective of the service user. Perversely, it is also possible to deliver a poor service and pass the audit. You have to ask yourself, "Who are we here for?" Personally I would rather fail an internal audit and know that the service user's needs had been met, rather than the other way round.

Apart from audits preventing people from doing something more useful with their time, their existence encourages a disproportionate focus on compliance with technical criteria instead of dealing with an incident and doing the right thing. Such regimes can cause unhealthy competition aimed at beating other departments' audit results, and result in friction between the auditors and the audited. Professor John Clarke of the Open University notes the effect that disproportionate inspection can have on morale and the feelings of mistrust that arise amongst those being audited. He states that the "high cost/low trust mix... (of a)...competitive, intrusive and interventionist mode of scrutiny creates potentially antagonistic relationships".[11]

The key to effective audit and inspection is *proportionality*. It may be appropriate to incorporate inspection into high-risk processes, such as the manufacture of nuclear reactor components; indeed, it could be argued that there should be 100% inspection of all such items. Conversely, if the potential loss from a possible error is minimal, then the inspection process can be proportionately reduced or even stopped. Effort should be directed towards the process instead, to improve it and reduce variation. This is the *only* way to reduce errors.

Where audit and inspection regimes are disproportionate (or unnecessary in the first place), this drives waste into the system and reduces overall efficiency. Note that in his Fourteen Points,[12] Deming tells us to, "cease *dependence* on mass inspection" (my italics). Inspection regimes have their place but in service organisations they are never a substitute for getting it right in the first place. *Reliance* on audit and inspection misses the point. As Harold S. Dodge puts it, "You can not inspect quality into a product".[13]

---

11   Clarke (2003) pp.153-154

12   *op. cit* (pp. 23-96)

13   Deming (1986) p.29

Annual Appraisals and Performance Ratings

One widespread technique associated with traditional performance management is the dreaded annual appraisal that ranks workers against set criteria (or against each other) to determine whether their contribution is of a sufficient standard or quantity. These reviews go by different names, but common titles are Performance Development Review or Personal Development Review (PDR). Some appraisals link perceived levels of performance to pay, and if a worker is deemed less effective than his or her peers he or she may be refused access to pay increments.

In the police, I think it's fair to say that the PDR process attracts varying levels of credibility and importance. Some officers take the view that it is simply a bureaucratic yearly process which appears to achieve little, if anything. I once described mine as an annual request for an advanced driving course, which, following submission, lived undisturbed in a drawer in the personnel department for another year. I never got the course. Am I bitter? Of course not.

Where PDRs are not taken particularly seriously by managers at least they are relatively benign. In cases where they are used to reward or punish workers, we move swiftly into extremely unpleasant territory. The first thing to remember is that a group of workers operating in the same system who, theoretically, are equally capable and hardworking, will still exhibit a degree of variation in their output. This is true for machine operators who repeat the same action day in, day out; so consider how much more pertinent it is for police officers or other workers who handle a wide range of variable demand types.

Now, let's assume that the range of data relating to whatever outputs these workers produce is plotted on a chart. (In the police example, the first hurdle would be to define a meaningful measure of performance, of course.) It is likely that the plotted results would show 'normal distribution' or the 'bell curve' pattern.[14] In other words, most individual values in a range of data tend to naturally group towards the centre.

If we were plotting the average IQ of college students, for example, most people would be positioned towards the middle of the range of values, with a few very intelligent individuals towards one end of the distribution and those with the lowest IQs towards the other. If we were plotting the

---

14   For a succinct explanation of the main aspects of normal distribution, see: Niles (2012)

number of 'stop and searches' conducted in a given period, most officers would have conducted a similar (mid-range) amount, with a few officers conducting a lot that period and others conducting hardly any. It is also likely that if the same group of officers were assessed in the same way at a different point in time, different individuals would be positioned towards each extreme of the distribution pattern. This is because of variation.

Figure 5.1 is a typical 'bell curve'. Please note that not all bell curve distributions are exactly symmetrical or in the same proportions as this one – they may be positioned more to the right or left of the centre of the horizontal axis, or be flatter or more pointed than the one shown.

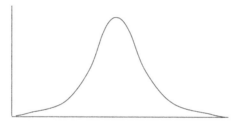

Figure 5.1: A bell curve

Let's imagine that the results of comparing workers' outputs are used to reward and punish those at the extremes. Suppose that management decree that the top 10% and bottom 10% should be singled out for special treatment. (Designating in advance that a proportion of a sample will fall into a particular category in this manner is known as *forced distribution*).

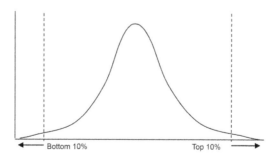

Figure 5.2: A bell curve with forced distribution (top and bottom 10%)

Below is another example of forced distribution where 50% of candidates must pass and 50% must fail a test, regardless of the volume of candidates or the actual number of correct answers. Some of the old police promotion exams used this method to determine success or failure. Everyone taking the exam always hoped the other candidates would be slightly dimmer than they were so they had a better chance of passing. If you encountered a particularly brainy crop of peers one year you knew it was going to be harder to pass.

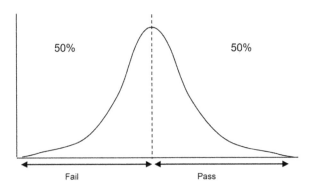

Figure 5.3: A bell curve with forced distribution (50% pass/50% fail)

Not the Laughing Policeman

Under forced distribution, individuals who have limited or no control over the system will be ranked and dealt with differently depending on what variation was doing at that time. Some will be praised; others stigmatised and labelled as 'poor performers'. Many companies have 'employee of the month schemes and I have even known of 'team of the month' awards. Deming argues that these schemes are essentially little more than lotteries that attribute praise randomly at the expense of team ethos and a cohesive system.

Conversely, those identified as 'poor performers' may be placed on action plans (or 'development' plans as they are sometimes euphemistically called). Apart from the stigma of this label, they may also be prohibited from progressing along a pay scale. Branded as failures, they will certainly be feeling demoralised and bewildered. Let's be clear that even in experimental conditions where the subjects have absolutely no influence on the outputs they produce, there *will* be variation that guarantees a bell curve, leaving some in the top 10% and others in the bottom 10%.[15] How can this be right?

In Tom Winsor's 2012 review into police pay and conditions, this very method has been proposed for adoption as part of the police PDR process. In his own words:

> ...if the annual appraisals of 100 members of staff are being moderated under a forced distribution system, the best ten appraisals must be ranked as exceptional, the next best 40 must be ranked as above average, the next 40 must be ranked as below average, and the bottom ten must be ranked as poor performers.[16]

How is it beneficial to automatically categorise 50% of the workforce as 'below average', or worse? (This will be recorded on people's personal files of course – who wants that on their file?) You will recall that we covered the folly of relying on averages earlier on in this book – there's always going to be about 50% of people/data/things below average! This can be seen by looking at stable SPC charts as well as the bell curve.

Winsor's recommendation goes on to exhort police managers to initiate unsatisfactory performance procedures against the 'least effective 10% of performers'.[17] This is despite the fact that some individuals who fall into the lower 10% bracket may actually be competent and performing at a higher rate than others in comparable work units elsewhere. It is entirely conceivable that some of the 'least effective 10% of performers' on one team may actually out-perform officers on another team who do not fall into the bottom 10%. How unfair is that? The result is that officers who produce comparable outputs on different teams are classified and treated differently. Some attract intense management scrutiny and could be prevented from progressing along the pay scale; others survive as merely 'below average'. Phew!

It isn't only the police who are being targeted by this sort of proposal. In June 2012, the Cabinet Secretary, Francis Maude, announced plans to inflict a similar scheme on civil service workers.[18] The proposals centre on private sector ideology to make the service 'more business-like', with annual appraisals that would identify the 'worst performing' 10% of staff

---

15   See Deming's 'Red Beads Experiment' and more on this theory in Deming (1994) pp.154-171

16   Winsor (2012) p.507

17   *ibid* p.637

18   BBC (2012) Francis Maude: Shake-Up 'Not Attack On Civil Service'. [Online] http://www.bbc. co.uk/news/uk-politics-18494800

through forced distribution. These individuals then risk being sacked if they do not 'improve' within a year. (The 'top' 25% of staff would be awarded a bonus – another perverse incentive, guaranteed to spark destructive internal competition.)

Couched in the predictable, emotive rhetoric of encouraging a 'better service' and 'enhancing accountability', the proposal was mute on the dysfunctional behaviour it would be likely to trigger. Oddly enough, even the minister seemed to falter on why 10% was chosen, admitting that the cut-off point was, "...by its very nature relatively arbitrary". (No, it's *totally* arbitrary!) Maude also affirmed the Government's intention to press on with the approach, despite its shortcomings and distinguished record of failure, announcing:

> It has often been tried. Far too rarely has it worked but we are going to have another go.[19]

That's the spirit. Has anyone thought there might be a *reason* why it has consistently failed in the past?

PRP: Performance-Related Pain

When pay is conditional on the results of performance appraisals, the spectre of Performance-Related Pay (PRP) raises its head. Winsor argues, "...that high performers should be paid more than those who perform adequately, and higher again than those who perform poorly".[20] How are these terms defined? How can police performance be measured effectively?

My fear is that easy-to-measure outputs such as numbers of arrests, detections, traffic tickets or intelligence submissions will assume primacy under this method and unquantifiable activity, such as being supportive and sympathetic to the family members of someone killed in a traffic accident, will not be brought into the narrative. Even when using arrests as a measure, it is worth noting that an arrest for drunk and disorderly (D&D) counts the same as an arrest for murder. The arrest for murder may have come about as a result of years of work and during that time there will have been hundreds of D&D prisoners scooped up.

---

19   *ibid*
20   Winsor (2012) p.499

Winsor argues that PRP schemes encourage 'improved goal-setting' (i.e. targets!) and 'strengthened appraisal systems', but acknowledges that there are negative consequences associated with performance-related pay, particularly:

- An unnatural focus on specific tasks

- Strategic behaviour ('gaming')

- Demotivation

- Lower job satisfaction

- An adverse effect on teamwork

- Lack of trust in the appraisal.[21]

In relation to incorporating forced distribution into the appraisal process, he refers to the controversy caused by its aggressive use within General Electric and suggests the following solution to combat its negative effects:

> Forced distribution does not have to be used as aggressively as it was used in General Electric.[22]

This is simply another example of what Russ Ackoff calls "Doing the wrong thing righter".[23]

Current Appraisal Models Ignore Systemic Considerations

Workers can only influence a relatively small proportion of the system that they are operating in. As discussed towards the end of Chapter Three, police officers are not helpless passengers who are unable to contribute towards individual performance but, in some circumstances, they can still only affect the 6% of special causes that Deming suggests. Is it right, then, that PDRs focus solely on workers as isolated 'components' driven by individual objectives rather than as contributors towards the overall system?

My answer to this is a resounding 'no', yet conventional management practice relies on yearly individual appraisals. Deming describes the effect this has on the workers:

---

21   *ibid* pp.489-490

22   *ibid* p.507

23   Ackoff (2004)

It leaves people bitter, crushed, bruised, battered, desolate, dejected…unable to comprehend why they are inferior. It is unfair, as it ascribes to people in a group differences that may be caused totally by the system that they work in.[24]

A major failing of the current model is that it rejects the notion that people have different skill sets. For example, on a police team you will have officers who are particularly good at sniffing out criminals, along with others who can act as a calming influence in volatile situations. There will be natural leaders within the group and others who are particularly skilled at devising intelligence-led operations, as well as some who are adept at building strong working relationships with partner agencies. That's what a team is all about. It's a system. All the components work together to achieve the overall aim. To then categorise individuals using perhaps just three ratings levels (for example, 'exceeds requirements', 'meets requirements' or 'needs development'), or to squeeze them into performance classifications using forced distribution is destructive and counterproductive. The only possible effects of these methods are demoralised individuals and damaged team cohesion. At best the system might stagnate; at worse it can be completely undermined and rendered useless.

In circumstances where an individual needs additional help and support, or if there is a genuinely lazy officer on a team with a bad attitude who goes round upsetting the public and colleagues, managers should address this directly with the individual concerned. A disruptive team member who is not challenged by managers can destabilise a team, especially when the others see no action being taken about his or her behaviour. This undermines team cohesion and can destroy confidence in the legitimacy of the manager. A one-size-fits-all yearly process is not the route for tackling this type of problem; it should be about intervening at the time to deal with the unacceptable behaviour and to rebuild team relationships.

As it is, the annual appraisal system is a powerful weapon in the hands of a manager who wants to ensure conformity in his or her team. If the manager judges individual effectiveness by the number of arrests, detections or stop and search forms, then guess what all but the strongest of subordinates will do to survive? Can you blame those who keep quiet and dutifully toe the party line under these circumstances? Those who do

---

24   Deming (1986) p.102

not 'get with the programme' can easily be marginalised and branded as displaying questionable commitment to organisational goals. A write up on their PDR, or perhaps an action plan, should do the trick – "This officer is not a team player/does not demonstrate commitment/submits a less-than-average number of stop and search forms" etc. Bye bye pay increment.

The current system of appraisals should be replaced with ongoing and open dialogue between managers and team members. Discussions should be about enhancing teamwork, not servicing an annual form-filling exercise that is based on blunt and rigid performance grading, or which involves classifications by forced distribution. This is divisive, destabilising and discourages teamwork – my *Three Ds* of performance appraisals. The aim of assessing performance in any context should be improvement of the system and attainment of purpose rather than a handy stick to beat the workers with. The inclusion of a punitive element within performance appraisals is not going to benefit anyone; neither will performance-related pay.

And so to Targets...

The performance management techniques we have looked at so far are capable of damaging the system in their own right, but nothing comes close to good old numerical targets. Despite the widespread belief that they were an aberration confined to the 1990s and early 2000s, let me assure you that they are very much alive and well today, in policing and beyond. The next section will begin to examine why targets are so central to performance management systems, and to consider some common misconceptions about their efficacy. I will then take you on a journey through some of the deep theoretical assumptions that underlie traditional performance management models and numerical targets in particular. The concepts explored during this chapter will then be expanded on in Chapter Six, where I will focus on the *consequences* of target-driven performance management. Overall, what I intend to demonstrate is threefold:

1. All numerical targets are arbitrary; in other words there is no reliable scientific method for setting them in the first place.

2. Target-driven performance management doesn't work. It damages the system, adversely affects behaviour, distorts outputs and damages morale.

3. The adverse consequences of target-driven performance management are unavoidable. No numerical target is immune from causing 'gaming' and other dysfunctional behaviour.

Let me begin by examining the case for the Defence. Proponents of target-driven performance management contend that targets enhance managerial responsibility, operational focus, and are a useful tool for motivating workers.[25] (This is based on the assumption that workers *need* to be motivated by some external lever. We will look at extrinsic versus intrinsic motivation later.) They believe that because they are so widely used and relied upon, it would be utter lunacy to abandon them – the alternative might be nothing short of anarchy.

Supporters agree that targets provide a means of setting clear goals, tracking performance, enhancing accountability and defining an intended organisational 'direction of travel'. They would say that workers need targets to keep them focused and that they are a necessary and crucial component of effective performance management. Any unintended consequences are the fault of bad or subversive individuals, rather than an inevitable by-product of the targets' existence.

Even moderate thinkers can fall into the trap of believing that targets are appropriate if certain conditions apply. For example:

*   The targets are designed carefully
*   The areas subject to targets are selected carefully
*   Only a few targets are set
*   Target-driven performance management systems are implemented properly.

At first these conditions may appear to be plausible safeguards. Even the most ardent supporter of target-driven performance management would not want to see a multitude of targets upon targets, burdensome reporting requirements, and organisational inertia that stifles effectiveness and harms service delivery. The problem is that whilst the four rules above may seem logical and attractive, they are all fundamentally flawed. By way of a quick rebuttal, the chief flaws in these pro-targets arguments are highlighted below.

*   Targets are appropriate if the targets are designed carefully.

---

25   See for example: Boyne and Chen (2006) pp.455-477; Capon, Farley, and Hubert (1987); Jennings and Haist (2004)

Some argue that it is possible to set targets using statistical methods.[26] The problem is that no one has ever devised a rigorous scientific method to do it; ultimately the 'science' amounts to little more than adding or subtracting a few per cent from last year's figure, or even just choosing a numerical value at random.

- Targets are appropriate if the areas subject to targets are selected carefully.

The assumption here is that so long as the right areas are made subject to targets, then targets could be appropriate. Whilst there is a case for selecting evidence-based performance indicators,[27] there is never a case for attaching a numerical target to the indicator.

- Targets are appropriate if only a few targets are set.

'Doing the wrong thing righter' anyone? Or, as John Seddon puts it, "Doing less of the wrong thing is not doing the right thing".[28]

- Targets are appropriate if target-driven performance management systems are implemented properly.

This supposition rests on the notion that workers are generally bad, unmotivated and need to be tightly controlled. The statement is also vague about 'properly' – what does this mean? Is it possible to implement target-driven performance management properly? Is there a known method for preventing 'gaming' and the other dysfunctional behaviours that universally flow from target-driven performance management systems? There will be more about this unpleasant phenomenon in the next chapter.

I don't believe that those who advocate or impose targets mean any harm. Why would managers question the methodology behind target-setting if it has been commonplace in their organisations for years? Certainly within the police, numerical targets have a long (and chequered) history. Senior officers have risen through the ranks surrounded by targets; both subject to them and responsible for applying them. Achieving targets aids promotion prospects, and this ingrains the targets doctrine further and encourages a vicious circle. For these managers, faced with no obvious alternative and no evidence of the destruction caused by numerical targets, it is easy to see why their application has continued.

---

26 See for example: Bird *et al.* (2005)
27 Heinrich and Marschke (2010)
28 Seddon (2008) p.106

It would be a bold move for a traditional manager to discard target-driven performance management if it was all they had ever known and trusted in. It could be quite an uncomfortable epiphany to realise that they had been wrong for all those years (and been rewarded for being wrong). Nevertheless, for a manager to embrace a new way of doing things, even at a late stage, would command well-deserved respect. It's never too late.

Why All Numerical Targets Are Arbitrary

One of the main tenets of the pro-targets argument that needs deconstructing is the notion that it can ever be possible to set a numerical target using a scientific or statistically robust method.

Here goes then… Even with the best will in the world there is no reliable method of determining where a numerical target can be set. It doesn't matter if a manager genuinely believes that a target will motivate staff, improve performance, or have some other undefined benefit, it just can't be done and the target will not deliver whatever benefit the manager hoped for. This is not the fault of the workers or the system – it's because it's impossible, full stop. Someone will work out a way of correctly predicting the National Lottery numbers ahead of an accepted scientific method of setting a numerical target.

Let's approach this conundrum from the perspective of a manager who wants to set a target. We'll stick with a police theme; let's say reducing crime rates. (We know that crime rates are influenced by a host of external factors, but for the purpose of this exercise they are as good an example as any.) The first step is to figure out a starting point from which to work. A natural starting point would be to understand what the current crime rate is. And an even better starting point would be to look at the crime rate using an SPC chart.

One of the most common (and arbitrary) target-setting methods is to pluck an aspirational figure straight out of the air without any understanding of data patterns or the capabilities of relevant processes. This method is easy – it simply involves choosing a figure to become the target because it sounds nice. "Wouldn't it be great to reduce crime by 10%?" Surely no one would argue against such a noble ambition (and anyone who questions the proposed 10% crime reduction target must be a heretic). This logic reminds me of a question that Deming asked of delegates: "Are you in favour of quality?"[29] No one is going to say 'no' are they?

A slight (but equally useless) variation on this theme is to look at what last year's figure was and work from there. Let's say that the total number of crimes recorded last year in a particular area was 10,000. An often-used method for determining the forthcoming year's target is to compare this figure with the year before that and see what the difference was between them. If the previous year's total was 10,300 crimes this would represent a decrease of 300 crimes between those two years, or 2.9%. Managers might therefore decide that this is an achievable reduction to aim for during the forthcoming year, and decide to set the target at 2.9%, or more likely 3% (3% sounds nicer, but both targets are still completely arbitrary).

What happens, though, if recorded crime two years ago was lower than last year? Say it was 9,850 offences, then compared to the 10,000 recorded last year this would represent an *increase* of 150 offences, or 1.5%. What now? Should managers set the reduction target at 1.5% to aim to get crime back to where it was, accept that crime is rising so try to keep a lid on it with a 0% reduction target, or (more likely) choose an arbitrary figure greater than 1.5% to aim for an overall reduction. Maybe 3% again? Even better, why not use the lower figure from two years ago as the benchmark, and set the reduction target at 3% below that?

It should immediately be apparent that these methods are based on nothing more than binary comparisons (along with a bit of blind number selection). Depending on whether total recorded crime two years ago was greater or lesser than last year, the actual decrease in the number of offences deemed acceptable for the forthcoming year's target is different. In the first case, by achieving a 3% reduction on 10,000 offences, this would amount to 9,700 offences (600 less than two years ago, or 450 less than the average of the two years combined). In the second case the target of 9,700 offences represents a reduction of 150 offences on two years ago, (or 225 less than the average of the two years combined). Which is right?

What if the average number of offences derived from three consecutive years was used as a baseline? Or four? Or every leap year? Is this better? Is it right? Which of the different projected amounts of crime for the forthcoming year is an acceptable level of crime to tolerate? Why?

---

29   Latzko and Saunders (2002) p.16

Stretching Credibility

Another related 'method' for setting targets occurs when managers question whether an apparently achievable reduction such as 3% is testing enough. This results in the creation of what is known as a 'stretch target'. No-one can claim that stretch targets are based on any logic whatsoever. The approach simply involves topping up the original target with a few more per cent, thereby creating a 'more challenging' target of 5%, 8%, or 10% again. No method, no science, just pure fantasy.

Target-setting has echoes of the funnel experiment, as the process involves changing an aim based on moving variables. It is perhaps the ultimate form of tampering. Despite this, I know that managers who endorse targets genuinely believe in them and implement them in the hope that they will improve performance. In the policing context, where numbers on charts often relate to significant events in people's lives, it is natural to want to reduce such occurrences by designing the organisation to be effective at achieving this. The problems begin when the quest is mired by well-intentioned but unscientific methods.

Target-setting also fails to take into account the capabilities of the system or available knowledge. It does not aid prediction or foster improvement. Furthermore, the mere presence of a target (or even a general goal, such as 'to reduce crime') is completely meaningless if there is no defined method for achieving it. Management has primary responsibility for acting on the system – simply setting an arbitrary target then sitting back and expecting the workers to achieve it is not going to work.

So what else can be done? Perhaps looking at SPC charts might tell us something. If a particular manager felt that the binary comparison starting point outlined above was an unsound approach this would be encouraging, but how could SPC charts help? Well they can demonstrate graphically why it is impossible to set a numerical target at all, despite (or maybe because of) the greater amount of available data to consider. This is illustrated below.

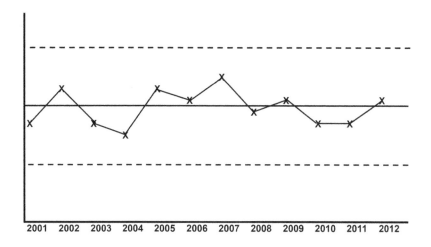

Figure 5.4: Crime rate SPC chart

This SPC chart displays yearly total recorded crime going back to 2001. (The numbers that would normally appear on the vertical axis are not important for the purposes of this example.) The first thing you notice is that the chart is in a state of statistical control; that is, data are stable and there are no signals. The manner in which the chart visually displays the data makes it apparent that there is no mileage in trying to set targets using binary comparisons to last year, or the year before.

In fact, you may as well choose any of the data points and make a binary comparison with that to determine the reduction target for next year. But why would 2012, or 2011, or any other of the yearly totals be considered a suitable benchmark to work from? All of these data points are subject to variation – there is absolutely no sense in choosing any of them as a potential comparator. Even if there were a basis for doing so, the second hurdle is calculating what the actual percentage reduction should be against this unstable 'benchmark'. How can anyone calibrate future performance against a moving variable?

As we have seen so far, the most relied-upon traditional method seems to be the 'finger in the air' approach. This approach is symptomatic of the irrational belief that we can influence future performance by picking a random snapshot of the past, making a binary comparison then choosing a random percentage to create a target. Whether you pick a 'good' year or a 'bad' year as the benchmark will influence whether your arbitrary numerical target is achieved or not. Effectively, what managers are doing by setting targets against any of these data points is akin to drawing a line in the sand to act as a boundary against the tide. The tide will ignore you!

Using an analogy from the funnel experiment (see Chapter Four), this is what would happen to the pattern of marble drops in Rule One if management designate the 'X' in the diagram below as a target.

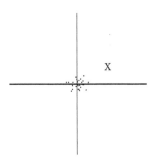

Figure 5.5: Funnel experiment – Rule One with target

The data doesn't know the target is there. The system will continue to produce outputs within the range of its capability so that no matter how many times the marble is dropped under Rule One conditions, it will always produce results within the same degree of common cause variation as seen above. The introduction of a target has absolutely no effect on the variation. If managers want the marble to fall closer to the 'X', or for variation to be narrowed, they will have to change system conditions. There is no point exhorting the workers to try harder, or telling the marble to roll towards the 'X'. Without systemic adjustment, the parameters are set in stone and disregard such follies as man-made targets.

Plan to Fail

A further peculiar quirk of defining numerical targets is the implied obverse of what the target aims to achieve. By this I mean that to state an intention to achieve a 5% reduction in recorded crime is to admit that we don't think we can do any better than this. In terms of detected offences (i.e. crimes solved), when the public see a detection target of 11% for vehicle crime, is this supposed to fill them with confidence? This is equivalent to saying that the police aim for 89% of vehicle crime to remain undetected. Or, if the police's public satisfaction target is 88%, this means we anticipate (and therefore by default, acquiesce) that 12% of the public will be dissatisfied with our service! Why would any organisation write acceptable levels of failure into their delivery plans?

Using the 11% detection target for vehicle crime as an example, why does anyone think that it is possible to precisely weigh the amount of effort required to produce an 11% reduction? Who puts in 11% effort when chasing a car thief? If management believe it is possible to achieve an 11% reduction that's great, but how likely is it that the actual reduction may turn out to be 10.9%, or 13% or 6%? If the organisation really could assume total control of vehicle crime reduction so as to be confident of achieving 11%, then why stop there? In fact, where would you stop? 15%, 25%, 80%?

Wherever the benchmark is set when striving to address crime, my view is that 100% is the only 'target' worth aiming for. Realistically, 100% may never be achieved for reasons already discussed, but what additional benefit is gained from designating arbitrary targets along the way? The danger of setting a target of 11% is that once it has been achieved the pressure is off and the focus that would have remained had the aim been 100% will vanish. If what managers really mean is that the target is *at least* 11% so as to encourage efforts to continue once the target is met, then why have the 11% target at all?

I almost admire the dogged determination of those managers who press on stoically in the face of this sort of simple logic, insistent that they can find a way of setting a numerical target despite all the evidence to the contrary. Imagine what that determination could achieve if it was put to more productive use. Anyway, whichever approach is chosen to set a target, we will now look at what becomes apparent when targets are plotted on an SPC chart.

How SPC Charts Can Show Why Targets Are Pointless

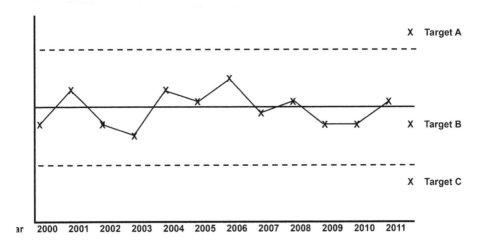

Figure 5.6: Crime rate SPC chart with targets

The above SPC chart shows three potential targets, 'A', 'B' and 'C'. Regardless of which magic potion was used to work out their value, each target is destined to be ineffective for the following reasons:

Target 'A' is set above the upper control limit, and if this chart represents the crime rate then it means that an unusually high volume of crime is acceptable. In reality, this target would never be set as it is far too easy to achieve! As the data point falls outside of the control limits, it is unlikely to occur anyway. For those who believe that targets motivate workers, the position of Target 'A' is such that there is no incentive to maintain current levels of output; this target could therefore even present a risk that performance will *deteriorate* to meet it. (Of course, if the chart were tracking detection rates, or some other 'positive' measure, then the opposite applies and the target would have been set unrealistically high.)

Target 'B' falls between the control limits so, as the process is already stable, sometimes it will be met and sometimes it won't, regardless of effort. How demoralising must it be to do your best, yet fail to meet an arbitrary target that is set somewhere in the range of expected variation? What about when individuals' targets are set in these circumstances – that some workers will be lucky and others won't, despite constant effort? This is an excellent way of demotivating the workforce and pitting people against each other. The overall system suffers every time.

128

Target 'C' is the opposite of Target 'A' inasmuch as it has been set below the lower control limit. If this target was a reduction target for crime rates, all the evidence points towards it being completely unattainable as it falls beyond the capability of the process. There is no point pressuring the workers to work harder. Crime will not be reduced to this degree unless the process itself is improved. Ordering staff to produce plans, report back about what they are doing, or holding individuals to account will make no difference to the control limits.

The only way to influence the crime rate data is to work on the process which, as we know, is the primary responsibility of management. Setting a target anywhere on this chart will not make the slightest bit of difference to the predictable range of data, as it does not affect (much less improve) the process one iota. The data don't know it is there! Furthermore, targets tell us nothing about the system parameters or predictable future performance. Put simply, the target-setting methods demonstrated above are irrational, and devoid of any logic or science.

The Sickness of Targets

By chance, I recently found an example of such a meaningless and arbitrary target in the local paper. In an article about police sickness rates, the *Staffordshire Newsletter* reported that, "Staffordshire Police has set a target of 8.5 days off sick for each of its employees in 2011/12".[30] Does anyone think this will make any difference? At the time of writing I haven't had a day off sick in ten years. In contrast, an officer I work with has been off sick for the last eight months, following a sudden heart attack and a quadruple bypass operation. I exceeded the target year-on-year; my colleague has blown his entire sickness 'quota' in one go, through no fault of his own.

How can such a target be meaningful to anyone? Do managers think that once an officer has accrued 7.5 days sickness in a twelve month period he or she will try a bit harder not to be sick for more than one more day? When management aggregates a team's sickness rates, all it takes is for one genuine case, such as that of my colleague, to obliterate the entire team's target, even if no one else has had a day off through sickness. Conversely, if unscrupulous individuals are intent on taking time off sick when they are not actually sick, then a management target of 8.5 days is not going to stop them. While we're at it, where does 8.5 days come from anyway?

---

30   *Staffordshire Newsletter*. 12th January, 2012 p.17

The $64,000 Question

Next time you are in a meeting where you are being held to account against a numerical target, throw this little hand grenade into the room:

"Why is that the target and how was it set?"

This question is guaranteed to elicit confusion, maybe even anger. No one will be able to give you a proper answer but at least the experience will have ensured your sanity remains intact for another day. Even better, your question might make people think. If you do get a response it will probably be along the lines of, "Because that's what the boss wants", or "Because it's in the plan".

Even when someone tries to set a target for all the right reasons this doesn't change the fact that it just can't be done. Furthermore, to base targets on the current output of a process is to admit defeat. It is like accepting that we can't do any better; that the process or system must already be at capacity. The fact is that the system or process is probably capable of a lot more, but is clogged up with waste. The only way to find out is to understand what the data are telling you and then work to improve the system. This approach is diametrically opposed to the traditional response of reacting blindly to common cause variation (tampering), berating the workers (coercion) and designating arbitrary numerical targets (superstition).

I reiterate that the only target worth striving for is 100%. Realistically, the police are never going to eliminate all crime or catch 100% of criminals for a variety of reasons, but that should not stop us aiming far beyond the artificial constraints of the arbitrary numerical targets we are subjected to. Inserting a random value into a range of data and designating it as a target has no benefit whatsoever. Ironically, managers could be pleasantly surprised to discover that by abandoning arbitrary numerical targets and adopting a systemic approach to performance management instead, a great deal more can be achieved than the paltry single-figure percentage adjustments they strive for.

> Managers! Take note: there is no known scientific method for setting a numerical target. Divert your efforts into something useful!

The Heart of the Matter

This next section is about the *why* of targets. Before we look at the consequences of target-driven performance management I think it is important to understand why targets are so favoured and what conditions they thrive in. In order to do this, I am going to start this section by posing three questions:

1. Why are targets such a prominent feature of performance management?

2. What are the underlying theoretical assumptions behind the established mode of performance management?

3. What does target-driven performance management tell us about organisational culture?

These questions are at the very heart of understanding why target-driven performance management is so pervasive. Once managers understand the theoretical assumptions that underpin command and control ideology, they can begin to appreciate why it is so damaging. It could even be the first step to acknowledging why the systems-orientated alternative is so much better.

To examine this more closely, here's a story from the Dark Ages, followed by some theory, then a history lesson, and then some more theory:

Principal Principles – Agency Theory

In mediaeval times the King wished to collect taxes and delegated the responsibility to the Lords of the Manor across the country in return for a proportion of the taxes collected. The Lords of the Manor then delegated the responsibility to agents to collect these taxes on their behalf. This meant that the Lords could concentrate on more important things.

At that time the exact population was unknown, and it occurred to the Lords that the untrustworthy agents might take the opportunity to pocket some of the taxes they collected, either by under-reporting the total amount of people taxed or by charging whatever they wanted and keeping the difference. For this reason the agents were closely monitored and required to produce detailed accounts of their tax-collecting activities.

This tale is an example of the type of arrangement that is known as a 'Principal-Agent' relationship. The principal is the one who delegates the work (and checks up on the worker), and the agent is the one who does the work in return for some reward. The theory that emerges as a result of the study of principal-agent relationships is known as 'Agency Theory'. A helpful definition is as follows:

> Agency relationships are created when one party, the *principal*, enters into a contractual agreement with a second party, the *agent*, and delegates to the latter responsibility for carrying out a function or set of tasks on the principal's behalf.[31]

The principal-agent model suffers from inbuilt disadvantages. It is impossible for the principal to know the exact amount of work the agent is doing, and if the agent also possesses greater technical expertise than the principal, this places the agent at a further advantage. For example, a mobile electrician could tell his boss that a particular wiring job cannot be done in less than four hours. If the boss does not have the same degree of electrical expertise, or is not in a position to watch the entire operation, he has no choice but to rely on what his employee tells him. The agent therefore has an advantage over the principal, caused by this imbalance of knowledge. In Agency Theory, this is known as *information asymmetry*. If the agent chose to do so, he could then use this knowledge gap to reduce effort or behave unethically without any real danger of being caught out by the principal. This condition is known as *moral hazard*.[32]

Some principals try to overcome information asymmetry by introducing policies that require large amounts of information to be reported to them about what the workers are doing. In policing, this often manifests itself in demands for written plans and task results that are routinely fed back to management. Managers do this because they feel they need to know about the minute detail of what workers are doing. The assumption is that, if this detail is not readily available, the workers must be up to no good, or at least not working as hard as they should be (i.e. moral hazard). Another tactic is to implement a barrage of audit and inspection to check up on levels of output, quality of work, as well as mistakes and defects.

Proponents of audit and inspection regimes believe that as workers know they are being monitored, they will work harder and make fewer mistakes. (Do you know anyone who goes to work with the intention of making mistakes? Me neither.) In really 'sophisticated' performance management systems, audit and inspection is often supplemented by reward and

---

31   Kassim and Menon (2003) pp121 - 139

32   For more on these specific points and Agency Theory in general, see: Van Slyke (2007); Caers *et al.* (2006); Stevens and Thevaranjan (2010) pp.25–139

punishment schemes and, in the worst cases, targets.[33] All are based on the assumption that externally-imposed carrots and sticks are important levers that can motivate workers.

These approaches ignore the possibility that workers may simply want to do a good job and are capable of feeling a sense of pride in their work. They also ignore the point that it is not the workers but the system that is mainly responsible for performance. As Deming points out, "The workers are handicapped by the system, and the system belongs to management".[34]

The principal-agent model is underpinned by the supposition that front line workers need to be controlled and require extrinsic motivation to do a decent job, and that individuals will always act in their own interests to the detriment of others, even if this is contrary to a prior agreement. Agency Theory is predicated on the notion that this type of behaviour is inevitable. (This argument is related to Rational Choice Theory, should you choose to delve further.[35])

Back to the Future

Fast forward a few hundred years to the 20th Century and not much had changed. The underlying model of organisational relationships was pretty much the same.[36] During the early 1900s, Frederick W. Taylor[37] conducted research into industrial working practices, which were based on methods similar to what we know now as 'time and motion studies'. He timed how long it took workers to complete a unit of work and compared individual workers' times against each other. This was in an attempt to calculate the optimum output per worker. His findings led to standardisation of working practices, output quotas, and reinforcement of what later became known as command and control ideology. Workers knew their place and managers became accustomed to controlling the activity of their charges through a mix of directives, measurement against standards, quotas, management reports and targets.

By the end of the 20th Century, this style of management was the unquestioned norm, particularly in the private sector, and from the 1980s onwards the devices of private sector performance management began to

---

33   See for example: Jensen and Meckling (1976); Walsh and Seward (1990)

34   Deming (1986) p.134

35   For more on the links between Rational Choice Theory and Agency Theory, see: Jensen and Meckling (1976); Albanese, Dacin, and Harris (1997a); Davis, Donaldson and Schoorman (1997) Davis, Donaldson and Schoorman (1997b)

36   Theory X and Theory Y resembles the principal-agent/principal-steward model. See Chapter 11.

37   Taylor (1911)

sneak across into public sector organisations. This was known as the New Public Management (NPM) reforms.[38] It was argued that many public sector institutions were unduly bureaucratic and inefficient and NPM would make the public sector more accountable and responsive. The aim was to make the public sector 'more businesslike' with the widespread installation of targets and other private-sector-style performance management alchemy, along with the notion of service users as 'customers', an emphasis on 'value for money' and a quasi competitive market ethos.

This transformation occurred despite well-founded reservations about the incompatibility of private and public sector cultures and purpose. For example, management expert Dr. Jim Armstrong argues cogently that the market theory on which the NPM reforms were based "...is not robust enough to embrace the full range of public sector activities such as governance and guarding public interest".[39] He also expresses concern at the effects of the myriad "... objectives, goals, framework documents, responsibility relationships, performance standards and outcomes"[40]. Most pointedly, he observes that the private sector model is imperfect even in its indigenous setting, so one wonders why reformers felt that its application to the public sector would be trouble-free. Whenever I hear the argument that public sector organisations should be made 'more businesslike' I always ask, 'Which business though?'

Despite these shortcomings, NPM reforms ploughed on, full steam ahead, and the police service was completely consumed by its ideology, as were many other public sector agencies. As the wholesale importation of private sector methods was a desperately ill fit for such not-for-profit public service organisations, reformers sought to enhance accountability through increased performance management instead. This has largely involved an extension of Taylor's blunt output-based measurement methodology into the complex policing world with its infinite variety of demand.[41] Round peg, square hole.

The study of Agency Theory and NPM reforms suggests that target-driven performance management is based on a sense of mistrust and the desire for managerial control. Metrics are used as a measure of productivity

---

38   For more on the NPM reforms, see: Hood (1991); Hood in Bekke, Perry, and Toonen, (1996) Hood (1998); Hughes (2003); McLaughlin, Muncie, and Hughes (2001); Pollitt and Bouckaert (2000).

39   Armstrong (1997) p.3

40   *ibid* pp. 6-7

41   Seddon (2003) p.31 and (2008) p.62 talks about the importance of designing the system so as to absorb variety.

and 'evidence' of efficiency. In public services, where profit is not the overarching aim of organisations, reformers have sought to instill quasi-market forces to drive performance and competition. Performance data is the currency, and we already know that simple inputs and outputs are easy to measure. Even in policing, where activity is difficult to quantify, these proxy measures of activity are seen by many as a barometer of legitimacy, demonstrating where taxpayers' money has gone and ostensibly heightening accountability.

It follows, therefore, that when the Principal-Agent model is the dominant theory underpinning organisational relationships, targets are considered to be a necessary tool for controlling the workers and motivating them.

Some Thoughts

The Principal-Agent construct is the dominant model within the British Police. Targets form one of the central pillars of the current mode of performance management because of prevailing organisational conditions; namely institutional mistrust and the assumption that workers require extrinsic motivation.

Notwithstanding the difficulties associated with quantifying police work,[42] the logic appears to be that once a simple performance measure has been identified (e.g. number of arrests per officer), then unless there is a target (or comparison between individuals, or both) the worker will be aimless and predisposed to underperform.

My view is this is not only wrong, but that it causes fractious relationships and disconnections throughout the system. It also generates unnecessary monitoring and measurement processes, as well as being counterproductive and damaging to morale. I'm reminded of one of Deming's perceptive observations that, "…if management stopped *de*motivating their employees then they wouldn't have to worry so much about motivating them".[43]

It's time to question the limits of accepted norms and push the boundaries. Who would have thought that someone could run a mile in less than four minutes, or that human beings would ever go into space? When the propeller-driven engine was at the height of aviation technology who could have imagined it would be eclipsed by the jet engine? Vinyl records and CDs? The list is endless. Progress is inevitable. Target-driven performance management has passed its sell-by date.

---

42   For more on the difficulties of quantifying outputs in the public sector generally, see: Caers *et al.* (2006); Pollitt (1999)

43   Neave (1990) p.200

Answer Sheet

Returning to the Heart of the Matter (p.131) I refer to the three questions that were posed and bullet-point my thoughts.

1. Why are targets such a prominent feature of performance management?

    - They have been applied for so long that target-driven performance management has become accepted practice.
    - They are easy to apply to things that are easy to measure.
    - They are consistent with the tenets of the Principal-Agent model.
    - They fit with the dominant NPM discourse.
    - They are seen as an effective tool for controlling staff.

2. What are the underlying theoretical assumptions behind the established mode of performance management?

    - Workers are lazy, dishonest and require control and direction.
    - People are extrinsically motivated rather than intrinsically motivated.
    - Targets are necessary to motivate workers.

3. What does target-driven performance management tell us about organisational culture?

    - Your boss doesn't trust you.

It's All About Trust

A recent conversation I had with a senior police manager went something like this:

> *Senior manager:* "I need a written plan."
> *Me:* "Why do you need it?"
> *Senior manager:* "So I know what your staff are doing about X".
> *Me:* "Why do you need to know?"
> *Senior manager:* "Because I'm a senior manager."
> *Me:* "Well I'm comfortable my staff are taking appropriate action about X."
> *Senior manager:* "But that's like you're trusting them to deal with it without asking for precise details."
> *Me:* "That's exactly what I'm doing."

CHAPTER SIX

Targets and Their Unintended Consequences

In recent years there has been a discernible shift in the public's opinion
of targets. With well-publicised examples of how they drive the wrong
sorts of behaviour and generate unnecessary bureaucracy,[1] it seemed that
target-driven performance management was also beginning to fall out of
favour with Government officials and senior policy makers. Gradually,
the extensive raft of public sector targets that had proliferated during the
darkest days of New Public Management (NPM) appeared to ebb slightly.
Some of them even disappeared completely.

In police management meetings, targets were seldom mentioned and
were less overt in performance documents. Senior managers spoke openly
about the drawbacks of target-driven performance management and,
instead, encouraged officers to 'do the right thing'. For a while it seemed
as though the policing world was becoming a happier, target-free place.

But don't be fooled. Targets have not gone away.

What This Isn't About

I want to assure you that this is not going to be a general moan about
performance management or measurement. The subject under scrutiny here
is purely *targets*. I believe that both priorities and measures are important
features of an effective performance management system.

Priorities are (or at least *should be*) intrinsically linked to purpose. If
we don't understand what the organisational purpose is, we cannot define
priorities and thereby ensure that effort is focused in the right areas.
Evidence-based prioritisation maximises the effectiveness of operational
responses.

Measures are also a critical component of an effective performance
management system. Once purpose-derived priorities have been identified,

---

1   A particularly powerful example was the scandal over quality of care at Stafford General Hospital. A series of inquiries found that targets had contributed to unnecessary deaths amongst patients.
See: Alberti (2009); Colin-Thomé (2009); Healthcare Commission (2009)

the next stage in understanding the system is to use measures to inform method. This should involve intelligently interpreting data drawn from the measures, using approaches such as SPC. The result is that knowledge is gained, enabling management to work on improving the system, and so the virtuous cycle continues. There is absolutely no argument against priorities or measures, as long as they are the right ones. It is *targets* that are the problem.

The Bad Old Days

Now that that disclaimer is out of the way, let's begin by looking at how the NPM reforms spawned targets and embedded them in the psyche of public sector organisations. During the height of what became known as New Labour's 'Targets and Terror'[2] regime of the late 1990s and early 2000s, targets were everywhere; overt, bold, demanding, all-powerful. Following the 1998 Comprehensive Spending Review, 366 national Public Service Agreement targets (PSAs)[3] were introduced, which included further tiers of 600 additional performance targets.[4] These dominated the public sector over the next few years and characterised the intrusive, interventionist mode of government control over the sector.

Targets set at the national level (such as PSAs) had the propensity to multiply exponentially as they descended through various levels and sub-categories on their way to the frontline. Broad, high level objectives routinely mutated into a tangle of confusing, contradictory targets at the operational level.[5] For example, one study produced evidence that national PSAs were converted to '…an average of 26 indicators per PSA' at the local level.[6]

During this period, no part of the public sector escaped the imposition of targets. In 2001, the Prime Minister's Delivery Unit (PMDU) was inaugurated to monitor and drive performance in around twenty key public sector targets.[7] Headed by Michael Barber, the PMDU reported directly to the Prime Minister, and was responsible for scrutinising public

---

2   'Targets and Terror' was a phrase originally associated with the Soviet regime of the 1930s, but was famously likened to the recent targets regime in the NHS by Bevan and Hood (2006) pp.517-538
3   See: James (2004) pp.397-419; Micheli and Neely (2010) pp.592-600
4   See: Chief Secretary to the Treasury. (1998a); Chief Secretary to the Treasury. (1998b)
5   See for example: Hood (2006) pp 515-521; Hood and Dixon (2010) pp.281-298; Jackson (2011) pp.13-26
6   Micheli and Neely (2010) p.597
7   Hood and Dixon (2010) pp.281-298

service performance against numerical targets and standards, publishing comparative data, and holding managers personally to account. Barber labeled the approach, 'Deliverology'.[8]

The police service certainly received its share of attention from the target-mongers. In 2002, the Police Reform Act empowered the Home Secretary to set annual performance targets for the police.[9] Forces were subsequently beholden to a range of numerical targets largely relating to the reduction and detection of crime, but also in a broad range of other areas, such as budgets and attendance levels. National targets were supplemented by force-level targets, which were supplemented by local targets, which were supplemented by team targets, which were sometimes then supplemented by individual targets. High level objectives would be published in force-level and local policing plans, and the exact numerical targets would look something like the following list, taken from an actual local policing plan:

- Reduce crime by at least 2%
- Detect at least 28% of offences
- Obtain at least 63 football banning orders
- At least 90% of non-emergency calls to be answered within 40 seconds
- At least 18% of police officers promoted to be female
- Detect at least 147 offensive weapon offences
- Detect at least 7% of graffiti offences
- Achieve at least 14.5 detections per officer.[10]

How did they come up with these numbers? No one knows.

When is a Target Not a Target?

The official line during the last few years has been that reliance on numerical targets is waning and there is a greater emphasis on officer discretion and common sense. Nevertheless, this apparent quiet retreat is not as encouraging as it might first appear to the untrained eye.

A couple of 'distraction techniques' have emerged, which appear to have been designed to shunt targets conveniently out of the spotlight whilst absolutely retaining them. Both methods are equally cunning, yet easy to spot once you know what you're looking for. They are:

---

8   Crace (2007)
9   Home Office (2002) Chapter 30
10   British Transport Police (2008)

1. Have fewer targets

2. Call targets something else.

The first technique is actually nothing more than simply doing less of the wrong thing. This sophisticated approach to hiding targets involves publicly decrying the multitude of numerical targets that the police have previously been subjected to, in favour of installing fewer targets; perhaps just one. Two Home Secretaries have used this method in recent years; the first occasion being when Labour's 'single confidence measure', was introduced following the 2008 Policing Green Paper. The then Home Secretary, Jacqui Smith, announced, "...*in future there will only be a single top-down target for police forces – on improving public confidence.*"[11] This target was subsequently rescinded in June 2010 by the Conservative Home Secretary, Theresa May, who replaced it with another single top-down target – 'to reduce crime'. During a speech in which she heavily criticised centralised targets, May declared:

> "*In scrapping the confidence target and the policing pledge, I couldn't be any clearer about your mission: it isn't a 30-point plan; it is to cut crime. No more, and no less*".[12]

Notwithstanding the fact that the purpose of the police service is not *only* to increase confidence or reduce crime (what about protecting vulnerable people, dealing with fatal road traffic collisions, delivering death messages in the middle of the night, searching for lost children, guarding murder scenes, mounting counter-terrorism operations, arbitrating in neighbour disputes, policing large demonstrations and football matches, providing security for Home Secretaries during official engagements, etc?), there are a couple of basic flaws in these attempts at creating a workable single target:

- Each of these 'single top-down targets' holds the police unilaterally responsible for something that is not totally within the service's ability to control i.e. public confidence can be affected by past experiences, the influence of the media, as well as varying degrees of understanding and expectations from the public about what the

---

11   Home Office (2008b)

12   Greenwood (2010)

police can or should deal with. Crime reduction, as we have seen, is also affected by numerous external factors such as substance abuse, economic drivers, and so on.

- It is pure fantasy to believe that such a broad aspiration 'to reduce crime' will ever be permitted to exist without tiers of numerical targets propping them up. If 'to reduce crime' is now the single national target, then the obvious question to ask is, by how much? Obviously, this is impossible to predict, much less set a hard numerical target for, but it won't stop it from happening.

The second technique to keep the word 'targets' off the public menu is to simply camouflage them as something else: 'milestones'[13] or 'headline goals',[14] for example.

The systematic misrepresentation of public sector targets applies to other agencies as well. I recently had cause to write to the Department of Health, following treatment in the Accident and Emergency (A&E) department of my local hospital. As ever, the people who work there seemed to be doing their best to help me, but just before four hours had elapsed I found myself at the centre of a flurry of activity and admitted to a ward for about an hour whilst an assessment was carried out. The doctor informed me that the only reason the assessment had been carried out on the ward rather than in the A&E department was because they "needed to get me out of there due to the four hour target".

When I subsequently raised concerns about this target with the Department of Health (DoH) and pointed out the dysfunctional behaviour it had caused, they pointed me in the direction of their shiny new range of 'clinical quality indicators', which, they claimed, were nothing like targets. I researched DoH guidance and found the DoH's four hour 'non-target' under the header of a 'performance management trigger'. It defines a time threshold for patients to be admitted, transferred or discharged from A&E, and reads as follows:

> A 95th percentile wait above 4 hours for admitted patients and with the same threshold for non-admitted.[15]

---

13 Collins (2011)
14 Brindle (2012)
15 Department of Health (2010)

Further into the guidance document I found this ominous little gem lurking:

A 95th percentile wait above four hours may trigger intervention...[16]

So...it's a 'clinical quality indicator' and not a target. Sounds like a target to me. Efforts at re-branding numerical targets by giving them a different name do not fool everyone; indeed some official documentation inadvertently leaves pretty blatant clues about the origins of 'milestones' *et al* and their similarity to traditional numerical targets. Look closely at the wording of another actual strategic policing plan:

The plan identifies a number of strategic priorities, which are linked to actions and milestones that ensure effective delivery. Measurement of progress will be through key performance indicators with challenging targets".[17]

Targets never went away. Although they may not officially exist anymore, they are so entrenched in police performance management culture that very few senior managers seem to be able to let go of them. In many cases, it is not just senior managers that cling to the target culture, but frontline supervisors as well. This is a terrible shame, and signifies the extent to which the rot has set in. Apart from the impossibility of scientifically setting a numerical target, every single numerical target brings with it a range of unpalatable side effects.

Targets Always Change Behaviour

Target-driven performance management always affects behaviour. This is evidenced by research and underpinned by theory, and we shall examine this first before looking at some real life examples. In a seminal paper on the effect of performance targets, Professors Gwyn Bevan of the London School of Economics and Christopher Hood of Oxford University argue:

Governance by targets rests on the assumption that targets change the behaviour of individuals and organisations.[18]

Supporters of target-driven performance management hope and believe that targets will change people's behaviour for the better, focusing efforts

16   *ibid* p.22
17   West Midlands Police Authority. (2008a)
18   Bevan and Hood (2006) pp.517-538

on organisational objectives and thereby achieving results. My experience is that a behaviour change is indeed inevitable, although the type of behaviour that results is rarely conducive to these aspirations. Goodhart's eponymous Law warns:

> Any observed statistical regularity will tend to collapse once pressure is placed upon it for control purposes.[19]

In other words, targets destabilise those processes subject to targets. Destabilise the processes and the whole system will destabilise. Donald Wheeler is more specific about the likely effects of target-driven performance management, suggesting that when people are pressured to meet a target one (or more) of three reactions ensue:

1. They work to improve the system

2. They distort the system

3. They distort the data.[20]

Supporters of target-driven performance management would anticipate that the first outcome is the most likely, but what management often fails to appreciate is that no matter how desperately workers want to improve the system and do the right thing for the service user, their influence is limited. It is management that owns the lion's share of the responsibility and capability to improve the system.

The reality is that when individuals are put under pressure to meet targets anything can (and does) happen. This does not mean that those who subvert the system are necessarily bad people; they are just trying to survive in a hostile environment – an environment where management inflicts unrealistic expectations upon them. I argue that targets inevitably promote perverse incentives and behaviours and the net result is that costs increase, morale is adversely affected, service delivery is sub-optimised and the overall system is damaged. This is not a mere possibility. It is not a threat. It is a *guarantee*.

This section will examine why these types of behaviours occur, and why the consequences are an absolute cast-iron certainty.

---

19   Goodhart (1975)
20   Wheeler (2000) p.20

Gaming

The types of behaviour that result from the imposition of targets are wide-ranging, but tend to fall into certain recognised categories. The most common of these is the phenomenon known as 'gaming', [21] which can be defined as, "...reactive subversion such as 'hitting the target and missing the point' or reducing performance where targets do not apply."[22]

Bevan and Hood identify three main types of gaming:

1. 'Ratchet effects' – where next year's targets are based on last year's performance, resulting in a perverse incentive for managers to under-report current performance in order to secure a less demanding target for next year.

2. 'Threshold effects' – where performance across different functions is reported as a whole. This has the effect of disguising poor individual or departmental performance and encourages high performance to deteriorate to the norm.

3. 'Output distortions' – where targets are achieved at the expense of important but unmeasured aspects of performance.[23]

Other consequences of target-based performance management are:

- Tunnel vision – where managers select some targets (usually the easiest to achieve or measure) and ignore others.

- Sub-optimisation – where managers operate in such a way that serves their own operation but damages the performance of the overall system.

- Myopia – where managers focus on achievable short-term objectives at the expense of longer-term aims.

- Ossification – where a performance indicator has become outdated but has not been removed or revised, and energy is still directed towards achieving it.[24]

---

21 See for example: Deming (1986); Deming (1994); Seddon (2003); Seddon (2008)
22 Bevan and Hood (2006) p.523
23 Adapted from Bevan and Hood (2006)
24 Adapted from: Smith (1990) pp.53-72; Pidd (2005) pp.482-493

It's Not Just a Police Problem

Examples of these effects were witnessed across the public sector throughout the NPM period and continue to this day. Wherever numerical targets exist, one or more of these effects will not be far away. Bevan and Hood's research concentrated on the effect of targets in the NHS, where they exposed examples of patients being left waiting in ambulances outside A&E departments until the hospital was confident that they could be seen within the stipulated target time. Tactics included trolleys in corridors being classed as 'beds', so as to outwit the target time for admissions, and special rooms 'appearing' next to A&E waiting rooms that weren't classed as waiting rooms, so that waiting time there did not count against the clock.[25] The research also found that there was no correlation between performance, awarded in star ratings, and the quality of clinical care provided by hospitals.

Separate research indicates that the four hour A&E target caused a disproportionate rate of admissions immediately prior to the four hour point in *all but one* hospital in England.[26] The distortion amidst the data typifies gaming activity and signifies decisions being driven by fear of missing the target (as in my personal experience at my local A&E department). Interestingly, the only hospital that ignored the target was found to have delivered a *better* service at *lower* cost.

Even the infamous 48-hour target for GP's appointments (intended so no one would have to wait more than 48 hours to see their GP) had the perverse effect of preventing prospective patients making an appointment any time outside of the next 48 hours.[27] Patients could not phone up on a Monday to book an appointment with their GP on the Friday of that week; they had to ring on a Wednesday or Thursday instead.

Other public sector organisations have suffered similar experiences.[28] One of the most notable examples is that of the education sector. As a direct consequence of target-driven performance management, instances of 'teaching to the test' occurred as educational establishments desperately tried to avoid the stigma of being positioned towards the bottom of

---

25   Bevan and Hood (2006)
26   Longman, H. (2011)
27   Hood (2006) pp.515-521
28   For a comprehensive review of dysfunctional behaviour caused by targets in health and education, see: Rothstein (2008)

government league tables.[29] Richard Bird, a former head teacher and legal consultant to the Association of School and College Leaders, argues:

> The skills of beating examination systems have not been lost to teachers today. Question-spotting; framework-providing; technique-coaching are all alive and well and producing their misleading results.[30]

Separate research identified that the pressure to meet targets has led to teachers concentrating '…on a narrow band of marginal students who were close to target thresholds…' at the expense of other students. Others point towards output distortions (see above) occurring as a direct result of target-driven performance management within education, resulting in neglect of those domains of education that are not subject to targets.

The Impact of Targets on Policing

How does target-driven performance management affect the police service? A good starting point is to look at how targets influence the way in which organisational priorities are designated or, rather, how targets skew policy and operational activity. The effects of targets become apparent if we examine the amount of importance that is placed on particular crime types.

For example, house burglaries, robberies and vehicle thefts are classed as 'Serious Acquisitive Crime' and are the subject of their own special targets. This means that the Serious Acquisitive Crime category is constantly in the management's spotlight when it comes to performance against targets.

Police officers already want to catch burglars – it's in the blood; so it's debatable whether the existence of an arbitrary numerical target will spur any frontline bobby to want to catch burglars that little bit more. Problems arise when placing a target on one classification of burglary inadvertently elevates its importance to the detriment of other equally serious offences (including other 'types' of burglary). Let's have a look at why this is the case.

The correct classification for what any member of the public would think of as being a house burglary is known in my force as 'Burglary Dwelling

---

29   For more on the effects of target-driven performance management in the education sector, see: Loveday (2005) pp.97-102; Hood (2006) pp.515-521; Heinrich and Marschke (2010) pp.183-208
30   Bird, R. (2008)
31   Hood (2006) p.518
32   See: Jacob (2005); Heinrich (2008)

House' (BDH). This classification extends to garages that are linked to the house by an integral door. Conversely, an identical garage that is not linked to the house (even if it used to have an integral door that has now been bricked up) is considered as a distinct structure in law and, if it is burgled, the correct crime classification is 'Burglary Other Building' (BOB). (Different police forces use different acronyms. For example, Cheshire has BIADs and BOTIADs – Burglary In A Dwelling and Burglary Other Than In A Dwelling. Bit of trivia there for you.) Now imagine two houses next to each other with identical attached garages, but where only one has an integral door to the house. If both garages are broken into during the same night and property to an identical value is stolen, the two victims will receive a differential service if there is a target-driven bias towards Burglary Dwelling House offences. Although no actual house was entered, the victim whose burglary is classified as BDH will receive an enhanced service – a faster response, CID attendance, extensive house-to-house enquiries and forensic scene examiners checking for fingerprints or DNA evidence. In contrast, his or her neighbours could be given a crime number over the phone, or if they are lucky might receive a visit from a local bobby sometime during the next few days. Theoretically, this could still apply if a pot of paint was the only item taken during the BDH and a £30,000 car was taken during the BOB offence.[33]

Common sense would dictate that they should be investigated as linked incidents, but the reality is that without intervention from someone who is prepared to deviate from policy, the burglaries would be treated differently, with each enquiry being routed to a different department to deal with in isolation.

These invisible dividing lines (which do not exist to the victims of crime) are a symptom of a disjointed system that operates through departments performing functional specialisms in silos. Targets that result in the prioritisation of certain offence types, or internal classifications that determine differential levels of service, impart no benefit to the service user. The overall consequences to the system are similar to those caused by thematic tampering (Chapter Four).

---

33 This example was presented by Chief Inspector Nick Bailey at the Vanguard Policing In Austerity conference, Birmingham, 13th September 2011.

The Ground-Level Impact

In the 2012 RSA research paper, 'Reflexive Coppers', the authors highlight targets as being one of the main barriers to the provision of a quality service. In their words:

> Like all public services, the police service has experienced years of 'target culture', obliging police to face inwards and upwards, reporting to management in quantitative terms, rather than outwards to communities seeking quality.[34]

Other researchers have consistently found this situation to be the norm. Former Chief Constable Peter Neyroud and Dr. Emma Disley of the RAND Corporation, for example, acknowledge the pressure caused by targets and warn of its consequences for the effective investigation of serious criminal offences:

> ...pressure to meet targets encourages managers to focus on volume crime investigations which are less resource intensive, at the expense of proper investigations of more serious crimes.[35]

In extreme cases, proactively targeting a particular offence type (e.g. prostitution or drug activity) can have the undesirable consequence of *increasing* recorded crime. This paradox was recognised by the Centre for Crime and Justice Studies in a report that noted:

> It is a moot point whether it made sense for the government to set a target to reduce police recorded robbery in the first place, given that increases might well reflect enhanced police action in this area. Ironically, the government's target on street crime has risked creating a perverse incentive for police forces to avoid identifying and recording robbery offences.[36]

There is also the risk that as confidence in police ability to deal with such offences increases, the public are more likely to report incidents that might not have been reported previously. This would then give the impression that the crime rate is increasing, which damages public confidence (a policing target), increases the fear of crime (another target) and prevents crime reduction targets from being met.

---

34 Rowson, Lindley, and Stanko, (2012)
35 Neyroud and Disley (2007) p.563
36 Centre for Crime and Justice Studies (2007)

Aside from the effect of targets directly influencing policies or priorities, their impact is felt in almost all corners of operational policing, and this affects the behaviour of individuals in a multitude of ways. Police officers are human beings just like you and me. (I happen to be both.) When placed in a situation where the attainment of targets becomes the primary objective, not even police officers are immune to the pressure to meet them.

A classic example of how targets can dictate the way in which officers on the ground respond to crime is in what many officers would recognise as the 'Section Five versus Drunk and Disorderly' debate. Both offences can apply to drunken and abusive behaviour in the street, both can attract an arrest, a night in the cells and an £80 fixed penalty. But, Section Five of the Public Order Act 1986 is classed as a crime, whereas being Drunk and Disorderly is not.

If you have ever witnessed drunken and abusive revellers in a city centre at 2am on a Saturday night it can be quite unpleasant and can spoil the night for everyone else who is just out for a good time. It's right that the police should intervene to stop this sort of behaviour, and make an arrest if that is deemed to be appropriate.

The problem is this: Section Five counts towards detection targets, whereas being Drunk and Disorderly does not. So, if the police are under pressure to meet detection targets then officers can be incentivised to make arrests under the Public Order Act offence.[37] Of course, this works in reverse if the focus for a local commander is to reduce crime; officers can be persuaded to deal with an identical incident by arresting under Drunk and Disorderly.

There are consequences for the arrested person. If officers are incentivised to arrest for Section Five then someone who behaves like a drunken fool rather than a nasty aggressive drunk, may well end up with a criminal record as a result. Conversely, an aggressive, abusive, threatening drunkard, who would be most appropriately dealt with under Section Five, could be treated leniently because of organisational pressures. Either way, the problem can be traced back to the target. The decision should, of course, be down to the officer on the street to use his or her professional judgement to determine which offence is most appropriate.

'Gaming' in *how* crimes are recorded (or not recorded) is another problem. John Seddon's work with police forces leads him to state, 'There

---

37   'We Are Making Ludicrous Arrests Just to Meet our Targets' *The Times* (2007) [Online] http://www.timesonline.co.uk/tol/news/uk/crime/article1790515.ece

have been many examples of police officers reclassifying offences in order to meet targets – for example, reclassifying shop theft as burglary'.[38] Depending on whether a target focuses on crime reduction or crime detection will determine whether officers are encouraged to under-record a particular offence type (where there is little chance of detecting it) or over-record it (where there is an easy arrest).

How to Beat The System

So, how else do resourceful human beings respond when they are pressured to meet targets? Well, police performance charts that count things, such as the number of intelligence logs submitted per team, provide a good example of how targets can be achieved despite failing to achieve purpose. If teams are pitted against each other to produce more intelligence logs, no one wants to be in the spotlight for being at the bottom of the league table. Common tricks can include:

- Submitting an intelligence log for the most mundane piece of information (e.g. 'The kids have been hanging around by the shops again').

- Breaking one piece of information into multiple pieces to enable the submission of several logs for the same piece of intelligence (e.g. Log 1: "John Smith is associating with Frank Jones". Log 2: "John Smith and Frank Jones stole a car, registration number ABC123 three days ago". Log 3: "Vehicle registration number ABC123 was involved in a burglary two days ago").

- Duplicating information already captured by another process (e.g. submitting an intelligence log as well as a stop and search form after conducting a search in the street).

- Two officers working together, who both submit an intelligence log about the same incident.

Of course, the result of this sort of activity is that the volume of intelligence logs increases, and the intelligence department will have to wade through an excessive amount of submissions that are of limited or no use. Not only does this cause delays by clogging the system, but any intelligence of real value risks being lost in the 'noise'. (Aside from

---

38   Seddon (2008) pp.124-125

the perverse effects caused by the target, counting intelligence logs is meaningless anyway, as they are merely an *input*, rather than an outcome in their own right.)

One Sergeant who took part in the research conducted for this book summed up the situation as follows:

> *"Recently we had a target that all officers would submit a set amount of intelligence reports. The result was that the system and intel office were drowning in a sea of pointless intel reports. We moved from quality to quantity".*

These perverse outcomes are neatly summed up by Professors James Fesler of Yale University and Donald Kettl of the University of Maryland:

> Excessive controls multiply requirements for review of proposed actions, increase red tape, and delay action. So much energy can be spent attempting to control administrative activities, in fact, that little time or money is left to do the job at hand.[39]

In other words, the system is crippled. Surely this is the exact opposite of what management set out to achieve?

The desperate efforts of those under the cosh who are trying to avoid unscientific and ultra-critical exposure somewhere near the foot of a league table are not a peculiarity of just the local performance management scene either. Sensationalist headlines such as 'UK's worst police forces named'[40] do nothing but further ingrain the targets mentality at a national level and increase pressure on entire organisations that are deemed to be 'failing'. Schools and hospitals have also found themselves in this invidious position over the last few years,[41] despite the fact that research has shown that league table methodology is inherently unstable and causes potentially damaging effects.[42] Separate research also indicates that an organisation's position within a league table does not necessarily bear any relation to its actual performance.[43]

Despite this, police forces across the country are compared against each other using the league table approach. Indeed the established mode

---

39   Fesler and Kettl (1991) p.321
40   'UK's Worst Police Forces Named.' *Daily Mail* (2006) [Online] http://www.dailymail.co.uk/news/article-412255/UKs-worst-police-forces-named.html
41   See: Loveday (2005); Hood, C. (2006) pp.515-521
42   See: Goldstein and Spiegelhalter (1996) pp.13-26
43   Bevan and Hood (2006) pp.17-538

of comparison for police forces nationally is a performance management tool called iQuanta.[44] This compares forces' crime data and aggregates performance into simplistic descriptors, such as 'Clearly improving', 'No apparent change' and 'Clearly deteriorating'. These determinations are presented next to 'up' and 'down' arrows (binary comparisons, again). The 'up' arrow is green of course. The method used makes it impossible to identify signals. How anyone can say performance is 'clearly improving' or 'clearly deteriorating' is, therefore, beyond me. You can imagine the effect the label 'Clearly deteriorating' has on senior managers.

The Human Cost

The consequences of target-driven performance management extend beyond merely causing an internal 'bump in the carpet' elsewhere in the system. The ubiquitous nature of policing targets damages organisational trust, professional judgement and frontline discretion. In extreme cases it can be responsible for affecting the psychological well-being of officers who are unable to reconcile the true organisational purpose of policing with the artificial incentives and implicit sanctions of a working environment dominated by targets.

The authors of the RSA report 'Reflexive Coppers' highlight the tension that is generated when officers who simply want to do the right thing are caught up in an organisational environment dominated by targets:

> A job that is 'figures driven' creates pressure to report on situations and manage relationships in a way that creates the desired figures, which does not rest easily with professional goals to serve and protect the public.[45]

This takes us right back to the notion of purpose. What is the purpose of the police? It certainly isn't to feed internal performance indicators, or to service politicians' desire for arbitrary numerical targets to be met.

Whether the pressure to meet targets involves mainly carrots, sticks or both, the results are often the same. The following quotes from officers in different forces are typical:

---

44   Here's a recent, randomly selected iQuanta document: Rutland CSP (2012) [Online] http://www. rutland.gov.uk/pdf/Late%20Paper%202_Crime%20Forecast_Agenda%206.pdf
45   Rowson, Lindley and Stanko (2012) p.19

"Every officer at the police station where I work is set targets for arrests per week. Pressure is brought to bear on officers to bring in arrests because the team then receives a point."[46]

"There is bullying in the police to hit the targets we allegedly don't have."[47]

"I seem to spend all my time chasing performance targets rather than actually doing the job..."[48]

"Every week I have to fill in a coded spreadsheet for my Inspector detailing how many arrests I've made, how many tickets I've given out, the number of stops or searches I have made, how many intel submissions I've made".[49]

"At the end of every single shift I get asked for my figures".[50]

"We have a performance board in our station. It shows "UP" and "DOWN" arrows, in red (bad) and green (good) and % figures".

A wealth of evidence suggests that the culture of organisations which rely on tight control and compliance mechanisms adversely affects worker motivation, and lowers productivity – the precise opposite of what management would have wanted. Morale is sapped and those subject to management scrutiny and control can feel dehumanised.[51] Furthermore, the inflexible, process-driven approach that results from target-driven performance management fatally restricts innovation, constrains professionalism, and turns the workforce into virtual automatons.[52] In extreme cases excessive controls and 'micromanagement' not only demoralise workers, but can even turn them against the system.[53]

Performance measurement expert, Dr. Dean Spitzer succinctly notes the relationship between targets and their effect on the working environment, as below:

---

46   'Target Men.' *The Spectator.* (2011) . [Online] http://www.spectator.co.uk/essays/all/6975453/target-men.thtml

47   Copperfield (2012) p.172

48   HMIC (2008) (p.97)

49   *ibid* p.174

50   *ibid*, p.180

51   See: Weber (1930); Weber (1947); Western (2007)

52   De Bruijn (2007)

53   Etzioni (1964)

Hitting targets leads to a command-and-control orientation and compliance, especially where there are rewards or penalties associated with it. In such an environment, everything is focused on hitting the desired number – often by whatever means are available...[54]

Unethical Behaviour

At one end of the scale, targets create an incentive to focus efforts on 'easy' arrests and detections at the expense of more complex or problematic investigations or areas of policing that do not generate outputs that count towards the target.[55] As one officer explained, "... it's not all that surprising if we put more effort into detecting the easier stuff. Picking the low hanging fruit".[56] Another good analogy is "...counting the ants while the elephants march by".[57]

At the other end of the scale, there is a risk that pressure from management to achieve targets can increase the likelihood of unethical activity. For example, research into the effect of the New York Police Department's (NYPD) target-driven performance management system (known as COMPSTAT) uncovered cases of heavy-handed policing that occurred purely as a result of officers desperately trying to meet quotas for arrests and tickets.[58]

Furthermore, in the UK, a recent report in the media suggested that officers were 'fiddling' response times to meet the targets for emergency incidents.[59] Would people be tempted to do this if there was no pressure to meet targets? Being a fast response driver myself, I know the only motivation when responding to an emergency incident is to get there as quickly and safely as possible. 'Protect and Serve', remember?

The pressure to meet targets could, in extreme cases, result in people's human rights being infringed through unnecessary arrests or unlawful searches. One officer wrote:

---

54   Spitzer (2007) pp.42-43
55   Examples of officers concentrating on 'easy' arrests to meet targets have been widely reported in the press. These three articles are fairly typical: Leapman (2007); Tendler (2007); Monro (2008)
56   Copperfield (2012) p.164
57   Inspector, 15 years' service, Eastern Force. Research conducted by the author.
58   Eterno and Silverman (2012)
59   Whitehead (2010)

We were recently told that our BCU *[Basic Command Unit – in essence, a police division]* PACE 1s *[stop and searches]* had fallen to an unacceptable level on our internal force league table and that we needed to stop-search more people. Bearing in mind we can only stop people on reasonable suspicion that they are committing or have committed criminal acts, surely the only way you can stop *more* people on reasonable suspicion that they are committing criminal acts is if you *see* more people of whom you have reasonable suspicion that they are committing criminal acts?[60]

In his 2008 Review of Policing, Sir Ronnie Flanagan highlighted similar risks, emphasising the increased possibility of people being unnecessarily criminalised:

The consequences of poor professional judgement, combined with existing performance management arrangements, are that officers are encouraged to criminalise people for behaviour which may have caused offence but the underlying behaviour would be better dealt with in a different way.[61]

His words do not suggest that officers were making *unlawful* arrests, just that the pressure to meet targets and feed internal performance management requirements had trumped common sense and doing the right thing. The effect of restricting the exercise of frontline professional judgement, combined with the pressure to meet targets, has led to several embarrassing news reports and incredulity from the general public. The following are just some examples:

- A child in Kent was arrested for removing a slice of cucumber from a sandwich and throwing it at another child.[62]

- A 70-year-old Cheshire pensioner (who had never been in trouble with the police) was arrested for criminal damage after he was accused of cutting back a neighbour's conifers too vigorously.[63]

---

60 Copperfield (2012) p.192
61 Flanagan (2008) p.57
62 Wright (2007)
63 Barratt (2007)

- A 13-year-old boy in the West Midlands (who had also never been in trouble) was arrested and formally reprimanded for assault, after throwing a water bomb at another youngster as a prank.[64]

One reporter neatly summed up the net effect of these types of incidents on public confidence, observing:

> The result is that the law-abiding public who are normally the staunchest supporters of the police are becoming terminally disenchanted with them.[65]

It's a clear case of 'Lose-Lose' for everyone concerned.

The Link Between Targets and Sub-Optimisation

Earlier on we looked at the concept of sub-optimisation, where one part of the system is optimised (has resources pumped into it) at the expense of the others. As we know, when other departments are adversely affected then the overall system suffers. The presence of targets or performance indicators in one part of the system will mean that those working within that department will do everything they can to meet the target (and avoid adverse management scrutiny), even at the expense of other departments.

For example, if call handlers are pressured by targets, the calls might have to be rushed and vital information could be missed. The control room operators could end up despatching response units to incidents without all the information the officers require to make a full assessment of what they might encounter when they arrive. The call handlers meet their target ('win') at the expense of the response unit officers who arrive at the incident appearing unprepared or unprofessional ('lose'). If crucial information is missed, such as a good description of a man with a knife, then members of the public and officers might be exposed to increased risk and the offender could get away ('lose'). This is what happens when individual components work against each other. The overall system loses.

A particular type of sub-optimisation, which I call *time-based sub-optimisation,* is different to other forms of sub-optimisation inasmuch as it does not involve departments working against each other. It involves departments working against themselves because of time-based targets.

---

64   West Midlands Police (2008) p.33
65   Phillips (2007)

One of the most obvious forms of time-based sub-optimisation comes about as a result of annual budget targets. The limitations of the annual budget cycle are well documented by the likes of Allen Schick and Christopher Pollitt,[66] who argue that this traditional cycle introduces artificial parameters into what is essentially a longer-term process and that the budget should run concurrently alongside other facets of the system. The annual nature of traditional budgeting is renowned for causing miserly restraint throughout the financial year, then, in the last few weeks, the purse strings tend to be relaxed and organisations splash out on new furniture and anything else that can be purchased to prevent the end-of-year budget showing an underspend. There are 2 main drivers for the way in which this budget is currently allocated – 1) a fear of a dressing down from management for overspending, and 2) a fear of being allocated a reduced budget for the subsequent year (any underspend cannot be carried over to the next year).

A common method to try to control any negative outcome is to allocate a proportion of the budget to departments on a monthly basis (e.g. 50 hours overtime being permissible per month). But natural variation dictates that in some months the expenditure will amount to more than 50 hours and some months it will be less than 50 hours.

Traditional budgeting 'tricks' can include holding back from entering expenses until the beginning of the next quarter, or rushing contracts or product just ahead of the cut-off date to achieve quarterly targets. But, what happens when events can't be controlled – and criminals use up some of the monthly budget without checking with management first? When I was a Sergeant I bore the brunt of a dressing down for a monthly overspend, after six officers incurred two hours of overtime each following the arrest of four criminals who had stolen a car. Rather than congratulating the officers for a job well done, the Duty Inspector was furious about the dent in his monthly overtime target.

End of Month Detections Scramble

Another classic example of time-based sub-optimisation is when someone in management realises that their division only needs a few more detected offences to be registered before the end of the year to meet the detection target. In a burst of activity, big operations are dreamt up in an attempt to

---

66   See: Schick (1998); Pollitt (1999)

arrest as many people as possible; this of course abstracts officers from other important duties, causing gaps elsewhere in the system. Audits and reviews are commissioned to try to identify investigations that might be on the cusp of finalisation; crime records are trawled to check if the correct boxes have been ticked, thereby ensuring the detection can be properly registered (some boxes are occasionally missed when the matter is filed), and admin are sometimes paid overtime to make sure that all available detections are entered into the system before close of play. Is any of this value work? Does any of it make a difference to the victim of crime?

This time-based sub-optimisation is akin to a situation where a long distance runner sets out to run twelve miles, but rather than set a steady pace throughout, inexplicably sprints the last two hundred yards of each mile. This technique will tire the runner and result in uneven performance, as well as a slower overall time. The same is true for the ongoing investigations that an officer manages. If left alone, the officer will prioritise workload and get more done throughout the year. Compared to the sub-optimised approach, which emphasises sudden bursts of activity without looking at the long-term picture, the average end-to-end time for investigations will be vastly reduced.

The extra work caused by this interference and sub-optimisation (e.g. getting rushed investigations back on track or re-attending to duties that officers were taken away from) has a knock-on effect on fresh investigations. Of course, when it comes to the end of next month, if the division is a few detections short of the target, the situation repeats itself, generating a cumulative effect on officers' ability to effectively manage their ongoing investigations.

The target might or might not have been hit. What is certain is that the system has been sub-optimised and overall performance will have suffered.

Nearest Available Officer

Sometimes the most powerful way to demonstrate how target-driven performance management causes damage to the overall system is to look at a real life example, where the result is so obviously perverse and undesirable that it completely exposes the flawed thinking behind target-setting. I particularly like this example because it shows how targets influence decision-making, leading to waste and nonsensical operational deployments that fly in the face of common sense.

First of all, here's a bit of background. UK police forces currently use a communications system called 'Airwave', a modern day version of the old police radio. Some forces have activated GPS tracking across their network, so that each individual Airwave terminal can be located and tracked. Control room staff can see on a screen where everyone is, which is helpful when deciding which unit to send to which job. It can also improve officers' safety, plus in the event that an entire team ever decided to park up somewhere and go to sleep whilst on night duty, this would show up as a big red glowing dot on the map. It would not take long for the Sergeant to find them…

The important factor to consider here is the effect of response time targets on control room operators' behaviour. In order to understand this I will first outline what police response time targets are all about. UK police forces use a grading system to categorise reported incidents. Although different forces use different terminology for the categories, the principles are pretty much the same, and result in tiered classifications based on perceived risk and urgency. These classifications determine how quickly and what type of police response ensues. The categories usually run along the lines of:

- Grade One: Immediate threat to life, crime in progress, or offender on scene.

- Grade Two: Early attendance desirable due to the nature of the incident, effect on the caller, or need to secure evidence/start a prompt investigation.

- Grade Three: Non-urgent incident where attendance is required but which falls outside of the above categories.

- Grade Four: Non-urgent incident where attendance can be scheduled for a mutually agreeable time.

- Grade Five: No attendance required; e.g. incident can be dealt with on the telephone.

It is the norm for response time targets to be set against both Grade One and Grade Two incidents; for example in West Midlands Police, the Grade One response classification attracts a target that states officers must arrive within 15 minutes of the call being received.[67] (This was revised from a

---

67   *BBC* (2011) West Midlands Police to Increase 999 Response Times. [Online] http://www.bbc. co.uk/news/uk-england-birmingham-13154124

longstanding 10-minute target in April 2011). Grade Two incidents are subject to a 60-minute target, whilst no fixed target exists for the remaining tiers for incidents in the West Midlands. Other forces apply similar time-based targets; these may vary but follow the same tiered approach.

Prioritising Things is Necessary; Targets are Bad

I believe that the notion of prioritising calls is entirely logical. It would be ridiculous for a report of a schoolchild calling another schoolchild a naughty name on Facebook (yes, we get these calls!) to be treated as urgently as a bank robbery in progress. The problems arise, however, when the major influence on decision-making is the target, rather than determining the most appropriate response. (I also don't believe that an officer responding to an emergency with blue lights and sirens would go any faster or slower whether a Grade One target was 10 minutes, 15 minutes, or anything else. As previously discussed, the objective is always to get there as quickly and safely as possible – the target is irrelevant.)

Putting real emergencies to one side, Grade Two incidents are often more problematic to manage. Categorising incidents ignores variety, and there is a vast range of incidents that are classed as Grade Two. One would hope, therefore, that the control room operators would be able to use their professional judgement and despatch officers accordingly.

In reality, this is easier said than done. The pressure to meet the target is greatly intensified when it is made known that response times are reviewed by management on a daily basis and individuals are expected to provide an explanation for any occurrences where the target was not achieved. Say a relatively low-risk Grade Two incident is almost reaching the target threshold at the same time as another higher-risk Grade Two incident still has 55 minutes left on the clock. Human nature dictates that when the operator is under pressure to meet targets, it will often be the older Grade Two incident that is prioritised, regardless of its nature or relative risk. This isn't because control room staff are bad people – it is the result of a one-size-fits-all classification system, intensified by numerical targets and management scrutiny: a dangerous combination. The result is that meeting the target becomes a major influencing factor on decision-making.

A Comedy of Targets

Consider this true story. It began when a neighbourhood dispute, a Grade Two incident, was reported. The control room staff realised the clock was ticking and, at that specific moment in time, all the local units were busy. A quick look on the GPS screen confirmed that the nearest available resource, a firearms unit, was about 20 miles away, so in order to meet the target, this unit was despatched. Needless to say, firearms units are specialists who have a distinct role to perform. The appearance of armed officers at a low-level incident risks giving the impression of a disproportionate or overbearing police response, and this could have a negative impact on public confidence. The caller just wanted a word with her local beat bobby, who knew about the history behind the dispute, and was surprised to be faced with officers carrying loaded handguns on their belts.

Once the caller had recounted her story, it transpired that a criminal offence of threatening behaviour had been committed by her neighbour. The firearms officers had to complete a crime report, obtain statements, and compile associated paperwork. But then the firearms officers were faced with a dilemma – the alleged offender was next door and needed to be arrested. They were overtly armed, and force policy prevents them from becoming involved in non-firearms incidents that may involve confrontation or making 'run of the mill' arrests.

The logic behind this is that the presence of police firearms at such a 'pre-planned' arrest is unnecessary and disproportionate to the perceived threat; plus if the offender becomes belligerent and a grappling match ensues, there is a danger that a gun could go off, or be taken off an officer. Furthermore, they do not have the option of leaving their guns in the car, for obvious reasons. This meant that whilst they had done an excellent job of meeting the target, their usefulness in this particular situation had reached its limit. The only solution was to wait for a local unit to become available to make the arrest.

In this case, the deployment of the firearms officers was a reaction completely motivated by the need to meet the 60-minute response time target. Fortunately, there were no firearms incidents reported whilst the officers were abstracted from their core function but using this specialist unit caused inefficiency and damage to the overall system. When this approach is repeated throughout the day, the effect is multiplied and results in an impaired level of service to the public.

For me, the systems solution to effective despatch of police resources lies in trusting the professional judgement of the control room operators. I would remove all time-based targets and rely on a simple classification that records whether an incident is an emergency or not. If it is an emergency, then the appropriate resources are despatched to get there as quickly and safely as possible. Here, GPS can assist the control room staff in deciding which resources to send. If it isn't an emergency, then the response should be prioritised against all the other live incidents, taking into account the exact nature of the call, along with factors such as the seriousness of the incident, the vulnerability of the caller, and the anticipated benefits of a quick response.

It is still important to record actual response times so that managers can understand the capabilities of the system. Through intelligent interpretation of this data, using SPC charts, managers can identify opportunities for improving the system, as well as identify and act upon obstacles that adversely affect performance. (This could be as simple as relocating default patrol areas to locations where there is a predictably high demand, thereby reducing response times.) If the data indicate that there is an evidence base for the introduction of a systemic change, then it is appropriate to make it. No target will tell you this.

Conclusion

Targets are so ingrained in the organisational psyche that many managers, workers and observers accept them without question. This is precisely why it is so important to challenge targets and the traditional assumptions that are associated with them.

Target-driven performance management is based on an underlying desire to control the workers, along with a basic assumption that they are primarily driven by extrinsic motivators. Any short-term 'results' it squeezes out of the workers through the traditional blend of rewards, sanctions and fear are only ever achieved at great unseen expense. Targets *always* change behaviour, and invariably the behaviour they instigate is unpalatable and counterproductive. The long term cost is felt through sub-optimisation, gaming, and the catastrophic harm that is caused to the system. Target-driven performance management makes service delivery worse and is terminally damaging to worker motivation and morale.

Optimistic 'safeguards' and mitigations, such as attempting to carefully design targets or limit their application, are undermined by the fact that it is scientifically impossible to set a numerical target in the first place. I repeat – this means that, without exception, *all* numerical targets are completely arbitrary. Furthermore, the paltry single figure adjustments typical of numerical targets (e.g. to reduce crime by 5%) artificially constrain ambition and potential. The only 'target' worth striving towards is perfection.

In summary, I present my position on targets as a simple two-point statement:

1. All numerical targets are arbitrary.

2. No numerical target is immune from causing dysfunctional behaviour.

I therefore submit that targets are the single most pernicious element of conventional management practice and should be abandoned.

CHAPTER SEVEN

Waste Disposal

"The quickest, easiest and most cost effective way of instantly releasing capacity is to simply stop doing the wrong things."

When it comes to removing waste, this is probably the single most useful piece of advice I can give. It will save your organisation more time and money than you could ever imagine.

Taiichi Ohno, the man largely responsible for the Toyota Production System, famously highlighted the damaging effects of waste on the system and talked about it from three perspectives:

- *Muda* – the Japanese word for waste.

- *Muri* – meaning 'overburden', which leads to waste.

- *Mura* – meaning 'unevenness', which also causes waste.[1]

I have adopted a deliberately light touch on the use of Japanese words and Lean references in this book. As mentioned in the introduction, Ohno did not call his approach anything. He was concerned that giving his methods a title would risk codification, that practitioners might treat them as ready-made 'tools' or one-size-fits-all 'solutions'. Deming also warned that merely adopting others' methods (or exotic names) and then attempting to apply them without knowledge or proper understanding would not achieve the desired result, and would reduce the scope for ongoing development and improvement of the methods themselves. The 'off the shelf' technique does not work.

These three Japanese words, however, are an aid to understanding how waste causes inertia and damage to the system. John Bicheno, of the Lean Enterprise Research Centre, offers some helpful guidance on recognising *Muda, Muri* and *Mura*; "(*Muda*)…is waste – or, more correctly, it is non-

---

1   See: Ohno (1988); Womack and Jones (2003)

value adding activity."[2] This definition encompasses all types of waste, including that caused by *Muri* and *Mura*.

Put simply, *Muri* "…causes waste by 'overburdening' people and machines".[3] Examples of this type of waste include loading an unmanageable volume or type of work onto staff or having multiple conflicting priorities such that none of them can be properly addressed. Overburdening a workforce in this way will restrict innovation and lower the quality of work, thereby damaging workers' morale. We have seen examples of this latter type of *Muri* in the previous chapter, along with the devastating effects it can have on the individual and the system.

Mura is unevenness, i.e. the waste that is caused by disrupting flow. A good example is the waste introduced at the doctor's surgery when it is overwhelmed by a rush of people wanting to book appointments at 8am every morning. It causes stops and starts in processes, as well as bottlenecks and the sorts of problems associated with handovers, batching and queuing that we saw in Chapter One.

Don't worry too much about trying to remember these terms. Bicheno points out that they are all interlinked; "*Mura* causes *Muri* causes *Muda* causes *Mura* and so on".[4] Try to say that after a few pints! For the practical user who wants to get on with improving their system, just remember that waste is waste whatever guise it is found in – the important thing is that it be recognised, then reduced, or ideally eliminated.

What's The Value?

Everything has a cost, either financial, time-based or in terms of the amount of capacity required to process it. Furthermore, it is impossible for the system to cope with fresh demand if it is already operating at capacity.

Before an organisation even attempts to redesign its processes, it should take a long hard look at existing practices in order to identify and remove waste. This will be a giant leap in the right direction and is the fastest way to build capacity. Also, it's usually free.

A good way to identify waste is to assess activity against its 'value'. In Chapter One, I offered my definition of value activity as, "activity that contributes towards purpose". John Seddon talks about *value demand*. He offers the following simple definition and example:

---

2   Bicheno (2008) p.12
3   *ibid* p.12
4   *ibid* p.13

Value demand is 'demand we want', demand that the service is there to provide for. In the case of housing benefits, there are only two value demands: 'Can I make a claim? And 'My circumstances have changed'.[5]

It therefore follows that organisational activity which deals with *value demand* is *value activity*. Value demand for the police is much broader than in the housing benefits example and would include a variety of activities, such as arresting thieves, preventing harm to vulnerable people, or investigating serious traffic collisions. This is obvious value activity, but it is important not to dismiss activity where the value element is less obvious. For example, whilst the wages department in a large organisation does not confer any direct benefit on the customer or service user, it is nevertheless appropriate to categorise that department's function as value activity. If people don't get paid, they will eventually stop working, so purpose from the customer's perspective will not be met.

It may be helpful to consider these different levels of value activity as *direct value activity* and *indirect value activity*. If frontline activity is not augmented by necessary support functions then the system will collapse. Indirect value activities are essential to the health of organisations and systems. In the same way, it is important to understand that a department, function or individual may not output pure direct value activity all the time; for example, a police dog handler who is not tracking a suspect at a particular moment in time is still providing indirect value simply by being available for deployment. Conversely, in the very simplest of terms, anything that isn't value demand or direct/indirect value activity is, by default, waste. There is no getting away from it.

Plotting demand on an SPC chart aids understanding of the system's capabilities and leads to opportunities for improving its design. This can be difficult for public service organisations that deal with a wide range of demand, especially as a lot of it can be quite unpredictable. Nevertheless, there is always an argument for analysing and understanding incoming demand in order to assist in designing the system around it. This enables the system to operate more effectively and reduces waste.

---

5   Seddon (2003) p.32

Epic Fail

The antithesis to value demand is what John Seddon calls *failure demand*. Failure demand occurs because of "…a failure to do something or do something right for the customer".[6] Classic examples include:

- Phoning up a council department because you don't understand how to fill in a complex form they have sent to you.

- Calling your internet provider because your broadband has stopped working.

- Having to contact an investigating officer to find out what is happening with your case.

Although this results in tangible work for the official/employee/police officer at the other end of the phone or at the front desk, it does not constitute value activity for the organisation because it wouldn't be needed if the initial service was effective. Someone has to do all this work and their time is not free. Neither is the customer's time. I have had experience of having to resend documentation to government departments and banks because their original request was incomplete or they refused to accept useful additional information provided by me at the first point of contact because it wasn't on one of their forms. This is failure demand.

This type of scenario is caused because the 'official' correspondence consists of standardised forms, accompanied by standardised procedures, standardised timescales for replies and standardised service levels. Ohno promoted the benefits of some standardisation in the workplace,[7] but the context that he was referring to was chiefly the manufacturing environment. People, however, cannot be 'standardised'. The problems are compounded where the system design is reliant on functional departments – i.e. silos – as this introduces disconnections and handovers into the design. Standards may be met but the customer receives a terrible service and the system becomes infested with avoidable waste.

I recall receiving a letter from the Inland Revenue a few years ago, advising that I might have been overcharged on my National Insurance contributions. There was also a form to complete. The letter asked me to provide some 'further information' so they could make an assessment

---

6   *ibid* p.32
7   Ohno (1988)

about whether I was due a refund. The further information they wanted was (wait for it) – 'How much National Insurance have you paid during 2007–2008?'

I phoned them and pointed out that they already knew this as they had my money, so I couldn't understand why they had sent the request. I confirmed the exact amount I had paid and asked whether I was indeed due a refund. I was informed that they couldn't tell me over the phone, and that I would have to write down the amount I had paid and send the completed form to them. Of course, the form included a mandatory field for my name and address, which they also knew as they had written to me in the first place.

In the end I seem to remember receiving a few pounds by way of a refund, but I'm convinced that the time and effort invested at both ends made it an expensive exercise for the Inland Revenue, and therefore the taxpayer. A simpler (and cheaper) process would be to remotely adjust my tax code, or better still, just transfer the money directly into my bank account and send an email to let me know what they have done and why.

Another ridiculous case of failure demand occurred as a result of a letter I received from the DVLA warning me that I was liable to be fined for not having tax on my car. I phoned them in response and the conversation went a bit like this:

Me: "Why have I received this notice? I've always had tax on my car, as I do now".

DVLA person: "Our records show you haven't had tax on it for three months".

Me: "That's strange because I bought a tax disc from the Post Office three months ago when it was due, so it's still got nine months left to run. My car registration is ABC123, the serial number on the tax disc is 123456789, the date I bought it was 'X' and the Post Office I got it from was 'Y'".

DVLA person: "Oh well, it sounds like we have made an error in our records in that case".

Me: "No problem. I take it that's all sorted then?"

DVLA person: "No. You need to write all that on the form, attach a photocopy of the tax disc and post it to us, otherwise we can't update our records and you will be fined for not having tax on your car".

In the end I had no choice but to do as instructed and, typically, there was no stamped addressed envelope enclosed either. I attached a letter requesting reimbursement for the cost of my stamp. I never received a reply, but at least it made me feel better.

Those stories might have made you chuckle or roll your eyes. The reality is that these are problems with the systems. Consider the enormous magnitude of waste these institutions must generate for themselves when you multiply my experience by that of thousands of other customers, day after day after day…

Watch Your Waste

Failure demand precipitates a particularly unpleasant form of waste because it is completely avoidable. It is not, however, the only form of waste that blights organisations.

A common misconception among some managers is that all incoming work must be necessary. This is fundamentally wrong. In my experience, certain types of activity, processes and norms tend to become embedded over time and are accepted as 'what we do here'; they are acknowledged without question and, therefore, go unchallenged. Even where something instinctively doesn't quite seem to make sense, or its value to the service user isn't obvious, we still do it. This quiet acceptance leads to stagnation and waste.

An effective method of identifying and addressing waste is to rigorously question why an activity takes place and never accept any of the following answers as being sufficient justification for its existence:

- Because it's what we've always done.
- Because it's the policy.
- Because it's what the boss wants.

Asking 'why' is a crucial question when it comes to testing whether processes constitute value activity or not. This applies when assessing existing processes or designing new ones. Prevention is better than cure as they say; it is always better to stop waste from getting a foothold in the first place. Naturally, when a system is first examined for waste the initial response is likely to be focused on waste removal rather than prevention, but once the 'spring clean' is complete it is everybody's responsibility to stay alert and prevent any resurgence. Waste has a nasty habit of sneaking back in; it is a master of disguise.

Four Types of Waste

To help identify waste within any system or process, I have developed a simple typology, based on my own observations and interpretation of existing literature. You will probably recognise the following broad categories of waste within your own organisation. I'm not claiming that there is anything particularly new or revolutionary about my classifications – just that waste is easier to recognise when you apply the model. In my experience, these four types of waste are particularly evident within the policing environment. Waste Type One is encountered furthest upstream, whilst the others can happen at any stage in the process. Stay alert!

- **Waste Type One:**
  The things a system or process shouldn't become involved with at all.

- **Waste Type Two:**
  Activity undertaken to correct what wasn't done properly in the first place (rework and additional remedial work caused by failure demand).

- **Waste Type Three:**
  Other activity that does not contribute towards purpose.

- **Waste Type Four:**
  Disproportionate amounts of value activity.

Each will now be explored in turn and we will see how even value activity can beget waste if it occurs in the wrong setting or in the wrong proportions.

Waste Type One:

The things a system or process shouldn't become involved with at all.

Identifying and removing this type of waste begins with going as far upstream as possible – right to the 'doorway' of the system or process. Waste tends to grow once you let it in, so the first thing to do is to understand your system's demand profile and decide what type of input is compatible with the purpose of the system. If Machine 'A' is designed to take sheets of metal in order to produce automotive components, whilst Machine 'B' exists to form individual chocolate bars from a mass of molten chocolate, you wouldn't want either type of inappropriate raw material entering the wrong machine. The effect would be to clog up both machines (at least) and spectacularly fail to achieve purpose.

The police are often relied upon as 'the service of last resort', but this does not mean it is appropriate to absorb work that sits firmly within the ambit of other professional agencies. For example, it is commonplace for police officers to be expected to deal with civil disputes, mental health issues and other matters that are primarily the responsibility of social services or council departments. This happens a lot because the appropriate agency or department is not available out of hours and it seems to fall to the police to plug the gaps. A classic example is the noisy neighbour or party – I've lost count of the times that calls about noisy parties are routed to the police simply because the local authority's noise abatement officer is not on duty. (I'd have thought that predictable demand for noisy parties would peak on Friday and Saturday nights, but there you go.)

The situation is replicated throughout the country, with officers recounting their remarkably consistent experiences as follows:

> *"We will deal with EVERYTHING in a vain attempt not to be criticised. We simply cannot say no to anyone".*

> *"We constantly acquiesce to the NHS, Fire Service and Local Councils amongst others. Public safety is our remit, but it also falls to other agencies too".*

> *"Our partner agencies have grown very used to having us as a fall back option. Too often the mental health team get us to do welfare checks as they can't go themselves. They don't acknowledge the limited powers we have. Social services do the same usually at 4:30pm on a Friday, just before they go home for the weekend".*

"We are all subjected to swingeing cuts yet other organisations cut their services and dump the additional workload on the police and are often not there to support us out of hours".

The point here is not that callers should be ignored, but that the police service needs to re-evaluate its purpose and acknowledge occasions where a call should be dealt with by another agency. Officers often become embroiled in situations where they have no jurisdiction or expertise, such as at mental health assessments on private property, or retrieving errant youngsters who have 'absconded' from local authority care.

Both types of situation fall squarely within the remit of other professionals and the police service should not be expected to act as the lead agency in what are often complex and sensitive circumstances. Constant acquiescence leads to unrealistically raising the expectations of callers and officials from partner agencies alike.

Even more extreme are the examples of police officers being obliged to respond to incidents that should not be the responsibility of *any* agency to react to. I know of cases where officers have been despatched to incidents such as, "My brother won't let me have my turn on the X-box", and "My ex-boyfriend is doing the washing up and I don't want him to". Other reports that have appeared in the press include:

There's a spider in my living room.[8]

A teenager called police saying that his parents had re-decorated his room and he did not like it.[9]

A woman dialled 999 to report that she didn't have a £1 coin for her shopping trolley.[10]

These calls might seem ludicrous or even comical but it is not a laughing matter when operators, because of rigid policy requirements, are left with no option but to send someone. (For example, the X-box, washing up and decorating calls are all technically classed as 'domestic' incidents and therefore attract mandatory police attendance, along with the multitude of obligatory associated forms and referrals.)

An informed, empowered and trusted call taker should be in a position to use his or her professional judgement to determine which cases are appropriate for police attendance. This goes back to what I was talking

---

8   *Surrey Today* (2012)
9   Ledbury Community Portal (2010)
10   Malkin (2008)

about in Chapter One, when advocated putting expertise at the front end of the process. It is also compatible with the principles of determining proportionate responses, along with evidence-based prioritisation, as discussed in Chapter Four.

Attempting to take on board absolutely any type of demand regardless of whether it should be absorbed by that particular (or indeed *any*) organisation is indicative of a system that has lost sight of its purpose. It overburdens the 'machinery' through inputs it was not designed to handle (*Muri*). A system without a clear aim generates activity that is disconnected from purpose and simultaneously restricts capacity to handle value demand. The longer any 'unit' of inappropriate demand remains within the system or process, or the further it travels along the chain, the more waste it begets. Even a unit of demand that is entirely appropriate for one agency could be a terminal waste generator within a policing system and vice versa.

Feeding sheets of metal into a chocolate machine will cause problems.

Waste Type Two:

Activity undertaken to correct what wasn't done properly in the first place (rework and additional remedial work caused by failure demand).

We have already looked at failure demand, along with some of its causes, but what type of waste does it beget? Well, the first (and most common) of these is *rework*, which is the actual activity that has to be repeated to put things right. In addition to this, further *remedial work* is often needed in addition to the rework. This remedial work can be considered to be a secondary, additional type of waste that occurs *on top* of the rework required to put right whatever had gone wrong or been omitted in the first place. (In other words, you could say that all rework is caused by failure demand, but not all the extra activity that failure demand causes is rework). To explain this distinction, let's have a look at a quick example.

A woman takes her car into a garage to have a new exhaust fitted to it. The booking process and actual exhaust fitting would be classed as value activity, as they contribute directly towards purpose. If the operation was carried out in a timely and effective manner then the purpose of the system would have been achieved and we would have a happy customer. Now imagine that the exhaust falls off on the customer's way home; she phones up the garage to complain and arrange for the work to be carried out again.

To resolve the problem, the receptionist first has to go through the entire booking procedure for the customer's car to be booked into a fresh appointment to have the exhaust system refitted. The receptionist then has to record the woman's complaint and send it to head office for someone to register, investigate and respond. The next day, the car owner brings her car back in to the garage and the work is carried out, this time without any problems. A few days later she receives a letter from the complaints department apologising for the problems; this is accompanied by a bunch of flowers.

From the point that the woman phoned the garage to tell them her brand new exhaust had fallen off, every single subsequent unit of activity that occurred would be classed as waste under this category. The second booking procedure and exhaust fitting are examples of rework because they are simply repeats of stages that had already occurred.

However, the failure to fit the exhaust properly the first time round created extra activity that would not otherwise have been present at all in the process; the recording of the complaint details that the secretary made, the routing of the complaint to the relevant department, their own registration process, the complaint investigation itself, and finally the generation of the letter and delivery of the flowers. All this represents avoidable cost, both in company time and capacity, the economic cost associated with the flowers and the reputational cost that is unseen and immeasurable.

Rework and remedial work initiated by failure demand occur within the policing environment when victims of crime call up to find out what is happening with their case, or when failure to attend a relatively straightforward incident results in the situation escalating and more resources, time or effort are required to bring the situation under control. These situations can be avoided by responding appropriately in the first place, or by ensuring that the victim of crime understands what is going to happen next, as well as when and how they will be updated with progress. That's the thing you see – waste often starts off small and likes to grow. It drains capacity and prevents value activity from occurring elsewhere. It's always best to nip it in the bud.

In all settings, the way to eliminate the waste associated with failure demand is simple – get it right first time. Management bear the responsibility of designing and maintaining a system that promotes quality and assists the workers in achieving this aim. Ensuring that processes are kept as short as possible, with the minimum amount of handovers (or ideally none, if practicable), will result in faster end-to-end times and reduce the likelihood of this type of waste occurring. This approach goes hand-in-hand with the principle of trusted and empowered workers taking pride and ownership in their work, rather than relying on retrospective audit and inspection checking for defects, and demanding rework.

Deming mused that the practice of relying upon retrospective inspection to identify defects then returning product back for rework is analogous to scraping burnt toast.[11] It is more efficient to cook the toast properly in the first place. Preventing rework and remedial work is all about getting upstream processes under control, as opposed to installing downstream corrective interventions.

Centre of Excellence?

A final thought on the types of waste in this category is this: you will be aware that some companies and public sector organisations have specific departments dedicated to dealing with complaints. It strikes me as odd and somewhat defeatist that an organisation would deliberately install a department whose sole function is to handle waste that is caused by waste. Why not just address the causes of the waste?

Recently, after making a complaint to my bank, I received a letter from the 'Head of the Complaints Centre of Excellence'. Why would an organisation pride itself on the existence of this department by giving it such a lofty title? It's an admission of failure. Would you be proud to hold this particular job title? The bank has totally missed the point by creating such an important-sounding department that deals exclusively in failure demand! My message to the bank is this: Don't be excellent at handling complaints – get the system right and you won't have so many.

Waste Type Three:

Other activity that does not contribute towards purpose.

The third type of waste is the most insidious and parasitic. It tends to come about as a direct result of traditional command and control management, tampering or organisational introspection. Waste Type Three occurs when

---

11   Kotler, Lee and Farris (2008)

organisational focus becomes internalised and effort is directed towards servicing internal requirements ahead of achieving purpose for the service user. Common examples include disproportionate bureaucratic reporting requirements, unnecessary written plans, plus the mandated operational activity that is derived from non-evidence-based decision-making or rigid policy.

Capacity within any system or process is finite so activity should remain under constant review to ascertain whether it generates benefit for the service user. I believe that rigorous cost/benefit analysis must be applied to ensure that any activity under review contributes either directly towards purpose or towards the overall health of the system. Furthermore, a test of proportionality is critical when considering the necessity (or otherwise) of any given activity. Non-value activity must be identified and eliminated. Unfortunately, this doesn't always happen.

A classic example of the type of waste that saps capacity whilst delivering virtually no benefit for the service user is the obligatory meeting that drags on for hours, where one eventually walks out of the room uncertain about what, if anything, has been achieved. How many times have you have sat in a meeting and wondered "Why am I here?" Standing items that are no longer relevant remain on the agenda and issues of little or no currency are routinely discussed. No one seems to know why.

Moreover, new meetings (and pre-meetings) are created all the time, with their frequency and duration being arbitrarily determined from the outset (i.e. two hours, repeated every week, etc.) This triggers a series of questions: If it's a new meeting, how does anyone know in advance how regular it needs to be? How does the convenor know it needs to be diarised for two hours? If the meeting is important enough to shunt something else out of my schedule, what is the evidence base that justifies this and what should I stop doing to accommodate it? How will the meeting's effectiveness be evaluated? If the meeting has been convened to discuss relatively routine operational activity, how on earth did we ever manage that particular area of business before the meeting came into existence? If we stopped having the meeting all of a sudden, would the world fall apart? I doubt it.

My position on meetings is threefold:

1. There must be a clear purpose to the meeting.

2. The number of attendees and length of the meeting must be proportionate to what it seeks to achieve.

3. There must be clear decisions and outcomes that everybody understands and acts upon when they leave the room.

These points are on a poster on the wall of my office, under the header 'Rules for Meetings'. I stick to them and, as a result, the very few meetings I convene are purposeful, punchy and proportionate. (The Three Ps of meetings, if you like.)

In my experience, decisions made at meetings are particularly susceptible to generating waste. Too often, operational and policy decisions seem to be made without due regard to the evidence base, which is a sure fire way of driving waste into the system and causing sub-optimisation, whilst simultaneously failing to achieve management's intentions. A parallel would be the contrast between the scientific methods relied upon for clinical evaluation of new medication, versus the sometimes unstable basis for public policy decisions. This was recently summed up as follows:

> When drugs are launched, we expect rigorous testing, yet with government strategy we rely on anecdote or public mood when empirical study could offer better results.[12]

Myron Tribus emphasises the importance of analysing and understanding data in order to determine whether there is an evidence base that provides a mandate for activity. He draws attention to a simple typology drawn up by Professor Tsuda of Rikkyo University in Tokyo,[13] which is reproduced in part below. The table classifies meeting styles and their effects; this helps to demonstrate how a deeper understanding of data can enrich discussions and decision-making at meetings, thereby reducing the likelihood of knee-jerk reactions and the creation of waste.

---

12   Henderson (2012)
13   Tribus. in Wheeler (1998) p.13

Style of Decision-Making	Decision-Making	Diagnosis
1. Discussions without data	Decisions are based on politics, emotion, turf, etc	People do not want to see problems, so they deny their existence
2. Data are discussed, but only if they are favourable	Decisions are based on raw data without analysis – options accepted on boss's hunch	People see problems but are habituated to their presence.
3. Good and bad data are discussed and analysed	Decisions are based on data, analysis and options proposed by the presenters	People see problems but do not know what to do because the problems are systemic
4. Data are presented, analysed statistically, and options are also analysed, including the option of changing policies.	Decisions are based on analyses and data – options and policies are questioned	People want to see their problems and are quick to seek out data – they want to solve problems

Figure 7.1: Professor Tsuda's Classification Scheme for Organisations

The table depicts a hierarchy of meeting styles, arranged by degrees of effectiveness. Only the fourth classification represents an approach that is devoid of waste. Of note is the reference to 'turf' under the first classification – this highlights the link between this most wasteful of meeting styles and the sub-optimisation it causes. This approach is also responsible for causing inappropriate operational responses and tampering. In addition to this, there is the important acknowledgement of problems usually being a systemic issue, as seen under the 'diagnosis' column of the third meeting style. This is notable, as the likelihood of the system being responsible for the majority of system conditions is often overlooked. Furthermore, Professor Tsuda's typology emphasises that the effectiveness of organisational decision-making is dependent on the statistical analysis of data, rather than what Deming refers to as 'superstitious learning'.[14] This reminds us of the usefulness of the SPC approach that was explored in Chapters Two and Three.

---

14   Crawford (2003) p.11

Double Your Money

When it comes to reducing waste associated with meetings, there is a simple technique that can instantly halve costs and what's more – it's free.

First of all, let's assume that a particular meeting is necessary. The next step is to look at the frequency of the meeting. If the meeting is scheduled to occur on a weekly basis, is there scope for it to be rescheduled fortnightly? If so, there's an instant 50% saving. Attendees' preparation time, travelling time to and from the meeting, and time actually at the meeting is not without cost. What if the number of attendees could be halved as well? What if the meeting only needs to occur once a month? What if the meeting can address business in an hour instead of two hours? So far we are down to 6.25% of the original cost of the proposed meeting..

Restricting the number of attendees, length and frequency of the meeting, focuses the attention on the most important aspects only, and prevents deviation from the purpose of the meeting. It discourages 'waffling' and keeps discussion focused. The result should be a punchier and more effective dialogue that results in clear decisions and actions.

Taking this rigorous assessment of necessity to the next level, ask whether there is there a need for a follow up meeting at all, or whether actions can simply be left to their respective owners to carry out following a one-off meeting. Alternatively, if feedback on actions is genuinely necessary, can this be done directly following completion, rather than during a subsequent meeting?

These principles can also be applied to other areas of operational activity. The necessity of meetings or other activity (e.g. writing plans, patrolling a particular area etc.) should be assessed on a cost/benefit basis. (Note that 'cost' does not necessarily refer to financial cost. It could be the cost of time or the cost to another part of the system.) This notion is entirely consistent with the tenets of evidence-based decision-making and prioritisation.

The two following questions can be helpful in ascertaining the balance between costs and benefits:

- Does the value of the activity outweigh the anticipated costs involved?

- Does the likely outcome justify the resources invested in the activity?

For example, there may be an hour-long weekly meeting that reviews routine policing activity. If 15 senior and middle managers are required to attend, then including preparation and travelling time, the cost might be three hours per person. Without trying to introduce an average cost of wages per hour into the equation, this meeting would cost 15 people x 3 hours x 4 times per month = 180 hours per month. If the outcome of the meeting amounts to little more than the allocation of routine tasks that departments would carry out as part of normal business, then is this an effective use of resources and finances? What about if, God forbid, the meeting instigates fresh waste activity, such as to report back on the routine activity? Even worse, what if non-evidence based activity (i.e. tampering) is initiated at the meeting and management insist that this is also reported upon? Costs would spiral out of control.

In order to establish the effectiveness of an activity, such as a proposed series of meetings, it is necessary to determine what value is likely to be added as a result. This can also be done during (or at the conclusion of) the activity by reviewing progress with a view to identifying and rigorously weeding out any non-value elements. Shining a light in this way reveals unseen waste and literally opens the door to additional capacity.

It's Not Just About Meetings

Unnecessary or unproductive meetings are not, of course, the only source of waste in the non-value activity category. Introducing processes that mandate the creation of plans and strategies for even the most straightforward aspects of daily business drives more waste into the system and slows things down. Deming argues that much routine organisational activity is capable of thriving without the need for written instructions, noting:

> Sub-processes need not be clearly defined and documented: people may merely do what needs to be done.[15]

Organisational theorist Karl Weick goes further, cautioning that reliance on plans is a red herring that leads to misplaced confidence:

> Managers keep forgetting it is what they do, not what they plan that explains their success. They keep giving credit to the wrong thing – namely, the plan – and having made this error, they then spend more

---

15   Neave (1990) p.126

time planning and less time acting. They are astonished when more planning improves nothing.[16]

It follows that the top-down intrusion and micromanagement associated with conventional management styles and the devices of the Principal-Agent model (see Chapter Five) are particularly unnecessary and counterproductive in the context of daily business. The constant demands for plans and explanations for problems that simply do not exist (when analysed from an evidential perspective) generate more waste, as operational staff are subsequently required to follow prescriptive one-size-fits-all tactics to address the perceived issues. This type of approach ignores local context and expertise, resulting in even more waste. It also disempowers those who know best how to tackle the issues in their field – the workers.

The greatest impact of these written plans is that they work against the system and impair progress towards the very objectives they ostensibly promote. This is usually because management's insistence on them is not based on any real evidence. A friend of mine who happens to be an experienced and accomplished salesman told me recently of how his new boss has forced him and his colleagues to produce written plans detailing a schedule which lists exactly when he will contact individual clients over the next twelve months. Why? Because the boss said so.

The plan ignores variation, the possibility of new customers signing contracts during the next twelve months and the possibility of other customers exiting contracts (and therefore not requiring a weekly call during their allocated time slot). It also ignores the fact that it measures inputs (i.e. number of calls) which is irrelevant to purpose. It introduces an inflexible template that constrains initiative, limits performance and doesn't actually achieve anything for the company. It treats all customers as being the same. The requirement for these plans demonstrates a lack of understanding of the work and of what is important to the customer. It provides an example of micromanagement so intense as to attract ridicule from observers.

---

16 Weick (1995) p.55

Taxi Driver

An analogy that I use to demonstrate the effect of this type of management style is that of a taxi driver. Normally, unless you are dealing with the most unscrupulous of human beings, the process of travelling in a taxi is no more complicated than telling the driver where you want to go, then paying at the end of the journey. If you use the same company (or even driver) on a regular basis it is likely that mutual trust builds and you become confident that a direct route and fair price will be the norm. This arrangement is beneficial to both parties – the driver gains a regular customer and you can be assured of an efficient and cost effective service.

Now imagine if the type of conventional management we have discussed is thrown into the mix. The first thing the poor driver has to contend with is the demand for a written plan ahead of the commencement of the journey. (In this case the driver happens to be male, only because it saves me from constantly using the phrase 'he or she' throughout this section). Under this new style of management, the driver is now required to write down his intended route in advance and to show the manager a map of the journey. Only after this has been drawn up may he set off. Clearly the effect is that the end-to-end experience is longer, as we wait for the poor chap to write up his plan at the start. If the meter is running, it also costs the customer more. Most significantly, the plan adds no value whatsoever, as the driver still takes the same route.

That was bad enough, but consider the next level of this madness – the manager also demands updates about the driver's progress throughout the journey. This means that the driver has to pull over every few minutes and report back to the manager exactly where they are on the map he has drawn. The result? More delays because of this unnecessary reporting activity, resulting in extra cost, as well as a longer process with more stages that add no value to the customer's experience.

Next, the manager not only wants plans in advance and regular updates, but requires that the driver completes a report at the end of the journey that describes the route taken, the time it took, his average speed, along with any number of other useless pieces of information that might be in vogue that week. Again, this is of no benefit to anyone.

Finally, this particular manager insists on telling the taxi driver how to do his job. Consequently, we have a situation where a competent professional is told at the outset what route to take, how fast to drive, when to stop, when to start and so on. The manager does not know the taxi driver's job as well as he does, yet demands that he travel from 'A' to 'B' via 'Z'. The taxi driver knows of a quicker route but is powerless to intervene and must do as he is told. This also annoys the customer.

In extreme cases, the taxi driver may be admonished at the end of the journey for taking so long to get from 'A' to 'B', even though it was the manager's fault. Really confused managers may try to set an arbitrary time-based target for the driver to complete the journey within, but we won't go there.

The result of all this management interference is that huge amounts of waste are generated because of the non-value activity that has been introduced into the process. Costs increase, the end-to-end time is stretched beyond your wildest imagination and there is no actual benefit to anyone. From a wider systems perspective, so much of this driver's capacity is now swallowed up performing pointless tasks that he is unable to service other customers' needs. He also feels demoralised and his taxi has a shorter working life due to excess mileage, wear and tear. The taxi company is unable to cope with demand, loses customers and suffers reputational damage. It's a lose-lose situation for all concerned.

The solution is simple – just let him do his job. If he keeps getting lost, is regularly late, fails to keep appointments for pick-ups, or charges too much for his services he will go out of business. It's in his interests to do a good job. It's in everyone's interests to allow him to do so and to keep the whole process simple and free from waste

Best Efforts + Rigid Policy = Chaos

Another major cause of waste in this third category is inflexible policy and practice. Rigid parameters for operational responses and working practices are guaranteed waste generators. This is particularly true in the public services environment where there is a wide variety of demand. Unlike a manufacturing plant that produces identical metal components, it is impossible to predetermine parameters for a truly 'customer shaped' response when dealing with service users who present highly individualised requirements. Victims of crime or hospital patients, say, will bring with them unique experiences and needs, and responses that rely on inflexible ready-made templates will always be an ill fit.

A case study that illustrates this involves the current focus on anti-social behaviour (ASB). In 2007, the profile of ASB sky-rocketed following the tragic deaths of Fiona Pilkington and her daughter, who had experienced sustained ASB from local youths.[17] An investigation by the Independent

---

17   Police Errors Contributed to Suicide of Tormented Mother Fiona Pilkington, *The Guardian*. (2009). [Online] http://www.guardian.co.uk/uk/2009/sep/28/fiona-pilkington-suicide-mother-police]

Police Complaints Commission (IPCC) concluded that the response of the police and other agencies had been inadequate and uncoordinated. It identified procedural errors, missed opportunities and inadequately investigated criminal allegations. As a result, four officers were held personally accountable and faced misconduct proceedings.[18] Leicestershire Police and other forces vowed to review what could often be a disparate response to ASB cases in the hope that such a tragedy could be prevented in future.

Further influenced by critical media reporting, the national response was to designate ASB as a priority amongst other existing police priorities. This resulted in the introduction of what I consider to be well-intentioned but largely inflexible policies that fail to take into account the uniqueness of each ASB case. These policies rely on menu-driven questioning, matrices and scoring templates that are designed to generate a numerical score in an attempt to pinpoint a caller's degree of vulnerability, along with the precise degree of threat and risk associated with the incident. The opportunity to apply professional judgement is severely limited. Clearly, whatever system was in place previously had been ineffectual in preventing the tragedy, and it was right that it be reviewed, but my concern is that some new procedures focus primarily on initiating a rigid templated response to a wide variety of cases – and evidence demonstrates that this does not necessarily reduce risk or protect the vulnerable more effectively.[19]

First, there has never been a universally accepted definition of ASB. Incidents as diverse as the following have been know to fall under the ASB classification. (These examples are from personal knowledge.)

- Neighbours closing their kitchen cupboards too loudly.

- Youths walking through a shopping centre, but not actually doing anything wrong.

- Children playing football on the grass.

Current policies categorise a set of unique circumstances into predetermined classifications, which then generate predetermined types of response. Effectively, this means that a wide continuum of threat and risk is categorised through a series of arbitrary filters and handled as though cases are identical.

---

18 IPCC publishes Fiona Pilkington investigation report (20110 [Online] http://www.ipcc.gov.uk/news/Pages/pr_240511_pilkington.aspx

19 Broadhurst *et al.* (2010) pp.352-370

Secondly, the new templates are largely perception-based; in other words if a caller has a particularly low threshold to nuisance behaviour and interprets their experience in a distinctly negative way, this heavily influences the police response. Conversely, a person who doesn't want to be a nuisance might actually play down their experiences and so fail to generate a high enough score on the points system to warrant the degree of response they need. In 2010 I was able to demonstrate that literal interpretation of one such policy could lead to a blue light response to a dog pooing on a pavement. Of course it was never anyone's intention that this should happen – it's ridiculous – but the fact that the policy relies on numerical scoring, rather than the professional judgement of frontline expertise, meant that a certain configuration of factors could, hypothetically, produce this degree of police deployment.

Third, in each case officers are required to record and investigate the incident in the same fashion as if a crime had occurred. A huge amount of paperwork becomes obligatory as soon as an incident is classified as ASB, along with an intrusive and extensive audit and inspection regime. The auditing tends to focus on technical compliance with the policy, such as:

- Whether incidents have been classified correctly

- Whether the right type of reference number was generated

- Whether a series of predetermined responses were triggered

- Whether the correct paperwork was completed

- Whether anyone has made any mistakes.

This mode of inspection shifts the emphasis away from identifying whether purpose has been achieved and towards passing or failing the audit. Instances of audit failure (and subsequent rework) are possible even in cases where a member of the public has actually received an effective and bespoke service. (I know of cases where purpose has been achieved, yet the associated paperwork has failed the audit.) It also focuses effort on certain internally-biased aspects of the process, which could lead to the types of behaviours associated with targets.

All cases are subject to a supervisor's review on a weekly basis; the supervisor is then required to report back to senior management during weekly and monthly meetings. In some cases, the volume of paperwork, checking by supervisors, auditing and reporting back information to the centre exceeds the amount of activity associated with actual crime investigations.

None of this achieves anything for the member of the public who wants help to resolve their ASB problem. Naturally, the resources and time ploughed into this burgeoning area of business come at a cost, not least to other parts of the system. Capacity becomes so restricted that the ability of the organisation to deal with relatively straightforward matters is impaired, risking a buildup of unmet demand. By focusing effort on introverted recording activity and prioritising internal organisational requirements ahead of activity designed to achieve purpose, the system slowly grinds to a halt and the public will experience a diminished level of service. Workers can either spend time *doing* the job, or *writing about it*; there are only a certain number of hours in the day.

Whilst the sudden prioritisation of ASB and the resultant creation of policies were intended to identify and protect the most vulnerable, I question whether this aim is always achieved. The categorisation and sheer volume of work associated with ASB risks losing the genuine cases in the 'noise'; an inflexible policy-driven approach can obfuscate the cases where people need the most protection. Processes geared towards meeting internal reporting and classification requirements can often fail to achieve purpose from the service users' perspective.

Unfortunately, the approach does not look as though it is going to go away. As recently as May 2012, the Home Secretary announced new plans to 'force' police to investigate cases of ASB following complaints by five separate people, or three complaints by one person.[20] These trigger points and the centrally-driven directives that follow beg questions such as, "Where do the thresholds of 'five' and 'three' come from?" as well as raise concerns that the proposals will intensify the process-driven one-size-fits-all approach further. Will any of this really help the police service to help victims of ASB?

One Size Doesn't Fit All

A good way to expose the waste generated by rigid policies and standardised 'solutions' is to consider the problem using a theoretical 'one-size-fits-all problem box', as below.

---

20   Tubb (2012)

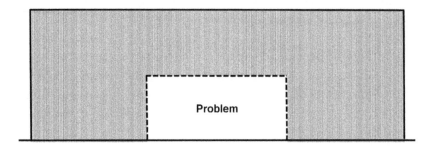

Figure 7.2: 'The One-Size-Fits-All Problem Box' – Configuration One

In this configuration we see that the one-size-fits-all box is easily able to contain the problem, but there remains an excessive amount of unused capacity, represented by the grey shaded area. This is akin to a disproportionately large response to a relatively small problem; a sledgehammer to crack a nut, if you like. (Remember the child being arrested for throwing water bombs from the last chapter?) This configuration would also be indicative of a hefty non-evidence-based response to a perceived problem that relies on standardised tactics (such as deploying a large number of officers into an area to conduct high visibility patrols) without understanding the extent of the issue at hand, or assessing the likely benefits of the tactic. In each case, waste is generated that robs other parts of the system of the capacity they require.

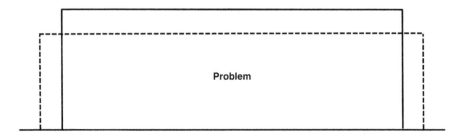

Figure 7.3: 'The One-Size-Fits-All Problem Box' – Configuration Two

In Configuration Two, the one-size-fits-all box is unable to contain the problem (the boundaries of which are shown by the dashed lines) due to its incompatible dimensions. There is sufficient overall capacity, which would be capable of containing a problem of equal volume, but the response is an ill fit due to its rigid design. In this case, apart from the waste that has been generated, the actual problem has not been solved. It is therefore likely to re-emerge, resulting in failure demand and a dissatisfied service user. An example could be that of police officers adhering strictly to a rigid policy or standardised menu of tactical options, when a degree of flexibility would enable them to fully resolve the issue at hand.

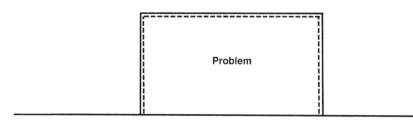

Figure 7.4: 'Not The One-Size-Fits-All Problem Box'

In this final configuration, featuring an 'adaptive problem box', we see that the box fits neatly around the problem, with no wasted capacity. This can only be achieved by understanding what is required from the service user and designing the response against demand. It is the superior alternative to the other configurations, and the key to effective and bespoke responses.

The One-Size-Fits-All Problem Box is a simplistic visual representation of how wasted capacity and ill-fitting template-driven responses cause waste.

In policing, Waste Type Three can be extremely wide-ranging, despite being easy to identify and eliminate (providing there is the will to do so). Apart from rigid policies and menu-driven responses, it often manifests itself in unnecessary bureaucracy, which impacts on the daily working lives of officers, sapping the system's capacity and restricting workers' ability to carry out value activity. Serving officers who took part in the research for this book comment on the problem, as below:

"I do get frustrated by the pyramid of bureaucracy heaped upon uniformed officers".

"We appear to spend more and more time telling non-operational staff what we intend to do, leaving less time for us to actually do it".

"The amount of paper records generated – which are never read again, save to satisfy the seemingly endless need to provide an audit trail – is a

huge waste of energy and focus".

"We need to cut bureaucracy... "

In his 2008 Review of Policing, Sir Ronnie Flanagan highlighted the endemic nature of this particular form of self-imposed institutional waste within the police service and contended that the key to surmounting it is through tackling the problem from a systemic perspective. As he put it,

> The impact of bureaucracy on staff is significant and we have an obligation to manage it as effectively as possible. Responding to this challenge means we need to look beyond the reform of individual forms, and address the systemic drivers of bureaucracy.[21]

He hit the nail on the head.

It's The Policy

You have heard me railing against prescriptive policy and one-size-fits-all solutions throughout this book. Does this mean that I am advocating a 'free-for-all' without limits, where everyone does just what they feel like? No, it doesn't. Especially in the police service, there are policies, procedures (and the law of course) that determine the extent and type of activity that can and should occur in response to specified sets of circumstances.

Whilst some policies are, in my opinion, excessively restrictive and bureaucratic, there are others that exist for absolutely legitimate reasons. For example, protocols on managing scenes of major incidents are designed to facilitate proven investigative methods. This means that those charged with gathering evidence from a murder scene will have an evidence-based framework from which to work.

In a similar manner, police pursuit policies preclude non-trained drivers from pursuing vehicles that fail to stop. These policies are intended to ensure that only appropriately-trained police drivers engage in pursuits, thereby maximising the likelihood of catching the offenders whilst maintaining public safety. In these sorts of circumstances, policy is necessary and proportionate.

In other cases, however, policies can unduly constrain those subjected to them. The ASB policies that we have just discussed are a good example of this. I argue that the key facets of an effective policy must be:

---

21   Flanagan (2008)

- Necessary

- Proportionate

- Evidence-based.

In other words, first of all there must be a genuine need for the policy. Ask yourself, "What would happen if this policy didn't exist?" If its absence would have little or no impact, then it isn't needed. (Clearly a new policy was necessary after the Pilkington case.)

Next, a policy must also be proportionate – does it rely on a sledgehammer to crack a nut? Is risk avoided, rather than managed? Is the policy realistic to implement and meaningful to those who will be expected to operate under its auspices? Finally, it must be evidence-based, otherwise even a policy born of genuine necessity will be incapable of achieving what it sets out to achieve – it would be little more than formalised tampering.

Policies must always incorporate a degree of flexibility around the edges and include an acceptance of variation. Proportionate policies encourage evidence-based good practice whilst preventing well-meaning but directionless activity. The combination of such frameworks and frontline professional judgement will facilitate learning and good practice. The test will always be whether a particular policy or procedure assists the workforce in achieving purpose. If it doesn't, it is waste and it will cause more waste.

In What I Have Done And In What I Have Failed To Do

Finally in this section, an interesting twist on Waste Type Three is the notion of *omissions*. So far we have looked at non-value *activity*; in other words, positive acts that contribute towards waste or which are innately wasteful themselves. When compiling my four types of waste I tried to ensure that nothing was missed, that all conceivable types of waste fitted into one of the categories; otherwise I must be prepared to revise my work. Theories are there to be tested, challenged and re-written after all.

Recently, whilst waiting in a queue at a supermarket checkout I had one of those little debates with myself about whether or not I should designate a fifth type of waste. I was considering whether waits and stoppages are a separate type of waste, or whether they fit into the non-value activity category. I thought about hold ups, idle time, queuing, and not undertaking value activity when capacity is available to do so. Waiting in the supermarket queue itself could be considered to be a sort of bottleneck – maybe this is why I began to wonder about such things. Initially it seemed that there was a clear distinction between the positive wasteful acts that we have considered so far and the lost opportunities, delays, inaction and inefficiencies that are equally culpable as sources of waste in processes and systems.

I was on the verge of designating a fifth type of waste when another voice entered the debate, arguing that non-value activity should include omissions. Why should there be a requirement for non-value activity to be a positive act? Even queuing (as I was doing at the time) is doing *something*, even if it isn't particularly 'active' activity. Just because a passive element is introduced into the mix, I don't necessarily think that it should be separated out from other non-value activity. I see non-value activity as comprising both positive and passive acts, as well as wasted capacity and omissions. So, by the time I was at the front of the queue I had made the decision to treat omissions, delays, waiting time *et al* as components of Waste Type Three.

Anyway, as I pointed out earlier – who cares how waste is classified? Just identify it and get rid of it.

Waste Type Four:

Disproportionate amounts of value activity.

This type of waste is different from the other three, as it focuses purely on *value activity*. It's true – you *can* have too much of a good thing. Doing too much of something in one area means that excessive capacity becomes consumed there, when resources might be utilised more beneficially elsewhere in the system. Just because an activity is certified value activity does not justify depleting excessive amounts of capacity to undertake it, particularly if cost/benefit analysis indicates that the anticipated benefit diminishes in proportion to cost after a certain point.

We need to understand the effect on the overall system. Optimising one part of it always comes at the expense of other parts (flattening a bump in the carpet here is likely to cause another bump to appear over there). The overall result is that sub-optimisation occurs and the whole system suffers.

The key to identifying and preventing Waste Type Four is by applying the principles of proportionality, using an evidence base as a starting point. Useful (but not exhaustive) questions that can assist may include:

- What is the extent of the problem?

- Is the perception of the problem backed up by data?

- What evidence is there that the proposed tactic will combat the problem?

- How do we assess the extent of the effectiveness of the proposed solution?

- What is the defined purpose of the suggested activity?

- How will we know when it is appropriate to disengage?

- What are the likely effects on other parts of the system if we go ahead and implement the tactic?

- Do the anticipated effects on other parts of the system justify implementing the proposed tactic?

As an example of good practice, let's assume that the issue at hand is determining the level of resources required to police a football match. The type of evidence that match commanders (a police term that does what it says on the tin) would need to consider could include: the anticipated number of fans; any history of animosity between the clubs; the time of day (evening games can tend to be more problematic due to the accessibility of alcohol); any intelligence that may exist to suggest there could be disorder; how many officers were required to police the fixture last time around and how effective that deployment was; and so on. Assuming that all these elements have been considered and it is decided that 100 officers would be needed, then commanders would next have to assess the likely effect of this deployment on other parts of the system.

Things to consider would begin with deciding where to draw the 100 officers from. Next, deciding whether it is better to pay overtime and rely on volunteers rather than remove officers from their usual duties. If so, will budgets allow this? If the overtime option is preferred then this means that the budget is no longer available for other requirements. What about a mix of overtime and duty time officers? How much of a hit can teams take if they are required to provide officers in duty time? What else might suffer? What are the reputational risks to the force and the threat to the public if insufficient officers are drawn from whatever source to police the event and mass disorder ensues? What is the priority? It's not easy, is it?

Anyway, assuming that 100 officers will be required and all systemic considerations have been taken into account, commanders need to resist the temptation to increase the deployment to 125 or 150 officers to 'make sure' the event is easily managed, or 'just in case'. The moment decision makers deviate from doing what the evidence base indicates is necessary there will be an adverse effect on the system and gaps will begin to appear elsewhere. True, an extra 50 officers would be a luxury that makes the event much easier to police, but at what cost? Response teams will be depleted and unable to effectively respond to demand, neighbourhood officers will be unable to keep their promises to attend community events, and others abstracted from their core roles will also be leaving their own workloads unattended. Furthermore, not all officers working at the football match will be gainfully employed on the day if there are too many of them. Some effects of deviation from the evidence-based approach will be measurable; others intangible. All will generate waste elsewhere in the system.

Similarly, if a neighbourhood policing team is planning a major crime prevention programme that involves visiting households and giving advice about how to prevent burglaries, as well as dishing out free alarms and marking property with ultra-violet markers, this must only be undertaken after assessing the evidence base and carrying out a cost/benefit analysis. It would be great to be able to 'carpet bomb' a whole area with this level of service, but if the data indicate that there isn't a significant burglary problem, then what is essentially value activity actually causes waste. The degree of anticipated benefit does not warrant the extent of the activity.

In the same way, say the evidence base suggested that a particular set of streets were vulnerable to burglaries. It would be great to provide this intensive crime prevention service to the *whole* estate, but it wouldn't be appropriate. Expanding value activity such as this beyond the parameters indicated by the evidence base, translates into a blunt and disproportionate response to the problem. Whilst officers are busy visiting households at the periphery of the estate, where there hasn't been a burglary since 1974, other genuine problems go unaddressed. The extra activity is also unlikely to have a direct effect on the burglaries either – if the evidence base suggests 75 houses within a defined burglary hotspot need additional protection (or 100 officers are required for a football match) then those are the parameters that must be adhered to – otherwise a situation occurs where no greater benefit will be realised, yet increased cost and waste is guaranteed. In a world where resources are finite, management must prioritise activity from the evidence, facts and data.

A final example is found by returning to inspection. As we have discussed, a proportionate degree of inspection can be appropriate in some circumstances, particularly if there is a significant degree of risk involved. (Deming argued we should *cease reliance* on inspection, not abandon it completely.) The right amount of inspection in the right circumstances is value activity. Conversely, disproportionate amounts of otherwise justifiable inspection, or indeed *any* inspection in circumstances where the level of risk does not justify it, equate to Waste Type Four.

Ooh, That Sounds Risky!

At the root of Waste Type Three and Four is the scourge of risk aversion. This is where managers or the prevailing organisational climate prefer the 'just in case' approach out of fear that something may go wrong at some point in the future. It discourages decision-making and risk management in favour of disproportionate one-size-fits-all responses, extensive written doctrine, rigid policies and retrospective criticism. It is responsible for knee-jerk reactions and tampering, which of course generate more waste. Meanwhile, frontline workers are forced to operate amidst a culture of back covering and the ever present fear of blame.

The relationship between risk aversion and waste within the police service was highlighted by Flanagan during his review in 2008. He observed:

> ...the unnecessary bureaucracy which can consume officers' time and divert them from more pressing priorities is very often a consequence of risk aversion.[22]

The endemic nature of the problem was also identified in a thematic review of police leadership conducted by Her Majesty's Inspectorate of Constabulary (HMIC) during the same year. The report highlighted the endemic nature of risk aversion and underlined some of its most harmful effects, such as the erosion of discretion and widespread reliance upon rigid policies.[23]

---

22   Flanagan (2008)
23   HMIC (2008)

The Flanagan and HMIC reports pricked the corporate conscience of the police service, yet, four years later, research conducted for this book indicates that risk aversion is still entrenched within the police psyche. One research respondent suggested that it was, in fact, the "predominant culture within the police" and proposed that the reason it was so widespread was, "...because senior managers don't trust more junior officers". Other officers involved in the research supported this perception – the following quotes are typical:

> *"Risk aversion governs most things that we do. There are ever more complex and time-consuming protocols for many types of incident that a common sense approach could easily negate".*

> *"Risk-aversion seems to increase the further up the rank structure a manager gets".*

One officer succinctly pinpointed the difference between risk *aversion* and risk *management*, insightfully making reference to the unique and sometimes unpredictable policing context:

> *"Policing is a risky business. We have to take risks as long as we don't place people at risk unduly. Risk assessment does not mean that we have to be risk averse, it is about managing the risk to minimise it".*

In a similar fashion to the way that 'best efforts', intended to protect victims of ASB, have led to unwieldy and impractical policies, the spectre of organisational risk aversion actually intensifies waste and causes organisational inertia. This leads to a culture where it is commonplace for officers to record huge amounts of information, with disproportionate checks and balances to an unnecessarily defensive degree, in a vain attempt to protect against potential criticism at some hypothetical point in the future. This is absolute waste.

I argue that proportionate risk management, through the application of professional judgement, is the antidote to risk aversion. It also follows that effective risk management is dependent on analysis of the facts (i.e. the evidence base). This leads to a culture of preparedness to act based on the available information, rather than simply falling back on policy, 'back covering', or even delaying (or avoiding) decisions. Such an ethos prevents the waste that is caused by introducing introspective non-value activity (Waste Type Three) or doing too much of a particular type of value activity (Waste Type Four). This necessary transition can only occur, however, in an organisational environment based on trust with a measured acceptance of a degree of risk and proportionality.

My Four Types Of Waste – A Summary

As a quick and easy pictorial reference to the four types of waste, I have devised a simple diagram which is reproduced below. It shows how the four types of waste can enter the system at various stages, thereby disrupting flow, eating up capacity and impairing effectiveness. The diagram also includes some straightforward pointers and solutions on how to avoid each type of waste.

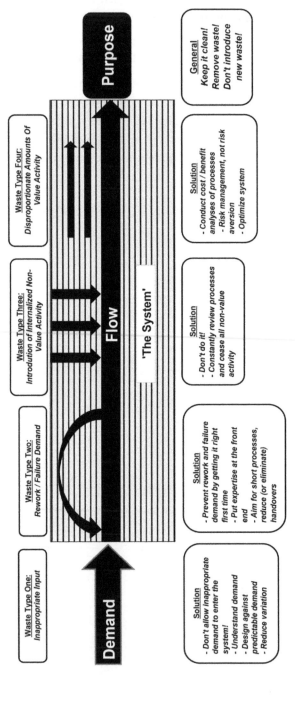

Figure 7.5: How the four types of waste impact on the system

By way of a quick run through, the first defence against waste is in understanding the purpose of the system and then identifying what type of demand it is intended to service. Designing the system or process against the predictable range of appropriate demand enables the correct types of input to be rapidly processed, whilst denying entry to inappropriate input. This staves off the potential problems that would emerge if unsuitable work units were to enter the system (or process) and progress along it, causing proliferation of waste as they go. The solution is like adopting the old policy of many a doorman – "If your name's not down, you're not coming in!"

Next, ensuring that processes are kept as short as possible, with expertise at the front end, a minimum number of handovers, and an emphasis on building in quality rather than trying to 'inspect it in', reduces the likelihood of failure demand. Keep flow even, break down barriers between departments and remove inappropriate incentives and internal competition. Do the right thing, understand the capabilities of the system or process, don't set arbitrary targets and Hey Presto – the numbers look after themselves and flow is accelerated.

So far so good. We now have the right kind of input being handled by a system that is designed to process it effectively, managed by those who understand the system's capabilities. The trusted and empowered workers within the system are merrily processing value demand and well on their way to achieving purpose. We now have a situation where waste is an endangered species within this system; the way it should be. The next trick is not to suddenly shoot oneself in the foot by introducing waste! Understanding variation, analysing data and only acting when an evidence base indicates a response is necessary, ensures that managers are on guard against the temptation to react inappropriately. It also negates the threat of tampering or reverting to the sorts of counterproductive devices of conventional management that we have discussed earlier.

By keeping self-generated waste out of the equation (e.g. unnecessary bureaucracy, plans, reports, reporting mechanisms, internalised audits, excessive meetings etc.) capacity is released to concentrate on value activity. The result is that purpose-driven work is processed more quickly and more effectively, unhindered by the self-destructive shackles of Waste Type Three. A further benefit is that the increased levels of available capacity serve to absorb any peaks amongst the variation present within ongoing work, and also reduce the likelihood of hold-ups, bottlenecks or delays. The icing on the cake is to keep all processes under constant review, strive to continuously improve them, and shut down any activity that does not contribute towards purpose, whenever and wherever it is found.

The final stage involves determining the amount of value activity that is necessary and proportionate to achieving purpose. Managers must use data and evidence to establish the optimal balance between cost and anticipated benefit. Sometimes this involves a degree of risk – if so, accept it, understand it and manage it. Don't try to avoid it. Do avoid sub-optimisation, however, and understand the system as a whole, including the interdependencies and interconnections that hold it together. Be aware that they may not always be obvious! Don't over-egg the pudding in one area of operations, or you will run out of eggs for another equally important pudding somewhere else in your 'systems bakery'.

Finally, don't go and hunt for waste to eradicate until you understand your demand profile and how your system operates. That would be flying blind.

In summary, please see the 'official' advice, below.

It's as simple as that.

If you follow these pointers, waste should be able to not enter and destroy your system.

CHAPTER EIGHT

Design Consequences

The previous chapter explained how to identify and understand different types of waste, and also considered a few aggravating factors such as risk aversion. In this chapter, I want to delve further into the underlying causes of waste and its effect on the system. Using case studies from the policing environment, I will also examine valiant yet fundamentally flawed techniques which managers sometimes apply in an attempt to remove waste or to increase capacity.

Overall, I intend to show that, aside from deep-seated cultural 'waste multipliers' such as risk aversion, *the overriding causes of waste within any system or process are its structural design and operating conditions.*

First, I want to look at how *not* to try to reduce waste or enhance capacity...

Method One: Salami Slicing

The salami slicing method is a widely adopted approach to downsizing in the name of (allegedly) becoming more cost-efficient. This method usually starts with a numerical target being set, either internally or by the government, such as a 20% budget reduction. Managers then strive to cut back operations (or departments, jobs, etc.) by the requisite proportion. Little regard is paid to the overall effect on the system or whether the percentage of cuts can even be sustained. 'Doing more for less' is the optimistic proclamation, but the reality is that cuts are often applied indiscriminately, with value activity being slashed in the same proportion as waste activity. No actual benefit is derived from the exercise; the inefficiencies that blighted the organisation beforehand are still there.

This is why the 'salami slicing' analogy is so appropriate. Simply positioning the knife 20% of the way along the salami and then cutting it will certainly achieve a 20% reduction, but at what hidden cost? The *best* that the organisation can hope for is that its new structure is smaller in overall size, but it will still be clogged with the same proportion of waste. If the cuts are made without any degree of insight, the organisation will actually be *less able* to cope with demand, having eliminated 20% of its previous capacity for handling value activity.

By setting a reduction target first, managers are starting from completely the wrong position. If you don't understand the purpose of the system, its interdependencies and the current proportion of waste it contains, then it is absolutely impossible to say whether a 20% reduction is achievable. It may well be that only 5% waste exists in a particular system so cutting it by 20% will destroy the system. Conversely, some parts of a system may contain 60% waste, so blindly cutting everything at the 20% mark means that a huge opportunity to reduce waste has been missed. It also leaves the new, smaller system with 60% waste in it!

The 'salami slicing' method is fundamentally flawed because it fails to differentiate between waste and value whilst the cuts are occurring. The proper way to reduce the size of a system is to look at what's *in* the salami and only remove the waste.

Method Two: Mopping the Floor

The other hopelessly ineffective (but popular) method of attempting to enhance operational capacity is analogous to increasing the number of people mopping a flooded floor, whilst ignoring the running tap that is causing the flood (the real problem). This approach is so counterproductive that it actually increases waste without ever solving the problem. It occurs most often because some managers make the assumption that all demand must be necessary (Waste Type 1).

This type of situation arises when managers see a particular department or function struggling with incoming demand. They immediately assume that this is because they are insufficiently resourced, so they divert resources from somewhere else to plug the gaps. The problem with this is that it ignores the possibility that the department or function is struggling because it is swamped with waste. It is also blind to the fact that 'somewhere else' will be depleted of resources as a result and is likely to start struggling with its own demand. Additional moppers end up being recruited from the sweeping department, leaving that department bereft and so on. This management reaction is typical where the system is organised into individual functional silos.

The mop approach is similar to some of the knee jerk responses and tampering that we examined previously. It is only ever capable of achieving a short-term solution at best (i.e. the floor isn't so flooded anymore – until the mopping stops, that is!). Meanwhile, other parts of the system creak under the strain and the overall result is a system that spins out of control or collapses.

The *only* way to deal with this situation is to turn off the tap. Go upstream, locate the source of the problem and *deal with it.* Mopping the floor is just an attempt at managing the symptoms. Once you have freed up the ten moppers you can redeploy them to value activity. The effect on the system of eliminating the non-value activity is that not only is the problem solved without any adverse effects, but, best of all, additional capacity has been created.

Design Faults

This latter approach is typical of some ill-informed conventional management practices. It sets off a chain reaction that begins with the assumption that all activity is value activity. We know that the answer to resolving these problems lies in adopting a whole system perspective and in acknowledging the fact that not all organisational activity is necessarily value activity.

Put simply, by reacting to isolated peaks in demand (rather than designing the system to meet demand) managers are doing nothing more than tampering with the system and barking up the wrong tree. The overwhelming proportion of any system's productivity comes about as a result of system design and conditions (not those working within it), and it should be obvious that deficiencies can only be remedied by addressing their systemic causes. Setting targets or berating the workers will not solve the problem; neither will arbitrary adjustments of resourcing levels or functional responsibilities. Vigour does not cure statistical impossibilities.

If, by analysing demand, understanding variation and gaining an appreciation of how work flows through relevant processes, managers discover that additional capacity is genuinely required in a particular area, they should only make adjustments with an awareness of the anticipated systemic effects. But, if processes do not need to be completely redesigned, the obvious first step of this 'adjustment programme' is to remove waste from existing processes. After this has been achieved, management's next obligation is to trace the sources of the waste and shut them down.

As discussed earlier, some sources of waste are relatively intangible and deep seated, such as cultural factors like risk aversion or a lack of organisational trust. These environmental conditions act as 'waste multipliers' and exacerbate existing organisational waste generators, such as duplication caused by complex filing systems or inflexible policies. Sometimes it's a 'chicken and egg' situation; no one can work out which came first – the inflexible policy or the organisational disposition of mistrust that required such a policy? These cultural causes can be difficult to tackle, so it may be more pragmatic to address the system design and operating conditions first before attempting to transform organisational culture. You never know, by demonstrating that you can achieve one mission, you might influence the other.

In my experience, sources of waste can be quickly traced to tangible design faults in the system, such as departments working in isolation, tight remits, restrictive policies, inappropriate incentives, internal competition, expertise positioned far from the front end and so on. The easiest way to 'turn off the tap' is to examine the design and operating conditions of the system to establish exactly how they generate waste. Moreover, this exercise provides the mandate to subsequently redesign parts of the system; the justification for doing so comes from the evidence base that this procedure uncovers.

Let's now have a look at this concept in more detail...

More Squads, More Remits, More Confusion

In policing there is a tendency to organise the work through specialist squads or tight departmental remits. When I joined the police I could deal with anyone I arrested, whether it was for assault, theft, house burglary, drugs possession, vehicle crime or anything else. Nowadays, there are specialist teams that exist purely to deal with a particular type of crime or incident. For instance, we have vehicle teams, burglary teams and robbery teams. Furthermore, in my force, detectives are currently based in separate local CID and force CID teams, as well as in Public Protection Units (PPU). These departments all deal with separate types of crimes or, in some circumstances, sub-groups of crimes.

Local CID operates under a policy that it will deal with robberies as long as they are not classed as 'commercial' robberies; if someone is threatened in the street and has £200 stolen, it will be local CID that investigates.

Conversely, if the robbery was committed in a shop and the £200 was the day's takings, this would be classed as a 'commercial' robbery and force CID would take on the enquiry. If the victim of a robbery was the ex-partner of the robber, then the PPU should technically deal with it because the matter would now be classed as a 'domestic' offence. Confusing, isn't it?

Similarly, uniformed officers will deal with low level assaults, local CID with slightly more serious assaults and force CID with the most serious assaults. PPU will sometimes argue that a serious domestic assault belongs with CID, whilst CID will contend that the domestic dimension of such an incident makes it the PPU's responsibility to investigate. Sometimes the determining factor is the precise level of injury sustained during an attack. Response and neighbourhood officers tend to pick up everything that falls just short of a particular threshold, or which doesn't fit neatly within the boundaries of a specific category.

In my experience, most criminals do not specialise. I know of offenders who will happily steal a car and break into a house. The same people will often involve themselves in drug-related offending, domestic abuse, shoplifting or street violence. But, whatever they are caught doing on a particular day will determine which team deals with them. Response officers are usually first on the scene, and then the problems begin:

- If they are a prolific burglar but have been arrested for vehicle crime on this occasion, the burglary team won't touch them.

- If they are one of the vehicle team's target criminals but have been caught with drugs, the vehicle crime team won't deal with them.

- If they are a renowned street robber, but have only beaten someone up and not stolen anything in the process, the robbery team won't get involved.

- If they are a high risk domestic abuse offender who has set about his or her ex-partner's new partner, then technically it's not a domestic abuse offence so the PPU won't get involved.

- These high risk offenders often receive extra attention from the offender management team, but when they've been arrested it is not usually in their remit to actually deal with the prisoner.[1]

---

1   Known criminals who present a risk are also managed by offender management teams who try to divert them from crime and implement 'control measures' such as home visits and induction into drugs clinics.

This situation sounds farcical, and it is. Even when officers based in specialist departments express a desire to become involved, they are often prevented from doing so by supervisors who stick to the department's precise policy remit. This can create tensions between departments and also leads to a perception of unhelpfulness. Actually, it is the fault of the fragmented system design and operating conditions, and not necessarily the individual. (As a Constable I recall catching someone in the act of handling stolen property and being admonished by my Sergeant because this type of crime wasn't within the group of offences that my team was supposed to be targeting! Silly me.)

Divide and Don't Conquer

Even in the most straightforward of cases (i.e. those that would not necessarily require the finely honed investigative acumen of a seasoned detective), this approach of dividing up responsibilities often results in mandatory handovers once an offender is arrested (typically by a frontline officer). In systems terms, the concept of separating out functions and handing over aspects of work between people or departments is known as *division of labour*. It results in arguments about what is in whose remit and how policy is interpreted, as well as a whole host of other side effects such as the reinforcement of silo working, fractious working relationships and sub-optimisation.

A common complaint amongst response officers in particular is that there are too many departments with tightly defined remits. Aside from the inherent waste associated with the obligatory handovers to such departments, this type of functionally-based operating model often results in work being rejected on the premise that it 'doesn't quite fit' a particular department's remit. The usual result is that frontline uniformed officers often have to take up the slack. This impacts on the capacity that is needed for an effective initial response to incidents.

Research conducted for this book found this to be a widespread problem in various forces. For example, one response team Sergeant quipped:

> *"Every department except response has a remit"*.

Other officers also alluded to the problem:

> *"It often seems to be the case that specialist departments appear to 'fob' jobs down to response teams when, at times, it's clearly a matter for another department to deal with"*.

"The general rule of thumb is that EVERY other department can pick and choose the incidents they attend and jobs they deal with. Response, however, do not have that option. Response officers in my station have dealt with a number of incidents that clearly fall within the remit of other departments; Section 18 assaults [Grievous Bodily Harm with Intent], sexual assaults, serious frauds, burglary dwellings, robberies and serious handling stolen goods come to mind".

I find these comments particularly interesting as they expose the ingrained (if begrudging) acknowledgement that policy is, indeed, the final arbiter. Whilst the officers appear unhappy about specialist departments apparently avoiding their responsibilities, they are implicitly stating that certain matters do not belong with their teams either. Effectively, the system design and behavioural norms that it generates have caused adversarial inter-departmental relationships. This is guaranteed to cause sub-optimisation and affect cooperation.

Again, this demonstrates the limitations of one-size-fits-all approaches and template-driven responses that rely on neat and precise combinations of factors; these rarely exist in real life. It is impossible to write policies that cover all conceivable eventualities. Tight remits and rigid policies cannot absorb the inevitable variety, and ill fits, gaps and anomalies will be commonplace.

Another officer spoke about the fractious relationships that result from teams operating as functional silos with tightly defined remits:

"We have that many different interview teams for different offences it becomes an argument as to who will be dealing with the prisoner".

In some cases, dependence on functional specialisms and tight remits can result in a perverse situation where frontline officers are stretched so thinly that they can barely cope with incoming demand, whilst prisoner handling team officers (or investigative specialists, such as the CID) are scratching around for work. It's like an hourglass where demand builds up at the top, then is gradually filtered through the narrow gap in the middle, before emerging into a world awash with under-utilised resources at the base. One officer described such an occurrence:

"Recently our Custody Intervention Team had more staff than on response! [There was only] one prisoner in the cells and, because he was not in the remit of the CIT, Response were expected to deal with it ... "

It is obvious that this type of situation will impact on the response team's ability to respond to fresh incidents. Meanwhile, the prisoner handlers remain under-utilised. On the one hand we see the response team being overloaded, resulting in capacity being unnecessarily depleted; on the other hand, the prisoner handling team are also using up available system capacity by being inactive. The result is that waste is driven into the system, flow is restricted and it becomes impossible to effectively manage incoming demand.

One officer made the following observation:

> *"My general view is that the smaller the teams, the tighter their remits, the more chafe points, the more specialised and the less useful the team".*

Well said that man!

Pincer Movement

The analogy of an hourglass is probably not a bad one, but when a system's structural design is top-heavy with internal waste generators, this causes an internal imbalance and the bizarre situation where the sand in the *bottom* of the hourglass starts fighting against gravity and tries to push *upwards* through the narrow middle section. Meanwhile, the externally-generated demand continues to push downwards. If the front end of the system is already too small to cope effectively with incoming demand, you can imagine the effect of the pressure from both sides. Officers talk about this phenomenon, about how 'back office' departments actually generate work for the frontline on top of the externally-generated demand that the system is intended to service.

> *"Uniformed officers are at the bottom of the pile. It's like an upside-down pyramid. You've got internal departments creating work for others to justify their own existence. The devil makes work for idle hands doesn't he? We've got enough on our plate already without having to perform tasks for people just so they can compile reports for management. It's sheer empire-building."*

> *"They are the people who arrive at 9am on a Monday and write 'constructive' advice on all relevant crimes. They are commonly thought to have lost their investigative and warranted powers on entry to the role and will not consider taking anything more than a directive role in investigations - tasking officers to make phone calls that they could easily make and grading the levels of risk to victims before dictating the response required with no hint of getting involved themselves."*

"I have to produce 'plans' for everything instead of just getting on with the job. Next month – more plans. What happens to the plans? What is the benefit in spending time writing them? How does another department trump my team so much as to be able to demand I write a plan for them or have to attend a meeting they set up? We don't create work for them!!"

"After I've been on patrol I have to come back into the station to enter on the computer which streets I've patrolled, how many cars I've stopped, what intelligence reports I've put in. What do they do with this information?"

"Some bright spark came up with the idea of 'prisoner monitoring forms'. This means every time we arrest someone we have to handwrite a four page form that contains information that is held on the custody computer, crime report and case file anyway! We get chased up if it isn't done. It's keeping someone in a job in an office somewhere."

Unless such internally-generated workload is based on an evidential need and has a tangible benefit then these additional tasks are little more than the evil offspring of optimistic tampering, and are, by definition, pure waste. (It's that insidious Waste Type Three again, in fact.)

If a particular task does need doing, then managers must weigh up the costs with the benefit, and then consider what resources are available and what the likely effects on the system will be. If the frontline has no spare capacity then it will not be able to absorb an additional workload without something else being dropped. This is dangerous enough where the extra work is value activity; in circumstances where it is not, it means that the officers who are expected to perform the task end up replacing value activity with non-value activity. As you can imagine, this is doubly destructive to the system.

Get the Balance Right

Organisational culture, internal politics and a desire to protect one's own area of operations all play a part in adding dysfunctional elements to a dysfunctional system design. Similar consequences will emerge in even the most clinical or theoretical of systems conditions. The underlying problem is the inbuilt generic instability of the *structural design* of the system. It is doomed from the outset.

To illustrate this, one Inspector summed up the design flaws inherent within the mandatory prisoner handover model that we discussed earlier:

"Response arrest the offender, and take him to custody. They then produce a handover package – which takes as long, if not longer, than actually dealing with the offender".

Whilst previous content has highlighted the inevitable consequences associated with the practice of mandatory prisoner handovers (such as fractious relationships), the above comment goes to the very heart of the problem of handovers in any system or process; namely, the end-to-end process is longer and inherently less efficient. This always has an adverse effect on the overall system, no matter how well people get on or want to help each other.

Before we examine this particular concept in cold scientific detail, let me first acknowledge that sometimes handovers are unavoidable. For example, officers could make an arrest 20 minutes before the end of a tour of duty. Extensive evidence collation ahead of interview might be required and it would not be practical for those officers to stay on duty for many hours to deal with the job themselves. Another example is where a suspect is too drunk to be interviewed. It would be unfair (and costly) to expect the arresting officer to wait around for the suspect to be sober enough to be dealt with, if the office would normally have gone off duty. Furthermore, in some cases the existence of particular specialist departments is entirely necessary. The Counter Terrorism Unit is trained in a unique line of work and it would be inappropriate to expect a response officer to manage an anti-terrorist investigation. Another example would be the Economic Crime Unit, which deals exclusively with complex and high value frauds. There are limits on what the omni-competent Police Constable on a response team can be expected to deal with. The presence of these very specialist units is not incompatible with the theory of building an effective system.

Theoretical arguments against division of labour must always be considered alongside the need to achieve the stated purpose of the system (e.g. to effectively prosecute terrorists or organised criminal gangs operating international multi-million pound fraud rackets). Any notion that such top-end specialist teams are somehow incompatible with systems thinking is predicated on a rigid ideology that ignores real life. Furthermore, any interpretation of systems thinking that suggests all the workers in a system must perform an identical role is a fallacy that translates into some sort of ill-conceived philosophy akin to 'Systems Communism'. As we saw in Chapter One, an effective system can comprise multiple functions and requires a variety of skill sets.

Where an understanding of predictable demand suggests that the presence of specialists is necessary, the key to their effective deployment is in determining the optimum proportion of these specialists. Too many and they become under-utilised; too few and they are unable to handle relevant demand. Both types of mismatch represent waste. After all, it would be ridiculous to invest thousands of pounds training all frontline officers as police helicopter observers if analysis of demand indicates that only 12 officers are required. The important thing is that the *right* amount of specialists are positioned within the operating model so that colleagues closer to the front end can pull on their expertise.

Division of labour and handovers are *always* bad when they exist unnecessarily. If expertise is at the front end it prevents the need for handovers and results in a shorter process. *Any* handover (whether necessary or avoidable) introduces an additional stage into the process and therefore slows it down. The skill is in knowing your system so that you can identify any handovers that are essential and then eliminate all the others.

More for Less?

Now the fun bit.

What with all the public sector cuts that are occurring at the moment, many police forces have redesigned their operating models. A common theme that I have seen is to reduce the size of the response teams and replace their numbers with thematic squads (e.g. vehicle crime teams) or generic prisoner handling teams. These latter teams exist to deal with people arrested as a result of response officers attending incidents. Proponents of this fragmented approach argue that the mandatory handover allows response officers to get back out on the streets more quickly, and that this compensates for the reduction in the size of response teams.

Let's look at whether this actually works using a real life example, followed by some simple maths.

A friend of mine, who works in a rural force where prisoner handovers are mandatory, recently had cause to arrest a shoplifter. Shoplifters are pretty much the most straightforward arrests that officers make, yet on this occasion the rigidity of the force policy defied all efforts to deal with the matter in a pro-systemic fashion. In this particular case, the individual concerned would have been eligible for a caution, meaning that extensive evidence collation for a court case would be unlikely to be required ahead of interview. Upon arrival at the custody block, my friend offered to deal with the prisoner himself but was told that policy dictated he must hand the matter over to the prisoner handling team after obtaining statements, CCTV evidence and completing handover documentation.

Handover documentation varies from force-to-force, but as a minimum it includes: the arresting officer's statement; statements from all witnesses; a narrative of the incident from start to finish; as well as printouts of all relevant documents relating to the case including a copy of the incident log; crime report and associated papers; a copy of the officer's pocket book entry; PNC (Police National Computer) print and details of any exhibits (i.e. CCTV disc). Along with this, there is almost always a pro-forma that lists all the papers attached to the handover package, and this requires a supervisor's signature. Once complete, the prisoner handling team Sergeant must read and check the contents then allocate it to a member of the team. The allocated officer then has to read the contents to understand the incident he or she will be dealing with. All this takes time. The prisoner handling team officer will then commence the post-arrest stage of the investigation.

The end-to-end process for this sequence of events is mapped below:

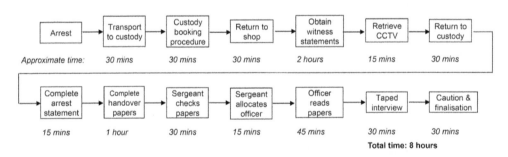

Figure 8.1: From arrest to case disposal (with mandatory handover)

Under this model, the arresting officer can only disengage from the matter once the Sergeant has checked the handover documentation, so he or she is off the streets for six hours. The model also has also caused the following side effects:

- Statements and CCTV evidence that will never be used in a court case have been obtained from members of the public. (Their time is not free!)

- A whole host of unnecessary paperwork and preparatory activity was instigated to meet the standard required to hand the job across to the prisoner handling team.

- Additional strain has been placed on available capacity in the custody block, as the shoplifter has to spend six hours waiting around in a cell before anyone is in a position to conduct an interview.

- More officers were drawn in to the process than was necessary (i.e. the prisoner handling officer and the prisoner handling team Sergeant - their time is not without cost either).

- The end-to-end time of the process was unnecessarily extended.

In contrast, had the arresting officer been permitted to deal with the incident from end-to-end, without involving the prisoner handling team, the process would look like this:

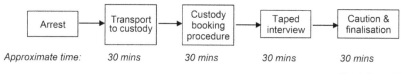

Figure 8.2: From arrest to case disposal (no handover)

The advantages of this model are obvious.

- A shorter, more efficient process.

- No handovers.

- Ownership retained throughout.

- Third parties (police and members of the public) are not unnecessarily drawn into the process.

- Minimal impact on custody block capacity.

- The arresting officer is back on patrol within two hours.

The purpose of introducing a prisoner handling team into the process was to increase the time response officers spend on the street, but by comparing the two models this has clearly had the unintended opposite effect. As well as the additional strain imposed on the custody block, this new model also causes a backlog in the control room (where jobs are allocated over the radio) because response officers are tied up for much longer than they should be. This means there are fewer officers left (on an already reduced response team) to deal with new incidents. These outstanding jobs then begin to stack up, waiting times for officer attendance also increase and the public experience a diminished level of service. This example illustrates the dangers of well-intentioned interference with a system before attempting to understand it.

But Surely that Was Just an Isolated and Extreme Case?

Dysfunctional system design and operating conditions (plus inflexible policies) can and do cause situations like this to arise. Even in cases where the anticipated end-to-end time is much shorter than in the above example, underlying theory dictates that handover-based processes will always be less efficient. Let's have a look at this concept in a bit more detail...

What follows is a hypothetical study on capacity and flow using 'before' and 'after' models relating to a police response team. In the 'before' model, the team consists of 20 officers who deal with their own cases from start to finish. For the purposes of the study, we will only look at capacity and flow in relation to those incidents that result in someone being arrested. We will also assume that each case is identical in terms of processing time, that demand is predictable and the officers involved are those new 'super officers' who do not require such distractions as refreshment breaks.

(It is accepted that in real life policing, demand can be unpredictable and flow is often uneven. In addition to this, each individual incident resulting in an arrest is different and officers also deal with a range of other incidents. However, I am discounting these factors here to keep this experiment 'clean', so that a direct comparison can be made between the two models – each model will operate under identical conditions to ensure fairness.)

Here are the parameters for the study:

- Officers on the team work a 10-hour tour of duty each day.

- The initial stage of dealing with an incident takes two hours (including travelling time).

- The post-arrest stage of dealing with an incident takes three hours.

- The assumption is that all activity that occurs during the initial attendance phase and the post-arrest phase is value activity.

(Any frontline officer will tell you that an average total time of five hours for finalising every aspect of an incident involving an arrest is optimistic, but I have chosen these timings to keep it simple and to deflect any accusations of exaggerating the problems which this type of operating model causes. What follows is a hypothetical *best case* scenario.)

Under the 'before' model, one officer on this response team can deal with two complete incidents during his or her tour of duty, as below:

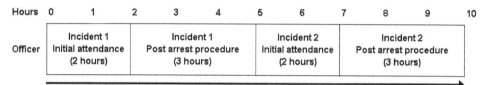

Figure 8.3: 'Before' model – single officer productivity chart

This model has the advantage of having no handovers and no 'idle' time. This means that the only activity which takes place under this model is value activity. There is no waste in the process. For a team of twenty officers, this means that the total team capacity is 40 incidents per tour of duty.

Now imagine that (as in the example involving the shoplifter), response policing has been remodelled and some officers have been channelled away from response policing to provide a dedicated prisoner handling facility. Given that there are a finite number of officers available, the whole point of redesigning police operating models should be to ensure that the newer configuration is the best possible design available. Managers will always want to extract the maximum amount of efficiency and effectiveness when redesigning any system. (Note: If you are a senior manager about to consider implementing this type of model, please, please read this section.)

Let's also assume that handovers from response officers to prisoner handling team officers take a mere 30 minutes, if they are both available to discuss the case whilst completing the necessary paperwork; If not, for the purposes of this study, it will take 30 minutes for the arresting officer to complete the handover paperwork and then another 30 minutes for the prisoner handling officer to read and understand it ahead of dealing with the arrested person. At least there should be no additional impact on the response officer if the prisoner handling officer is unavailable at the point that the handover documentation is compiled, as he or she can leave the completed paperwork and go back out to other incidents within 30 minutes.

(In reality, this is at the optimistic end of the scale, as any frontline response officer will tell you.)

Our team of 20 officers has now been split into one group of 10 officers who respond to incidents, plus a second group of 10 officers who do not respond to incidents but receive handovers from their colleagues. We will call this configuration the 'after' model.

Proponents of this type of operating model argue that although the initial response capability is reduced, those officers who are designated as response officers are available for deployment to new incidents much faster than if they were required to deal with incidents from start to finish. In this case, it means that they should be back out on the streets after two hours instead of five hours.

Here's what proponents believe the process would look like:

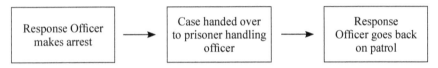

Figure 8.4: Prisoner handling model flowchart

At first glance it would appear that this can only be a good thing. But is it?

Smoke and Mirrors

The first point to consider is that whenever a handover is introduced into any process, it makes the process longer, without actually adding any value. In this case, because of the handover (30 minutes), one incident will now take a total of five and a half hours to deal with (or six hours if the prisoner handling officer has to read the handover documentation without speaking to the arresting officer). This is in contrast with the five hours per incident total that applied under the 'before' model. In both cases, the amount of actual value work in the process (i.e. the initial attendance and the post-arrest procedure) remains the same: two hours and three hours per stage, respectively.

All the handover does is to insert a new stage that wasn't there before. The *best* that can be hoped for is that the total end-to-end time for two consecutive incidents taken together is 11 hours, as below.

(Note: The timeline has been 'zoomed in' to show 30 minute intervals – this is purely to allow the handover stages to be depicted in correct proportion to the other stages. Handovers are marked 'H/O'.)

Figure 8.5: 'After' model – single officer productivity chart

This is interesting enough, but to really uncover the flaws in the 'after' model, we need to look at the overall relationship between the work conducted by the response officers and the prisoner handling officers. This goes back to the very heart of understanding systems and processes, as discussed in Chapter One. *Figure 8.5* simply depicts the chain of activities required to handle two consecutive cases; in other words, it only shows *what* happens, not *who* does what, *how* one part of the process is reliant on another, or the *effect* on the overall system. Appreciation of systemic interdependencies and the notion that what happens in one part of the system is likely to have an effect elsewhere in the system are critical considerations, necessary for gaining a level of understanding that goes beyond the obvious.

Now, consider that there are only 10 officers carrying out the core response role under the 'after' model, as opposed to 20 in the 'before' model. This of course means that the maximum capacity for initial incident management is 10 incidents at a time instead of 20, as previously. It follows that if more than 10 incidents are reported simultaneously, there would be insufficient capacity to manage them and jobs would begin to queue up. This restriction on available capacity at the front end of the process has resulted in the creation of a *bottleneck*. You may recall from Chapter One that bottlenecks dictate the speed of the process from that point on. This means that if demand ever exceeds capacity, even if the flow through the process then stabilises at that rate, the process will *always* be running with an inbuilt lag.

Anyway, to illustrate the best case scenario for the 'after' model, let's assume that the maximum amount of incidents that are reported together is only ever 10. (Never mind that the 'before' model could handle a demand rate of 20 incidents at a time.) Even now, with a stable input of one incident per response officer entering the process, let's see what happens when the interdependencies of the 'after' design are taken into consideration. To do this we will look at how the activity of response and prisoner handling officers occurs together within the process. As there are 10 response officers and 10 prisoner handling officers on the team, the simplest way to visualise this is by examining the activity conducted by one member of each half of the team, side by side.

Response Officer	Incident 1 Initial attendance (2 hours)	H/O (30 mins)	Incident 2 Initial attendance (2 hours)	H/O (30 mins)	Incident 3 Initial attendance (2 hours)	H/O (30 mins)	Incident 4 Initial attendance (2 hours)	H/O (30 mins)

Hours	0	0.5	1	1.5	2	2.5	3	3.5	4	4.5	5	5.5	6	6.5	7	7.5	8	8.5	9	9.5	10

Prisoner Handling Officer	Inactivity	H/O (30 mins)	Incident 1 Post arrest procedure (3 hours)	H/O (30 mins)	Incident 2 Post arrest procedure (3 hours)	H/O (30 mins)	Inc 3 (1st 30 mins)

Figure 8.6: 'After' model – response officer/prisoner handling officer dependencies

It can be seen here that the response officer is able to deal with the initial stage of four incidents and complete the related handover documentation during one 10 hour tour of duty. This means that the 10 response officers can deal with their portion of a total of 40 incidents per tour of duty. This is exactly the same as the amount of initial attendance at incidents that could be dealt with under the 'before model'; i.e. 20 response officers per team, dealing with 40 incidents per tour of duty. In that respect there does not appear to be any advantage in terms of the amount of capacity the team has available for initial attendance under the 'after' model. The suggestion that officers are being released from so-called 'back room activity' to attend more incidents is a either a smoke and mirrors trick or just bad maths. Moreover, 20% of each response officer's time is now spent completing handover documentation.

The rub really comes when the effect of the 'after' configuration is examined in relation to the flow of work and the way in which parts of the process have become disconnected from each other. *Figure 8.6* demonstrates this. After the first handover, the opportunity for face-to-face interaction during subsequent handovers is impeded by the fact that the two parallel processes slip out of sync. As the prisoner handling officer is unable to ask questions about the circumstances of the case, this increases the likelihood of misinterpretation of the material facts recorded in the paperwork, leading to an elevated risk of errors.

Now consider the effect of this model on the end-to-end times of individual cases. In the 'before' model, the maximum end-to-end time per incident was five hours. In the model depicted, the end-to-end time for Incident 4 would be eight and a half hours. This is because there was insufficient capacity within the model to even begin the post-arrest phase until three hours after the arresting officer had completed the handover package.

Whilst this study supposes that flow is constant and all incidents take the same amount of time to deal with, the reality is very different. Natural peaks and troughs in incoming demand mean that there is also an increased risk of inactivity being introduced into the process – prisoner handling officers can experience periods where they literally have nothing to do. This is waste. Aside from the issues surrounding the 'after' model's inability to cope with predictable demand, this configuration with strict functional boundaries increases the likelihood of one part of the process being under-utilised.

Why It All Went Wrong

The consequences of the 'after' model are significant. By breaking up the flow of activity and designating distinct roles to different officers, the 'surface' effect is minimal (i.e. the response officers can still handle the initial stages of 40 incidents per tour of duty) but the unseen effects on the overall system are devastating. Delays are now built into the model, which can only be seen by examining how the processes relating to the different roles affect each other. The 'after' model is spinning out of control, just like Rule Four of the Funnel Experiment (see Chapter 4). As the prisoner handling function cannot keep up with the rate of demand that the response function generates, the two processes slip further and further out of sync.

Figure 8.6 shows the drift that is evident between the points in the two processes where the handovers are positioned. The handovers become increasingly misaligned and the prisoner handling officer has to rely on trying to learn about the nature of the incident from a written account left by the response officer. One effect of this is that each prisoner has to wait longer and longer in the cell block before they can be dealt with, causing additional strain on the capacity of that department. (This is a good example of an unanticipated effect on another part of the system.) The structural design and operating conditions of the 'after' model guarantee that the two separate roles can never be synchronized, and that this will progressively worsen.

By the end of the 10 hour tour of duty, although four prisoners per response officer have been arrested, only two prisoners per prisoner handling officer will have been completely dealt with. This compares with the team operating under the 'before' model, that was capable of handling 40 complete incidents from start to finish during one 10 hour tour of duty.

Good Money After Bad

So, what to do now? Passing the incomplete work onto the next team that comes on duty means that the incoming prisoner handling team suffers reduced capacity from the outset and that there will be a delay before it can deal with the first batch of prisoners generated by its own response officers.

This bottleneck will cause more delays further down the line, and so on. At the end of that tour of duty, there will be even more unfinished jobs and prisoners waiting to be dealt with, and the vicious circle will intensify. Unless there is a let up in the initial rate of demand, the squeeze will get tighter with every tour of duty.

Management could consider pumping overtime at the situation, but this would mean that officers have to routinely stay on duty for lengthy periods to complete the work, plus this method would rapidly exhaust the budget (and the officers).This quick fix 'solution' does not actually resolves the systemic failings caused by the design fault.

Another option would be to try and operate the model until the point where demand exceeds capacity and then use some of the response officers to try and plug the gaps - response officers are taken away from their core role in order to perform 'back room' functions so there are fewer response officers on the streets. It follows that front end capacity is reduced, and incidents will stack up before a response officer is available to deal with them. In effect the bottleneck has just been further restricted and pushed further upstream without anyone actually addressing the cause of the problem. Both this approach and that of prisoners being routinely handed on to the next shift are commonplace in my experience.

This traditional management reaction of shunting work around rather than dealing with the root cause (i.e. a badly designed system) is not uncommon and has predictable consequences. Taking the above example as a starting point, what usually follows could be described as a 'destructive domino effect':

1. The prisoner handling officers become overwhelmed so some of their work is farmed out to response officers.

2. This means that there are fewer response officers available to deal with incoming incidents.

3. Incidents then stack up and there is no one to deal with them.

4. Managers panic about the volume of unresourced incidents and treat the situation as though it has occurred as the result of an unknown 'special cause' that is outside their control and not of their making.

5. Managers instruct other departments, such as neighbourhood policing teams, to stop what they are doing and start dealing with the excess volume of unresourced incidents.

6. The neighbourhood officers' own workload is neglected and begins to stack up because there is no one else to do it.

This could go on but what usually happens is that, in the short term, the excess volume of unresourced incidents is brought back down to 'an acceptable level' (whatever that is supposed to mean), and people talk about what a great team effort there must have been. Phrases like 'all hands to the pump' are heard. This is apt, as the approach is more like fire fighting than fire prevention. (It's exactly the same as the 'mop method' we looked at earlier.) The negative effects creep in later and are usually along the lines of the fabled 'Mrs Miggins' writing to the Chief Constable to complain that the local neighbourhood team aren't doing anything about the parking problems she reported. The local neighbourhood officers would probably love to help, but have been abstracted to 'more important' work, such as keeping a lid on the under-resourced incidents caused by the badly designed system.

Meanwhile, the neighbourhood teams' work has stacked up and thus begins a desperate game of 'catch up'. Ultimately the public are the losers. Management then start asking questions about why the neighbourhood teams have so many outstanding ongoing cases and why public satisfaction is down (usually compared to the last data point).

The other survival technique that can creep in involves the risk of corners being cut; officers might be tempted to rush procedures and paperwork to create space for the next prisoner. The possibility of this occurring does not mean that the officers are bad people – they are trying desperately to make the system work under conditions that prevent them from doing so. Such an approach will often manifest itself in standards of paperwork dropping, which of course is met with the predictable management response of blaming the workers. This is often coupled with the introduction of more stringent controls or inspection mechanisms intended to prevent standards from slipping. One response Sergeant who took part in the research for this book summed up the situation as follows:

> *"We are stretched too thin and juggling too many plates.*
> *Things get missed and we get criticised".*

All of the problems we have exposed so far are down to the system, and no amount of emergency patching will resolve the problem. Likewise, no amount of berating the workers or exhorting them to work harder will fix the problem. They are not the problem – the structural design and operating conditions of the system constitute the problem. In these circumstances, I firmly believe that if there are enough response officers to meet demand in the first place and the work is not divided, the system will be more effective and productive with none of these horrible side effects. There would be no accumulation of unresourced incidents (except if there was a riot or some other unpredictable major incident), no temptation for management to instigate mass-tampering, no angry letters to the Chief and no excuse for blaming individuals for what was an avoidable mess. It would also mean a much better service for the public. Everybody wins.

Assessment of the Models

Whichever way you look at it, when it comes to dealing with incidents that result in straightforward arrests, there does not seem to be a better system design than the 'before' model.

When a prisoner handling team (or even a thematic crime squad) doesn't appear to be coping all that well with demand (despite the best efforts of those on the team), the standard management response often seems to be no more scientific than, "Well let's take a couple more officers from somewhere else to increase the size of the team then". (Mops – taps!)

It is not possible to change one part of the system without affecting another part of it. (Bumps – Carpet!) Increasing the size of a prisoner handling team may give the initial impression of increased effectiveness in that area, but at what cost? This is another example of sub-optimisation. As the 'demand funnel' at the start of the process becomes ever more constricted it diminishes the effectiveness of the response function. The lessons here extend well beyond the realms of prisoner handling teams of course – this is just an example used to illustrate the point. Any system that is predicated on functional departments will be vulnerable to the same fate. The only way to build effective systems and processes is to design them against demand and look at the entire flow of work from start to finish, whilst adopting a whole system perspective.

I argue again that it is critical to get the front end right or everything that follows will misfire.

Shared Services – Shared Pain?

On a lighter note, here's another example of how a system's structural design and operating conditions can be responsible for waste. Once again, the main culprits are division of labour, handovers and inflexible processes. This one's a bit shorter. It might make you laugh, or wince, or both.

Like many large organisations, police forces usually have some form of Occupational Health department, where officers and staff can receive medical and rehabilitative care. Historically, employees who required the services of the Occupational Health department would deal directly with the staff who worked there. Appointments would be booked directly with the department, and if an officer required a follow up appointment this would be done face-to-face with the occupational health secretary at the time. The flowchart for the process would look something like this:

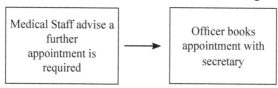

Figure 8.7: Occupational health flowchart (before)

Recently some forces centralised many support functions and introduced Shared Service Centres, or SSCs. The idea behind this was to create a corporate department that dealt primarily with personnel matters, resourcing and occupational health issues. The creation of SSCs involved redeploying staff from other departments to a call centre to deal with enquiries by phone and email. Operators would not necessarily possess any knowledge of the area of business that they would take enquiries about, so after registering a request, their role would be to issue a reference number and allocate a task to the relevant person or department. The person who possessed the relevant knowledge would then respond to the SSC, who would subsequently respond to the enquirer.

This change in the system affected the way that employees were required to book appointments with the Occupational Health department. If an officer needed to book a further appointment, often he or she could no longer do this face-to-face with the secretary. In the new procedure the officer must inform the secretary, who then has no option but to initiate a sequence of events that revolves around the SSC arranging the appointment via the officer's supervisor (who, of course, is not present). The flowchart for this new process looks something like this:

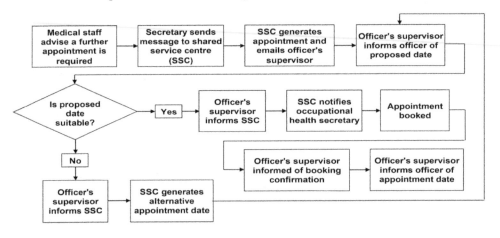

Figure 8.8: Occupational health flowchart (after)

The process now involves multiple additional stages and handovers that weren't present before. The end-to-end time is significantly longer, and the risk of rework and failure demand has increased, particularly if the proposed future appointment date is unsuitable, and the officer only finds out about this via his or her supervisor. To compound the situation, the model prevents an alternative date from being agreed face-to-face at the time with the secretary. If the officer's supervisor is on leave or isn't able to speak to the officer on the day the proposed date is notified this also causes delays. Once the date is agreed, the supervisor then has to advise the SSC that his or her officer has been notified, and there is a further delay until the date is finally confirmed because the SSC has to send out another email to confirm the booking! In any case, the introduction of the supervisor into the booking process represents a new (and unnecessary) feature of the process.

Other side effects include disempowerment of the secretary and the officer who needs the appointment. How would you feel as an adult if you were not allowed to book a GP's appointment yourself, but had to do it through an intermediary? What about the supervisor whose first question to the officer will always be, "Is this date suitable for you?". The process causes the supervisor unnecessary work. What about the secretary who would previously have determined a suitable appointment date and closed the transaction within moments? It could be considered that the entire involvement of the SSC in this process is avoidable and can be classed as waste.

I asked an SSC operator in one force about the new process and she informed me it was the 'criteria they have to follow', despite the fact that she and her colleagues felt that it was cumbersome and unrewarding. She told me that she missed the human contact and interaction that routinely occurred between officers and staff under the previous model. How demoralising must it be to be reduced to recording information and passing messages backwards and forwards via email and phone when you desperately want to provide a quality service for colleagues, and have the skills to do so?

Once again, the pattern repeats itself – a redesign of the system that removes the expertise from the front end, introduces large amounts of waste into what was an extremely straightforward process, and which operates less efficiently and costs more! It also single-handedly de-skills and demoralises good people who want to do their best but who are constrained by a rigid design and prescriptive policies.

When assessing whether any type of shared services function is of benefit, the clue is in the name – does the department actually deliver a 'service'?

If the only activity that takes place is the passing backwards and forwards of messages then the answer is 'no'. As with the example above, no value activity is taking place. If, on the other hand, a joint department existed that dealt with, say, human resources and information technology, where all the operators were skilled in these fields, it would mean that callers would actually have their queries dealt with *at the time* and not simply passed on. In these circumstances, such a shared services department could be a valuable asset because the expertise is at the front end.

It is probable that, in the light of public sector cuts, the rationale for creating SSCs was an attempt at reducing costs by centralising certain functions. The result is a spectacular own goal that adversely affects productivity and drives up costs. All the extra people and activity required to book a simple appointment are not working for free; all the passing of messages, duplication and efforts directed at handling the failure demand has a cost. What might have seemed to be a quick way of cutting back localised functions and replacing them with an all-singing, all-dancing single department is very likely to have a long term adverse (and expensive) effect on the overall system.

As John Seddon points out, "...cost management actually increases costs".[2]

Time to Wrap Things Up

Well, that's it on waste. I hope the theory contained within the last chapter and the case studies in this one have melded together effectively to provide an insight into this monolithic threat to effective systems.

I'm now going to finish this chapter on a similar note to the beginning of the previous chapter, and leave the final word to John Bicheno:

> Keep in mind that the most effective thing you can do to improve the effectiveness of an existing system is to free up capacity. This enables response time to be improved and initiates a virtuous cycle that steadily eliminates problems.[3]

2   Seddon (2003) p.101
3   Bicheno (2008) p.71

CHAPTER NINE

Fixing the system

There's a whole lot more to building a better system than just cutting out a bit of waste. Up to this point I have questioned some widely applied and accepted conventional management practices, and various mainstays of established performance management such as targets, traditional modes of comparison and written plans. You may be thinking, "It's all well and good criticising what we thought was the proper way of doing things; but that's just not constructive..." You'd be right (sort of).

In my defence I'd claim that it hasn't just been about exposing the management practices that irritate me. I have proposed some powerful alternatives, such as SPC and evidence-based policing models; I have highlighted the dangers of tampering, handovers and waste in all its horrible disguises; I have hinted that getting it right at the front end (and maybe even a bit of trust) will go a long way; I've begun to lay out a pathway that leads away from the horror.

What next though? How does one put it all together?

Well, the first stage involves breaking down the original model; the second involves rebuilding a better, stronger one. As Myron Tribus pointed out:

> A hypothesis or idea cannot just be destroyed: it must, in practice, be replaced by something else.[1]

So, it's time to build a systems-orientated model of management that will eclipse every aspect of the traditional format.

Fixing the system is easy - there are only two stages:

1. Stop doing the wrong things.

2. Start doing the right things.

We've spent quite a bit of time on Stage One; let's now concentrate on Stage Two...

---

1   As cited in: Neave (1990) p.352

Purpose – Measures – Method[2]

Purpose – Measures – Method: These three words are on a self-made poster that adorns the wall of my office. Used together, they act like a magic formula to ensure my managerial actions are always compatible with systems thinking. Each informs the other two: Measures must be derived from Purpose otherwise they skew operational activity. Method is dictated by Measures. Method should achieve Purpose.

We will now look at each of them in turn.

What's The Purpose?

Remember Deming's quote, "A system must have an aim"?[3] Well, the starting point for understanding or designing any system is always to go right back to the beginning. Why are we here? What is the police service for? Whom do we serve? Who is our real boss? What is the aim of the system? What is our *purpose*? I covered some of the thinking on this is Chapter One.

When attempting to understand or design any system it is important to define what it is there to do. I'm not advocating a poster campaign of fancy organisational slogans, but if we are certain about what a system is there for, we can quickly identify what the system is *not* there for. For example, a woman who dialled 999 and asked for the fire service to test her plug sockets had her request politely refused by the operator.[4] Without even needing to write down what the purpose of the fire service is (or the 999 system for that matter), it is obvious that this type of demand is inappropriate. By keeping it out, the system avoids becoming embroiled in the things it shouldn't become involved with at all (i.e. 'Waste Type One' in Chapter Seven).

Purpose is the reason *why* a particular activity happens and it must always be defined and understood from the customer's or service user's point of view (i.e. 'outside-in').[5] It is not some lofty corporate strapline that has been dreamt up on a management 'away day', and then subsequently imposed on the organisation. Purpose must always be derived from an understanding of the system's value demand (the demand that the service is there to provide). This ensures that any subsequent definition of purpose is

2   Seddon (2003) p.49; (2008) p.83
3   Deming (1994) p.50
4   Silverman (2012)
5   Seddon (2008) p.80

meaningful; it also enables the system to be designed around what matters to the end user. Bicheno suggests adopting a 'helicopter view'; i.e. looking at the system from above to identify overall purpose, without being too prescriptive or getting into lists.[6] This allows purpose to be understood and defined from a perspective that encapsulates the overarching aim of the system.

Such simple definitions of purpose in different types of settings could include:

- To pay the right people the right money as quickly as possible - Housing benefits.[7]

- To provide a regular, accessible and affordable means of public transport - Local bus service.

- To provide luxury accommodation- 5* Hotel.

To return to policing, the LAPD's well-known mission statement, "To protect and to serve", provides us with a broad, high-level definition of purpose for that organisation. It is obvious, however, that such statements are insufficient descriptors of the myriad policing activities that contribute towards organisational purpose; they are too vague to encapsulate exactly what needs to be done to meet the needs of the end user.

It can be more useful, therefore, to consider organisational purpose as being defined by a set of tiered definitions. The overarching purpose statement ('helicopter view') sits at the top of a pyramid comprising sub-definitions that are specific to different parts of the system. Each lower-level aim must be totally compatible with the high-level stated purpose of the organisation. To illustrate this, we will use the LAPD slogan as a generic statement for the police, and consider the purpose of some of the individual departments listed in Chapter One, *Figure 1.1*, all of which are necessary components of an effective policing system. Each department has a distinct role to play, but its purpose always aligns with the overall aim. This tiered concept can be seen in the 'purpose pyramid', below:

---

6   Bicheno (2008) p.20
7   Seddon (2008) p.79

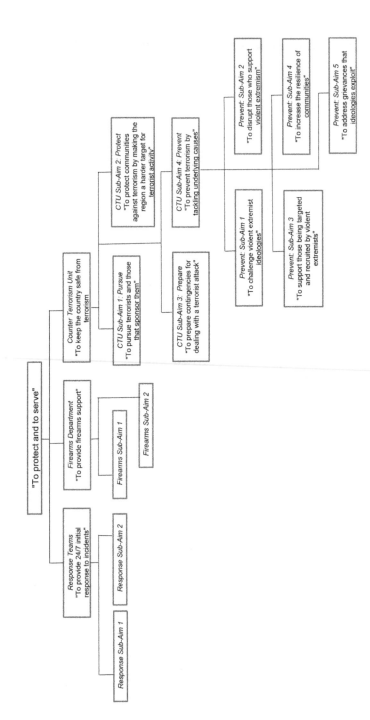

Figure 9.1: Purpose pyramid

Figure 9.1 illustrates how the high-level purpose statement "To protect and to serve" sits above departmental aims, which in turn sit above intra-departmental sub-aims. All are consistent with the overall stated purpose of the system, and all complement each other. I have concentrated on the Counter Terrorism Unit (CTU) to illustrate this, and outlined two sub-layers of purpose that exist within this department[8] (other policing departments would also exhibit similar sub-groups). You can imagine how complex a full organisational chart would be if all the departments originally listed in *Figure 1.1* had their defined aims and sub-aims included. The important thing is that individual strands of activity are always synchronised with the overarching organisational purpose; if they aren't, they shouldn't be there at all.

The Counter Terrorism Unit branches of the pyramid extend to subgroups within the 'Prevent' strand. Each 'mini purpose' resonates with others at the same level, as well as with the overarching 'Prevent' purpose statement, the stated departmental aim of the CTU, and of course the headline organisational purpose of "To protect and to serve". It is apparent that even the individual strands listed within the 'Prevent' category are entirely compatible with the overarching purpose at the organisational level. If no direct correlation can be made between them, then it would be safe to say that lower-level activity had deviated from overall purpose and should be stopped or realigned. On such a chart, you should always be able to identify a clear relationship between the high-level purpose statement and *any* individual sub-aim, no matter how many tiers down the pyramid it is positioned.

As well as defining multi-layered purpose statements in terms relevant to departmental sub-groups, it is also possible to categorise individual *themes* that sit underneath the overall broad statement of purpose. Using a police example again, this alternative thematic approach to defining purpose can also be presented in the form of a pyramid. In this version, the sub-layers transcend departmental boundaries and, as before, complement each other as well as the overall purpose statement. As ever, it is critical that purpose statements at every layer (whether departmental or thematic) originate from identifying what is important to the end user.

---

8   West Midlands Police (2012)

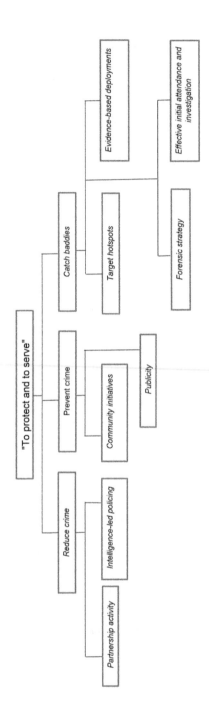

Figure 9.2: Thematic purpose pyramid

This thematic version of a 'purpose pyramid' illustrates how individual policing aims, priorities and themes can be derived from the high-level purpose statement and arranged into a logical structure beneath it. Each header has scope for expansion into its own set of sub-aims or thematic activity, if necessary. Once again, it is essential that the components of the pyramid complement each other and the activity generated is geared towards meeting purpose from the end-user's perspective.

Right, so that was an overview of purpose. Have a think about what *your* organisation's purpose would be if it were written down. What about the purpose of your department, or even your own role? Are they compatible with each other? Are they compatible with the organisation's stated purpose? Does the activity that occurs every day meet purpose from the customer's or service user's perspective?

Next we will look at measures. The way we measure things can define the character of an organisation. Depending on how it is done, measurement can either be a powerful lever for improvement or a suicide pill. Here's why...

Just For Good Measure

Why measure? Well, first and foremost, measurement is necessary to enable us to understand how the system is performing, to predict how it will continue to perform into the future, and to identify opportunities for improvement. Measurement is critical for ensuring that activity meets purpose, as well as for alerting us to warning signals about the emergence of hitherto unseen problems which could damage the system.

Measurement is present in multiple settings. Often the most obvious examples are taken for granted, such as speedometers, oil level indicators and temperature gauges on cars. These measurements are crucial to motoring – the temperature gauge, for example, performs a simple yet essential function. Without it, cars would overheat without any warning. It operates in the same way as an SPC chart – when the temperature is shown as being within the usual range, everything is fine, but when it creeps beyond the 'upper control limit' this is a signal that there is a problem requiring further investigation; otherwise there will be imminent adverse effects upon the system.

Measurement is often misunderstood and can evoke responses right across the spectrum, depending on who you speak to. For example, I know a lot of frontline bobbies who tend to dismiss performance measurement as a 'waste of time'. I disagree strongly with this sentiment, but completely understand why police performance measurement has such a bad reputation. The reason it is so widely derided is because, as we have seen in Chapters Two and Three, it is often done so very badly. The wrong things are measured and used as performance indicators (e.g. number of detections per officer), or the data derived from the measurement exercise are presented poorly (e.g. in league tables) and the results are used as a tool for managerial control. This is in direct contrast to the principles of using appropriate measures to learn about and improve the system.

A lot of people confuse measurement with targets. The pro-targets brigade often confuse the practice of measurement with that of target-setting and those on the receiving end are immediately suspicious of it. When people think that measurement is something it isn't, 'good' measurement can quickly earn itself a bad name through mistaken association with targets. Furthermore, measuring things, indicators, data and charts can sometimes be seen as a bit 'geeky'.

To illustrate how some managers can totally misunderstand measurement whilst adopting completely different perspectives, here are two excerpts from conversations I have had with some of my former senior managers...

> *Senior manager*: "Targets are important."
>
> *Me*: "I disagree. Targets always cause dysfunctional behaviour."
>
> *Senior manager*: "No, we need targets so that as a police service we ensure we concentrate on the most important things, like burglaries."
>
> *Me*: "I totally agree we should tackle burglaries, but we don't need to have a numerical target to do it. I think you're confusing 'targets' with 'priorities.'
>
> *Senior manager*: "But we need targets so we know how we're performing."
>
> *Me*: "Now you're confusing 'targets' with 'measures'."

And at the other end of the scale:

> *Senior manager:* "You are too concerned with charts and data!"
>
> *Me:* "You are not concerned enough with charts and data!"

I'd like to summarise my position on targets, priorities and measurement as follows:

- Priorities are important (when evidence based)

- Measurement (when done properly) is essential

- Numerical targets are always bad.

Right Measures, Measured Right!

So, now that we're clear on what measurement is and what it isn't, how should it be done? Well the first clue is in the title of this section: *Right Measures, Measured Right![9]* When it comes to measures, this is my snappy mantra that keeps me on track. When approaching the subject of measurement, the first thing that managers need to ensure is that the *right things* are being measured. To help identify what these are we need to be absolutely certain about purpose. Appropriate measures must be related to purpose, otherwise they risk becoming perverse incentives for activity that bears no relation to purpose. Non-value activity (i.e. waste) detracts from the system's capacity for value activity.

Performance measurement expert, Dr Dean Spitzer, highlights the importance of measuring the right things, pointing out:

> ...if you don't measure the right things, you won't be able to manage the right things, and you won't get the right results...[10]

By ensuring that the right measures are selected in the first place, the tasks of understanding the capabilities of the system and managing its performance will be made much easier. Managers will be able to make evidence-based decisions, as well as identify opportunities for making improvements. Conversely, if the wrong things are measured it is impossible to understand anything about the system's performance, or make informed decisions about any aspect of it. Sometimes, however, you will need to accept that some things can't be measured, such as in the case of crime prevention. The presence of an officer on a particular street at a particular time might prevent an offence from occurring, but ask yourself this – how do you measure something that hasn't happened?"

I want to give a quick overview of simple systems because it is an easy introduction to purpose-derived measures and to the difference between *primary* measures and *secondary* measures. So, for example, the purpose

---

9   My Mum and Dad will both tell me that this mantra should read 'Right Measures, Measured Properly'. I accept that would be better grammar, but probably less memorable.

10   Spitzer (2007) p.54

of a machine that produces metal discs could be defined as something like, *"To produce sufficient quantities of metal discs of the best possible quality for 'X' usage"*. Relevant purpose-derived *primary* measures could include things like:

- The number of discs the machine produces per hour/day

- The dimensions of a random sample of the discs produced

- The proportion of discs ultimately rejected as unusable

- The number of machine malfunctions reported.

Simple metrics such as these could be overlaid with data relating to the machine's operation (e.g. its operating temperature) and maintenance schedule (e.g. how much oil does it require and how regularly, or how frequently does a particular part need to be replaced?). This allows those responsible for the machine to triangulate data from multiple sources to obtain a balanced picture of its performance. Rather than relying on obscure or irrelevant measures, or just one measure in isolation (e.g. the number of discs the machine has produced within a given time frame), by interpreting the data from a raft of purpose-driven measures it becomes possible to gain an appreciation of actual performance and the factors that affect it.

Assessing performance from multiple perspectives involves using measures that are both clearly linked to purpose and those that, at first, appear less obviously associated with it. For example, the number of items produced could be considered to be a measure directly linked to purpose, whereas data about the operating temperature of the machine may appear to have a less obvious relationship with it. A measure that is blatantly linked to purpose could be classed as a *primary measure*, whilst one that is of value (i.e. a 'right' measure) but less obviously connected to purpose, could be considered to be a *secondary measure*.

The *secondary measure* relating to the machine's temperature may not put metal discs on the table of the customer, but it does allow the machinist to understand how the machine is operating, and it provides a warning of abnormal temperatures which could indicate there is a problem. The operator can make adjustments to ensure the machine runs smoothly and produces metal discs without breaking down. Therefore, it can be argued that the operating temperature measure (along with others that relate to maintenance) are valuable *secondary* measures that indirectly contribute towards purpose.

If management decided to measure only the number of discs produced, the result would be a very one-dimensional, incomplete and unstable indicator of performance, susceptible to misinterpretation and incapable of identifying external factors that could affect production. It could also drive inappropriate behaviours by creating an environment where the machine operator feels under pressure to produce as many units as possible within a given time frame. Overall, this single measure would fail to help those responsible for the machine to accurately identify its true capabilities or understand the factors that affect its performance. The temptation for some managers would be to rely upon this simplistic Taylorist 'Scientific Management' approach[11] (see Chapter Five) or, worse still, make the misguided assumption that the machine operator presents the greatest opportunity for improving performance rather than the machine.

Likewise, if management were to choose 'measures' such as the number of scratches on the exterior paintwork of the machine, this would tell them nothing about its performance. It would also generate work for those charged with counting and reporting them. The scratches, of course, would have absolutely no effect on the machine's performance.

The manner in which some police forces use measures relating to missing people is a good example of measures that do not improve performance. The raw figures are presented with the obligatory green and red rows of numbers that compare 'performance' data showing how many people have gone missing in each police division, along with the average number of missing person reports per day, and so on. Binary comparisons with the previous month's figures determine whether the text is displayed in red or green. Apart from the fact that there are so many external factors affecting the missing person rate, one has to wonder about the efficacy of these measures.

To ascertain the usefulness (or otherwise) of any type of measurement activity, assess it against the criteria specified at the start of this section. Therefore, in this case:

- Do the data tell us anything about the capabilities of the system? No.

---

11   Taylor (1911)

- Does it enable us to predict anything about the future missing person rate? No.

- Does it identify ways in which the system can be improved? No.

This is because the wrong measures have been chosen and are presented in an unusable format.

Measurement In The Policing Environment

In complex systems, determining appropriate measures can be difficult. Outputs can often be awkward to define and it is problematic to make the connection between cause and effect in respect of outcomes.[12] This is particularly true of the public sector. Counting the number of arrests per officer is easy, but it is less straightforward to gauge the precise impact on crime levels that an individual officer's activity has had. It is also misleading to attempt to directly attribute success against purpose to one piece of activity such as an arrest; this is because the arrest itself forms just one component of a successful investigation. If the overall purpose is to bring an offender to justice it is overly simplistic to isolate one such aspect of activity as being the sole definitive measure of performance. As we have seen earlier, it also drives dysfunctional behaviour by introducing perverse incentives and focusing attention on only one aspect of the system.

By adopting an holistic approach to performance (and other measurement) in policing, managers should never lose sight of the *purpose of the measurement* – i.e. to understand the system, aid prediction and improve things. It's safe to say that if the wrong things are being measured they will be easy to identify by applying this test and if the measures don't contribute towards any of these aims they should be scrapped. Police managers should use a mix of primary and secondary measures because success can be difficult to define or measure precisely within such a complex system as policing.

For example, if a broad policing aim is 'to reduce crime' (notwithstanding the multiple external influences that affect the crime rate) then it is perfectly logical that one of the things we should measure is the crime rate. This would be a *primary* measure. Consequently, if crime rate data is intelligently interpreted (as discussed in previous sections of the book), this helps managers to understand the system, predict the range within which the crime rate will continue (if there is no variation in influencing

---

12   See: Pollitt (1999)

factors) and, most importantly of all, identify opportunities for instigating evidence-based policing responses to reduce it – i.e. to meet purpose.

Underpinning this would be other measures that relate to how wider aspects of the policing system operate. An example of a *secondary* measure could be in data relating to the maintenance of police vehicles. By examining the data, managers can identify common faults and pinpoint predictable maintenance requirements; this enables them to design this aspect of the system around its demand profile. If this exercise reveals bottlenecks in service schedules, or peaks in particular mechanical defects by type, frequency or location, it makes sense to look deeper in order to smooth out the flow, thereby reducing waste and increasing efficiency. The result will be that more police vehicles are available to patrol the area and attend incidents. This type of measure meets the test of helping us to understand the system, predict how it will operate and identify opportunities to improve it. The result is that capacity is enhanced, which will contribute to achieving purpose from the service user's perspective – i.e. 'to reduce crime'.

As stated earlier, when it comes to devising appropriate measures, the trick is always to work back to purpose. If a chosen measure can be traced to purpose, the chances are that you are on the right track. In complex systems purpose can exist in various iterations and at multiple levels – and measurement processes often need to be quite sophisticated to reflect this. For example, although a criminal investigation might involve several departments (response officers, CID, custody staff, etc.), when devising appropriate measures it is important to consider what is important to the service user (i.e. the victim of crime) and ensure that the measures take into account the entire process.

I think it must now be clear that traditional measures, which rely on assessing functional departments in isolation, are flawed. Although a successful prosecution is a laudable aim, it is wrong to award 'points' for a detection to *one* individual or department when so many people have contributed towards this achievement. As we have seen in earlier chapters, there are also innate difficulties in relying upon detection rates as an accurate measure of performance, not least because of the multiple external factors that affect them.

I am sure that victims of crime want a speedy, efficient and effective service. Relevant purpose-derived measures of criminal investigations could, perhaps, centre on things like the total end-to-end time or number of handovers during the investigation process. Whilst not wishing to induce officers to rush their enquiries, if the end-to-end time of investigations were routinely charted this would show both the system's capability in this field of activity and areas for improvement. It might be the case that there are particular stages of the investigation process that suffer from bottlenecks or other delays. Likewise, it may become apparent that there are unnecessary handovers that slow the process down and introduce waste.

In a similar vein, a measure that records the number of reported incidents resolved at the first point of contact could be useful. Whilst many incidents will require attendance by officers (and potentially subsequent follow-ups), I know from experience that many straightforward enquiries can actually be resolved during that initial contact with the member of the public. Think back to the concepts discussed in Chapter One and, in particular, the benefits of short processes because expertise is positioned at the front end – the public receive a quicker and more effective service, and there is less need for follow-ups and handovers. It could be argued then, that (subject to rounded interpretation of course) this type of measure is of benefit as it, too, is directly linked to purpose from the service user's perspective.

All of these purpose-driven measures would present managers with an extremely useful insight into actual system performance. Only by using such measures can opportunities for systemic improvement be discovered. Contrast this with the 'tick box culture' of simply counting the number of detected offences at the end of the process.

Once You Have The Right Measures, Then What?

Once managers are satisfied that the right measures have been selected (i.e. those that are derived from purpose), the next thing to ensure is that measurement activity is accurate and the data are presented appropriately. It would be a terrible shame to carefully choose purpose-driven measures, only to use the data produced from measurement to populate the sort of 'this month versus last month' nonsense that we saw in Chapter Two. This brings us to the second part of the *Right Measures, Measured Right* mantra – i.e. *Measured Right*.

As we have seen in earlier chapters, poor appreciation of data is often the root cause of mistaken assumptions about performance. The data are presented in an opaque or misleading way (e.g. rows of numbers in a table) and are then used as a means to identify and punish 'poor performers', without actually doing anything to improve the system. Furthermore, ignorance of SPC and variation can cause managers to make erroneous assumptions based on imagined trends within benign data.

Data derived from measurement activities should only ever be used for those stated aims of understanding the system, predicting the future and improving the system. An ideal method for interpreting measurement data is through the use of SPC because it effectively filters out the noise and a true picture of performance is immediately visible, giving an indication of the capabilities of the system or process in question. It also offers a solid evidence base for predicting how data will continue to behave if no systemic adjustments are made, as well as providing a basis for action when signals are present.

To use the metal disc-making machine as an example, let's assume that management have adopted the measures suggested earlier and habitually plot the data on SPC charts. There will be an inevitable degree of variation amongst the discs produced and this will be reflected in data pertaining to their production, such as hourly output or the error rate. If the error rate is unacceptably high or if there are warning signals, then management can use this information to act, safe in the knowledge that they are not simply tampering. Similarly, if signals relating to errors coincide with signals relating to the machine's operating temperature or occur at certain points in the maintenance schedule, this provides management with an immediate avenue of inquiry. It may be the case that as a certain component wears, the dimensions of the discs are adversely affected, or the error rate might change in direct relation to the machine's operating temperature. Without choosing the right measures, or using the data properly, these correlations would be impossible to see.

In order to achieve effective measurement it is essential to consider the measurement process within the context in which it exists, and to appreciate its limitations. Even the right measures will be damaging if they are used as a beating stick or interpreted in isolation. Managers need to understand that measurement data are just a part of the overall narrative; they must be viewed from a systemic perspective, rather than as disconnected chunks of information. An environment that is conducive to systems thinking principles ensures that effective measurement practice is at the heart of an ethos of continuously seeking opportunities for improvement.

With these aims in mind, Spitzer talks about his concept of 'Four Keys'; conditions that he argues are necessary for effective measurement.[13] These are:

- Context
- Focus
- Integration
- Interactivity.

Context "…is everything that surrounds a task, including the social and psychological climate in which it is embedded".[14] If measurement occurs in a positive environment where people can see it being used to improve the system rather than to berate individuals, the effect can be astounding.

Focus simply relates to selecting the right measures. Spitzer points out that the sheer volume of irrelevant measures in many organisations actually dilutes performance measurement and leads to a lack of direction and focus. This is a similar concept to that of being forced to endure multiple and conflicting priorities – it becomes impossible to see what is important.

Integration reminds us of the systems thinking principles of interconnectivity and interdependence. Measures that apply to individual departments in isolation result in a silo mentality, along with unhealthy internalised conflict and competition. Conversely, cross-functional measures promote cooperative behaviours and lead to higher levels of collaboration and a greater likelihood of attaining purpose.

Interactivity in the context of measurement relates to what Spitzer calls the 'measurement socialisation process'. He argues that transformational performance measurement is "…not a static, technical process of identifying standard measures and collecting and analysing data on them. It is much more of a social process".[15]

Performance management expert, Donald Moynihan, makes a similar assertion and argues that dialogue, leadership and organisational culture are the key components of effective performance management.[16] Context and inclusiveness are also critical; rather than being chosen by managers and imposed from above, measures should be meaningful to those in the

---

13   Spitzer, D. R. (2007)
14   *ibid* p 52
15   *ibid* p.54
16   Moynihan (2008)

work. This ensures that they are "in the right hands" and are being used *by* and *for* frontline workers.

Final Pointers On Measurement

Especially in complex systems, or environments where it is difficult to quantify performance, measurement data do not represent the entire picture. The data must be interpreted in conjunction with the narrative that describes organisational activity, and with influencing factors and overall context. This is because, as Moynihan argues, performance information alone is subjective, ambiguous and incomplete.

What's important is that measurement is focused towards the right things; "It is better to imperfectly measure relevant dimensions than to perfectly measure irrelevant ones."[17] For this reason, measures must always be derived from purpose ('right measures') and there should be no inappropriate influences that skew activity (e.g. targets or perverse incentives).

There's Method In The Madness

Method (i.e. 'how to do it') is informed by purpose-derived measures. As the saying goes, "What gets measured gets done".[18] This reaffirms how important it is that the *right* measures are in place to guide activity. If the wrong measures are chosen, they will effectively supersede purpose, and replace true organisational purpose with a perverse *de facto* purpose.

Likewise, as we have seen, it is critical that the *right* measures be used in the *right way*. Even the right measures are capable of driving the wrong sorts of behaviour if they are used inappropriately (e.g. to make comparisons between teams or to demand answers about common cause variation present in the data). When this happens, method becomes disconnected from purpose and things go wrong. The links between purpose, measures and method must never be broken.

The beauty of having the right measures, used properly, is that they always inform method; this results in a virtuous cycle where the activity subject to measurement is directly related to purpose, thereby increasing the likelihood of achieving the aims of the system. If those responsible for determining method keep asking, "Does this activity contribute towards

---

17   Bommer *et al.* (1995) p.602
18   As cited in Lapsley (1999)

achieving purpose?" this should act as a guide to the appropriateness of the methods being adopted. If the answer is ever 'No', then the chosen method is nothing but waste.

Organisational activity will be most effective when a proposed method is aligned to purpose *and* the measures provide a mandate for evidence-based action. Contrast this with the horrors of blind tampering, knee-jerk reactions and the scattergun approach of the 'policy roulette wheel' seen in Chapter Four.

The Purpose-Measures-Method Lesson on a Postage Stamp

In short, you won't go far wrong when…

- *Purpose* is explicit and understood

- The right *measures* are derived from purpose and used insightfully

- The data from measurement are used to initiate a *method* that is justified by the evidence base.

Time for a Bit of Cycling

There are various cyclical models for process improvement. One of the most famous is Deming's PDSA cycle (also sometimes referred to as 'The Shewhart Cycle').[19] This is reproduced below:

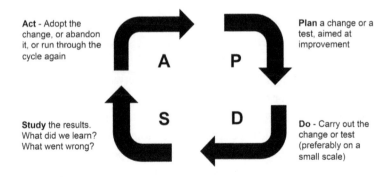

Act - Adopt the change, or abandon it, or run through the cycle again

Plan a change or a test, aimed at improvement

Study the results. What did we learn? What went wrong?

Do - Carry out the change or test (preferably on a small scale)

Figure 9.3: The PDSA Cycle

---

19   Deming (1994) p.132

The cycle is simple and self-explanatory; indeed, its strength is in its very simplicity. The cycle does not end after the 'act' stage – it is intended to be an ongoing process for improvement which encourages continuous adjustment and evaluation. Brian Joiner proposes a similar cycle, namely PDCA ('Plan – Do – Check – Act'), which operates in much the same fashion. (I'll leave you to visualise it). Joiner describes the stages of the PDCA cycle as follows:

P: Plan what you're going to do and how you will know if it works.

D: Do; carry out the plan.

C: Check; evaluate the outcome, learn from the results.

A: Take action.[20]

Both the PDSA and PDCA cycles can act as useful templates for understanding and improving processes. Joiner emphasises the importance of adapting the cycle to the situation and ensuring that its components are effectively integrated, as opposed to having different parts of the organisation carry out different components in isolation. This resonates in particular with Spitzer's arguments for context and integration (elements of his 'Four Keys'), demonstrating that the principles for effective measurement extend into other areas of systems thinking.

Although Joiner promotes PDCA in that sequence, he also suggests that it may be better to start at Check rather than at Plan (i.e. CAPD). This, he argues, is because:

Check is the driver for rapid *learning*. Without it, improvement is nearly impossible.[21]

Furthermore:

By getting conscientious about Check, by treating decisions as experiments from which we must learn, we get *all* the components of PDCA to fall into place.[22]

---

20   Joiner (1994) p.44

21   *ibid* p.47

22   *ibid* p.46

This brings me to my preferred process improvement cycle – John Seddon's Check – Plan – Do (CPD) cycle.[23] This cycle (which forms the bedrock of the Vanguard Method) is similar to the CAPD variant of Joiner's PDCA cycle, inasmuch as it starts with Check, but I like it because it distils the process improvement cycle down to its three essential components. The CPD cycle encourages constant review, adjustment and improvement. A version of it is reproduced below:

Figure 9.4: 'Check – Plan – Do'

Seddon elaborates on the stages of the cycle as follows:[24]

Check

- What is the purpose of this system?

- What are its core processes?

- Capability - what are the system and its processes predictably achieving?

- System conditions - why does the process or system behave in this way?

Plan

- What needs changing to improve performance?

- What action could be taken and with what predictable consequences?

23   Pell and Seddon (2012) p.xi
24   Seddon (2012)

- Against what measures should action be taken (to ensure the organisation learns)?

Do

- Take the planned action and monitor the consequences versus prediction and purpose.

The major difference between the CPD cycle and the PDSA and PDCA cycles is the starting point of Check. It is the only process improvement model of the three that always begins 'in the work'. This means that planning only occurs after an understanding of the system or process has been established. Such a configuration lends itself to evidence-based planning, making it a more robust model. Seddon summarises the Check phase as simply, "Get Knowledge". In his words:

> The purpose of Check is to do just that – get knowledge about the 'what and why' of current performance as a system.[25]

The importance of Check is such that under the Vanguard Method there are six defined phases for getting knowledge before even proceeding to the Plan and Do stages.[26] These phases comprise a comprehensive and logical sequence that ensures a solid understanding of the system or process in question. The six phases are outlined below:

1. *Purpose*: What is the purpose of this system?

As we have already discussed, the very first thing that must be understood about any system or process is its purpose. We have covered purpose in some detail already, and I don't intend to labour the point; suffice to say that when purpose is unknown or ill-defined, what you get is a right mess.

2. *Demand:* What are the types and frequencies of demand?

Unless predictable demand is fully understood it is impossible to design your system against it, and the only way to gain an accurate appreciation of demand is to study the work. To achieve this, there is no substitute for immersing yourself *in* the work and learning about it from within. This empirical approach (i.e. learning by doing and discovering) is more powerful than rational methods (i.e. learning by being told) because those

---

25   Seddon (2008) p.79
26   The section on the Vanguard Method and the six stages of Check is based on relevant content from: Pell and Seddon (2012) p.xi; Seddon (2008) pp.78-81

responsible for designing the system discover the current capabilities of the system for themselves. As Seddon puts it:

> Answering this question requires managers to *go to all the places where the organisation transacts with customers* and study demand in their terms: why do they call, what do they want, what would create value for them, what matters to them? It is impossible to move to the next stage without having a thorough understanding of the major types of value and failure demand and their predictability. Understanding predictability is essential. Designing for the unpredictable would make the system unnecessarily complex and costly.[27]

Once predictable demand is known, not only does it become possible to design your system to deal with it effectively, but the gulf between value and non-value demand will become self-evident. Understanding the demand profile also enables managers to optimise the system, thereby ensuring it is geared to handle predictable demand without overcompensating for infrequent or unforeseeable events. This prevents a risk-averse mentality from infecting the design stage and ensures that the amount of staff, equipment or skills decided upon is proportionate.

When an unusual type of demand occurs, frontline staff should be able to *pull* expertise from colleagues within the system, thereby resolving the problem for the customer or service user and, at the same, increasing their own skill base. This is a much more effective approach than simply palming off the problem to another department.

In short, getting knowledge about the demand profile enables managers to design bespoke systems and processes that consistently achieve purpose from the customer's (or service user's) perspective.

In policing terms, this exercise could involve examining the various types of demand that present themselves to the organisation. Initially, perhaps, it would be useful to identify the proportion of reported crime incidents, traffic incidents, general requests for advice, and so on. Often the most straightforward way of accessing demand is to go straight to where the majority of it enters the system (i.e. the police call centre) and simply listen to calls as they come in. It might also involve analysing when, where and how demand arises, in order to identify peak times or locations.

---

27   Seddon (2008) p.80

Cheshire Constabulary performed this exercise in 2010, reviewing 14,000 calls and another 8,000 requests for service that entered the system via post, police station front counters, email and face-to-face interactions with officers on patrol.[28] The exercise highlighted the fact that the force's systems were configured to categorise demand into neat little boxes at the earliest opportunity, without necessarily understanding what it was that the caller really needed. Chief Inspector Nick Bailey describes this situation as follows:

> The purpose of this system is to give a predetermined level of service based on the categorisation of the call which in turn is based on nationally recognised categories of crime and disorder.[29]

This discovery prompted the realisation that:

> At this stage, it was clear that our purpose, which our Policing Plan and literature say is to be focused on the public, was in reality focused on compliance and performance.[30]

As a result of this, Cheshire Constabulary reassessed its demand profile from the service users' perspective and realised that the calls for service were not so much about, "I would like to report being subjected to threatening behaviour under Section 4a of the Public Order Act 1986", but "The local youths are being a nuisance – can you come and have a word with them please?" As a result of appreciating demand from an 'outside in' perspective instead of a 'which box does this fit in?' perspective, Cheshire Constabulary found that there were several broad themes that prompted calls for service. These included jargon-free requests such as:

- "I want to report/give information about 'X'".
- "Please turn up/stop something from happening".
- "Please give me some advice/information".[31]

By getting in amongst incoming demand, the force realised what it really was that members of the public needed them to do, and established a true picture of demand. This allowed them to proceed to the next phase of Check.

---

28   Watson and Bailey 'No Soft Option: Changing Thinking Across an Entire Police Force'. In Pell and Seddon (2012) p.52
29   *ibid* p.50
30   *ibid* p.50
31   *ibid* p.53

3. Capability: **What is the system predictably achieving?**

After the type and frequency of predictable demand has been determined, the next step is to make an assessment of the capability of the system. Are there any parts of the system where bottlenecks or delays are evident? It may be that this exercise exposes a 'warts and all' picture of how the system is performing – if so, this is to be welcomed, as without a true picture of the *status quo* it will be impossible to know where to make adjustments.

This phase of Check may well expose hideous examples of waste. Chapters Seven and Eight explored waste in some detail so I don't intend to cover old ground, but when Cheshire Constabulary carried out this exercise it discovered much of what I have been griping about – the force estimated that about 40% of their demand was actually waste.[32] This was caused by the 'usual suspects'; i.e. burdensome internalised reporting requirements, failure demand and inefficient processes. It was obvious that the capability of the system was being severely hampered and that simply reducing the proportion of waste would instantly unleash significant capacity to handle value demand.

Precisely how much of an understanding of capability can be gained will be partly dependent on the type of measures already in place. If relevant measures are already in operation they will provide managers with an instant insight into the true capability of the system, thereby aiding future redesign. If, however, the only existing measures consist of the usual battery of fragmented, silo-based, dysfunctional metrics, which tell us nothing about the system, I'm afraid it's time to go back to the drawing board rather quickly to devise temporary measures that actually shed light on how the system is performing.

Although temporary, these diagnostic measures should be determined using the same principles as the long-term measures discussed in the Purpose – Measures – Method   section earlier. As you would expect, plotting the data from these measures using SPC will facilitate intelligent interpretation and avoid inadvertent tampering.

4. Flow: **'How does the work work?'**

After purpose, demand and capability are understood, the next stage is to examine how the work flows through the system. Process mapping (as mentioned in Chapter One) can be very useful here, but those embarking

---

32   *ibid* p.53

upon this phase of Check must identify what constitutes value from the customer's (or service user's) perspective and prioritise those processes for analysis.

An excellent way of learning about how work flows through the system is to start at the point where incoming demand is generated, then follow the work until the service has been completed successfully. It is also important to ensure that flow is contemplated and measured from an *end-to-end* perspective, not as it enters and leaves individual departments. This ensures that those conducting this phase of Check retain the 'helicopter view' of the system that we talked about earlier.

Cheshire Constabulary's work on Check uncovered a range of adverse factors that affected the flow of work in its system.[33] These are indicative of the current situation in other police forces and include:

- Handovers
- Targets
- Functional departments.

These factors introduced waste in the form of unnecessary stages in simple processes, perverse incentives and disconnects throughout the fabric of the system. By removing these obstacles, the force was able to significantly improve flow.

When considered in conjunction with the hard data gleaned from assessing the system's capability, this normative part of the Check exercise will produce actionable opportunities for systemic improvement. The approach will also identify levers for improvement within processes, as well as expose waste and highlight inefficiencies. Analysing and understanding flow elicits the evidence base for shorter, more efficient processes, a reduction in variation (i.e. flow is less 'bumpy') and a more effective system that is capable of meeting demand.

5. *Understanding system conditions:* Why does the system behave in this way?

When describing this phase of Check, Seddon talks specifically about understanding the system conditions responsible for the waste uncovered in the flow phase. However, 'understanding system conditions' has much

---

33   *ibid* pp.66-67

broader implications. Systems conditions are *everything that affect how a system behaves* – some of these are structural factors such as those cited by Seddon, namely:

> ...measures, roles, process design, procedures, information technology, structure, contracts...[34]

In addition to the 'physical' conditions listed above, there are a whole host of influences that define organisational culture and norms. These environmental conditions also have a significant impact on the system. Examples would include:

- Organisational norms

- Relationships

- Degrees of trust, autonomy and devolved responsibility;

- Position on risk management

- Assumptions about worker motivation.

This combination of 'physical' and 'environmental' conditions offers an insight into why the system behaves in a certain way. Adverse conditions of either type will inevitably generate waste and other unwelcome side-effects – and when they are identified they must be earmarked for removal during the subsequent Plan stage of the Check – Plan – Do cycle. It is also entirely possible that occurrences of particular systems conditions acting *positively* on the behaviour of the system (or part of the system) may be uncovered during this phase of Check. If this occurs it may provide an evidence base that justifies further study, with the possibility of reproducing these conditions in other parts of the system (subject to local context of course).

If you don't look, you'll never know.

6. *Management thinking:* Underlying assumptions about how the work is managed.

This phase of Check relates to gaining an understanding of the type of management norms, practices and overall organisational disposition that defines the system. In command and control organisations these assumptions usually manifest themselves in the form of coercive and prescriptive management practices that constrain the workers and restrict

---

34   Seddon (2008) p.81

innovation. There is the usual heavy reliance on targets and inspection as a means of trying to ensure 'quality', a dominant ethos of policy-based decision-making, as well as a wide range of other controls and incentives.

In systems thinking organisations, the management disposition is trust-orientated with an emphasis on devolved responsibility and the practice of professional judgement. The focus of operational activity is on doing the right thing, achieving purpose and meeting demand from the customer's or service user's perspective. Everything that occurs within the organisation is viewed from a 'whole system' perspective to ensure that work is managed in a cohesive fashion. There is a culture of openness, dialogue and learning, which fosters innovation and continuous improvement.

If, as a result of Check, enquirers discover that their organisation has features of this latter type of management, then they already have an environment that is receptive to what will be required during the Plan and Do stages of the cycle. If Check reveals that the organisation is permeated with management thinking synonymous with command and control ideology, there is a lot of work to do. The good news is that transformation is still possible.

Planning and Doing

Having just spent a lot of time on Check I suspect you may be bracing yourself for several pages on the remainder of the Check – Plan – Do cycle. Not so! The other two stages of the cycle are really just about taking action after getting knowledge during the first stage. Hence, Plan can be summarised as identifying levers for change, making adjustments to the system and devising appropriate measures that will inform method. The planning phase utilises the evidence base gleaned during the Check stage and redesigns the system, ready for action.

The Do stage is simply about initiating the planned action and monitoring its effect, using the purpose-derived measures specified during the Plan stage. If Check and Plan have been conducted thoroughly, then Do should be straightforward. If it is not possible to redesign the whole system in one go, it can be entirely appropriate to test the new model in one part of it, by way of experimentation.

In either case, checking actual progress against what was predicted will indicate whether the changes are having the anticipated effect. The methods undertaken as part of Do will be underpinned by relevant and useful measures to indicate whether purpose is being achieved. The effectiveness of the redesigned system can be evaluated against the measures; the data elicited will aid prediction about performance and provide an evidence base for further adjustments to the system if necessary. Oh wait, we're back at Check…

That's the way it works. It's a cycle.

Mine's a Double

The whole spirit of Purpose – Measures – Method and the Check – Plan – Do' cycle is underpinned by an ethos of continuous learning and improvement. Change is emergent and this is why Check keeps coming round as part of a continuous cycle, rather than as merely one stage of a linear model. The depth of learning that comes from the application of the cycle is dependent on the rigour with which it is applied, as well as the mindset of those applying it. A useful model for maximising the learning gleaned from the application of the CPD cycle is Chris Argyris's[35] theory of 'single and double loop learning'.

> Single loop learning occurs where there is a single feedback loop, with individuals modifying their actions according to the difference between expected and obtained outcomes. This is an ongoing error-correction process that continues until an acceptable level of knowledge or action is achieved.[36]

Single loop learning is advantageous but limited in its scope because it doesn't push the boundaries beyond what is already considered possible. *Double loop learning,* on the other hand, is about questioning the assumptions implicit in single loop learning. Spitzer sums up the notion as:

> In double loop learning, individuals question the very content of the learning, test those beliefs they have taken for granted, and challenge the expectations, values, and assumptions that led them to adopt the knowledge or engage in the actions in the first place.[37]

It's all about asking '*why?*'

- *Why* is that the accepted process for 'X'?
- *Why* can't employee 'Y' authorise such-and-such?
- *Why* does it take 'up to 10 working days' to complete 'Z'?

---

35   See: Argyris and Schön (1974); Argyris (1976)
36   Spitzer (2007) p.143
37   *ibid* p.143

- *Why* do you believe that tactic will solve the problem?
- *Why* is that the target?
- *Why* do you want the report?[38]

Anyone asking these sorts of questions as part of a CPD cycle (or even during normal conversations) should be prepared for a range of reactions from those who operate under the current model. Be prepared for your behaviour to be interpreted as any or all of the following:

- Being subversive
- Being negative
- Being a troublemaker
- Not being a team player.

C'est la vie. Challenging conventional wisdom, or 'the way things are done round here' isn't easy, which is why double loop learning is most difficult in environments where existing approaches are deep-rooted. The most difficult stage of adopting a systems thinking mindset is *unlearning* what you thought was the proper way of doing things. Nevertheless, double loop learning is the perfect discourse for the Check – Plan – Do cycle to operate within because it is about fundamentally challenging accepted learning and taking innovation to the next level. It transcends the boundaries of recognised thinking, is limitless, perpetual and transformational.

Summary

This chapter has concentrated on exploring the overarching principles of fixing the system. The first thing to do is *stop doing the wrong things*. As we saw from the last couple of chapters, simply removing waste is often an instantaneous and spectacular method of improving the system. Remember though, when it comes to designing a better system, waste removal is never the whole story.

Once you have slammed the brakes on the bad stuff, there is a real opportunity to completely transform the system into a bespoke entity that exists to truly achieve purpose. The Purpose – Measures – Method approach offers a structured framework that gets enquirers thinking about what the system is there to do and how it can be attained.

---

38   This particular question is on another self-made poster that adorns the wall of my office and is taken from: Scherkenbach (2001) p.137

Running alongside the Purpose – Measures – Method framework is the equally powerful Check – Plan – Do cycle. This offers a methodical and incisive model that ensures the system is fully understood and the right areas are acted upon. Taken together, the two models are at the very heart of changing the way we think about systems. This is the second stage of fixing the system that I alluded to at the start of the chapter – *start doing the right things*.

CHAPTER TEN

Tools of the Trade

The previous chapter concentrated on underlying principles and frameworks for fixing the system. This one will look at some actual methods and techniques for learning about the system and making improvements. It is not intended to be a comprehensive examination (or even a complete list) of approaches, but rather something to whet the appetite and demonstrate how certain techniques, principles and concepts can be useful when applied during the various stages of Check – Plan – Do and beyond.

There is a multitude of systems improvement disciplines out there such as Lean, Six Sigma and Lean Six Sigma[1] which emphasise the use of tools and codified methods. Furthermore, IT providers can supply software that automatically maps processes and analyses performance metrics. To managers hoping for instantaneous organisational improvements or improved productivity, such methods and technological solutions can be alluring. But there are pitfalls to watch out for. These approaches may appear attractive but if applied in isolation they can do more harm than good. As Deming warned, when it comes to transforming systems there is no such thing as 'instant pudding'.[2]

In defence of those who might be tempted by a tools-based approach, I believe that their objective is well-intentioned. It is easy for enthusiastic managers to be seduced by exotic-sounding methods, propagated by external practitioners who claim to be experts. On the other side of the coin, it can be equally tempting to dismiss the use of tools as being superfluous to systems thinking. Either view, taken to extremes, can be counter-productive.

My general position is that tools can be useful but they are not the answer. In the same way that managers copy good ideas from elsewhere without understanding the underlying theory, tools can become relied

---

1   See: Womack and Jones (2003); George, Rowlands and Kastle (2004)
2   Deming (1986) p.126

upon without taking organisational context into account. This results in ill-fitting models that cannot be adapted for local nuances. Another drawback is that tools can cause practitioners to focus excessively on the methods associated with redesigning systems or processes, without necessarily understanding the purpose of the system or conducting a comprehensive Check analysis. The most important limitation of the tools-based approach is that tools do not change management thinking – it is perfectly possible to implement tools-orientated change programmes in command and control organisations without altering their ethos or culture.

For example, lean methodology is particularly suited to identifying and removing waste, and its application may result in cashable savings and an initial impression that the programme had been successful. If, however, management thinking and norms remain the same as before, the organisation, in the case of the police force, will suffer from the usual tangle of targets, plans and management reports. In the long term, aspirations will not be fully realised and those within the organisation will feel disappointed and disillusioned.

The limited scope of the tools approach can damage people's faith in good process improvement techniques applied within an appropriate context. By perceived association, these failed change programmes can dent the reputation of systems thinking and harden the observer's opinions about the efficacy of such associated philosophies. Making token adjustments at the periphery misses the point. Shortening a process that should not be there in the first place is akin to what Seddon mischievously calls, "Doing the wrong thing *faster*".[3]

A chisel is just a chisel. It does not possess skill or insight. The person using the tool is the one who possesses the skill and ability. Selecting the right tool for the job also depends upon the knowledge and experience of the craftsperson. The chisel is not useful if it is used as a saw or hammer. A saw or hammer will not do the work of a chisel. No tool is a substitute for the creativity and vision of the human mind.

Process improvement tools are just inanimate objects. It is up to the user to select the appropriate ones and use them at the right time, in the right way. Those who understand the system as a whole will perceive tools as supplementary aids that can be of use in the right situation. They are not a substitute for thinking differently.

---

3   Seddon (2011)

SPC and Other Animals

The systems approach, however, can incorporate and benefit from the use of some tools if they are applied in the right circumstances. The classic example is SPC charts. I've harped on about how useful SPC charts are for intelligent interpretation of data, understanding the capabilities of the process, preventing knee-jerk reactions, predicting the future, encouraging evidence-based decision-making, and so on. I love them. The thing is though, even the mighty SPC beast is still just a tool. Although I would argue that SPC is integral to the systems approach, it still requires insight and the adoption of a systems perspective to achieve its full potential.

SPC does not have a brain of its own; it is only a very sophisticated 'chisel'. What use would an SPC chart be if the data it displayed pertained to the wrong measures? What if an organisation produced SPC charts for such a multitude of measures that it became impossible to prioritise what was important? How about if management constantly insisted on written plans, disproportionate meetings or voluminous reports about SPC charts? What if managers didn't understand how to interpret SPC data in the first place? What if they even tried to set targets within the data?

The point I'm making is that SPC may be the closest thing to a perfect tool, but it is still a tool. The results that can flow from its use are contingent on the craftsperson who uses it; this must be someone who understands its capabilities and limitations and who knows when and how to use it within the wider systems context.

Déjà vu

Back in Chapter One we looked at process mapping and critical path analysis. Both these methods are useful for learning about how processes operate; they are also particularly helpful in identifying bottlenecks and other waste because they draw attention to where the value activity is (and isn't) occurring. Process mapping is a good tactic to employ when when attempting to understand and analyse processes as part of the Check phase of the Check – Plan – Do cycle. Critical path analysis is particularly effective at highlighting the interdependencies that exist within and between processes. Both techniques are tried and tested methods that can be applied as part of a comprehensive system review and redesign programme. As we have covered them in some detail previously, I am not going to repeat myself here, but I wanted to remind you about where they fit in.

Process Cycle Efficiency

A useful tool that can identify opportunities for improving flow and reducing waste within processes is a method called Process Cycle Efficiency (PCE). The PCE of a process is presented as a percentage of value activity that occurs within it. It is calculated by simply dividing the time taken in value activity by the total end-to-end time of the process. Say, for example, that you want to have your car serviced and would like to collect it at soon as it is ready. You are asked to book it in at 9am and collect it at 1pm. The total end-to-end time is therefore four hours. Let's say that the garage mechanics conduct work on other vehicles before attending to your car. Only the time spent actually servicing your car can be classed as value activity and this takes two hours to complete.

Analysing this process to determine PCE would involve nothing more complicated than the following simple equation.

Time in value activity (2 hours) ÷ End-to-end time (4 hours) = 50%

The PCE in this process is 50%; the process contains 50% value activity and 50% waste. It is now management's responsibility to devise ways of reducing the waste and making the process more efficient. By understanding the capabilities of their system, the garage's managers can unlock ways to improve efficiency and speed up the end-to-end time for servicing vehicles. They may discover that there is a glut of demand at the beginning of the day (some garages, as well as other enterprises, deliberately overbook custom on the assumption that there will be last minute cancellations or delays; if there aren't any, this causes bottlenecks and unevenness in the flow – '*Mura*'). A solution could be to stagger incoming demand via an appointment system, thereby matching demand to capacity.

Alternatively, analysis of demand might find that the number of mechanics working at the garage is insufficient to cope with predictable demand, leading to recurrent delays and avoidable waste. The reason for the deficiency in this process's PCE is a capacity problem, rather than a flow problem. Assuming that two hours per service represents an efficient process in itself, then will be no mileage in pressurising the mechanics to work faster when servicing vehicles – this will generate corner-cutting and other unwelcome behaviour. Solutions could include increasing the workforce to handle predictable demand, or limiting the number of servicing jobs that could be booked. (The latter option of turning away business is not good practice, however).

PCE can be especially useful at highlighting inefficiencies when dealing with processes that are particularly complex, have multiple stages, or involve several departments or individuals. Where a unit of work passes through several departments it's easy to lose sight of the activity that takes place anywhere other than right under your nose. This problem is exacerbated by inter-departmental rivalries, rigid policies and performance frameworks that encourage functional silos. As a result, flow between departments becomes uneven and disconnections occur, generating waste and extending the end-to-end time.

Pareto

Pareto analysis is a statistical technique devised by Joseph M. Juran and named after Italian economist Vilfredo Pareto who observed that 80% of the land in Italy was owned by 20% of the people. Also, known as the 80/20 rule, the Pareto principle states that roughly 80% of the effects come from 20% of the causes.[4] For example:

- 80% of profits come from 20% of customers.

- 80% of crime is committed by 20% of people.

- 80% of problems in a system are caused by 20% of system conditions.

Pareto analysis is useful because it can help identify the biggest levers for improvement. For example, if demand is plotted on a Pareto chart it will be immediately clear what the most frequent types of demand are and thus where resources and effort should be focused. The approach is also useful for identifying problems because the Pareto chart will graphically highlight the greatest issues and thereby indicate where the greatest gains can be achieved.

Creating a Pareto chart is easy. The first thing you need to do is construct a table of values – in this case we will use data relating to mechanical defects on police vehicles. First, list the categories in order from the most frequently occurring to the least frequently occurring with the corresponding data in a column next to each header. Next, calculate the percentage value for each – this is achieved by dividing the data for an individual category

---

4   See: Juran (1962); Juran and Gryna (1970); Koch (2001) Or for a quick overview: Haughey, D. (2012)

by the overall total. Finally, add together the percentage values in a third column to show the cumulative percentage that emerges as the categories stack up. You will end up with something like this:

Category	Count	% of Total	Cumulative %
Gearbox Problems	176	35.5	35.5
Clutch Problems	123	24.8	60.3
Electrical Failure	59	11.9	72.2
Fuel Line Problems	40	8.0	80.2
Brake Problems	35	7.0	87.2
Cooling System Problems	19	3.8	91.0
Exhaust Problems	15	3.0	94.0
Steering Problems	9	1.8	95.8
Bodywork wear and tear	8	1.6	97.4
Window damage	5	1.0	98.4
Other damage	4	0.8	99.2
Uncategorised	4	0.8	100
Totals	497	100%	100%

Figure 10.1: Pareto data table – Police vehicle mechanical defects

Once you have the data table, it is easy to construct the actual chart. Simply order the categories from largest to smallest, left to right, and present each as a bar with the percentage value above it. Next, draw a curve that plots the cumulative percentage above the bars and Hey Presto - you have your Pareto chart. The chart that is derived from the above data table is displayed below:

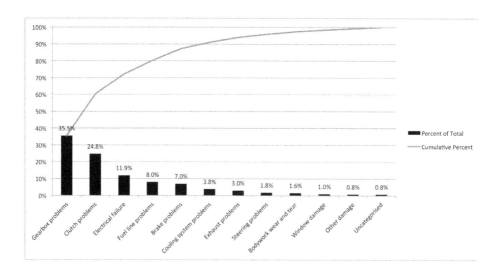

Figure 10.2: Pareto chart – Police vehicle mechanical defects

By ordering the types of defects from the most common to the least common by percentage, it becomes clear where the issues lie. The curve that plots the cumulative percentage makes it apparent where the greatest opportunities lie for preventing defects (i.e. the steepest part of the curve, to the left hand side of the chart). In this case, gearbox and clutch problems account for over 60% of total mechanical failures – this highlights the fact that the bulk of defects are concentrated in just two of twelve categories. Although there are multiple types of defects to the right hand side of where the 80/20 break would be (i.e. where the curve crosses the horizontal 80% line), these only account for a relatively small total percentage between them.

Further investigation into these issues might reveal that the types of vehicles being used have gearboxes and clutches that are not robust enough for 24/7 response policing. (Alternatively, it might be that the bobbies driving them routinely thrash the cars to death.) Either way, the data indicates that there is an evidence base for tackling these two issues as a priority over all the other mechanical problems. Whether this involves changing the cars, installing tougher gearboxes and clutches, or improving driver training, action taken here will significantly reduce the overall rate of mechanical defects.

By way of another example, Pareto analysis can be very useful when attempting to understand types of demand as part of the Check phase of Check – Plan – Do. This is illustrated in *Figure 10.3*, below:

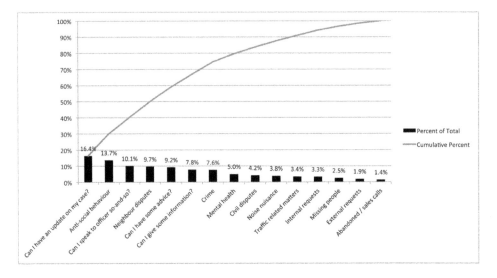

Figure 10.3: Pareto chart – Types of police demand

This chart plots types of demand in a hypothetical police area, where 1,000 calls for service have been analysed. In this case, there is a smaller degree of variation amongst the 15 categories. If you were to draw a vertical line where the cumulative percentage curve crosses the 80% marker, it would be positioned more centrally than on the vehicle defects chart. This just means that more categories make up the top 80% of data, resulting in a flatter curve.

What is interesting about this chart, however, is that it highlights the proportion of failure demand in the system. Note that the largest type of demand is caused by people trying to find out what is happening with their case (16.4%). There is also a significant chunk (10.1%) that relates to what is essentially a switchboard function ("Can I speak to officer so-and-so?"). These two categories alone account for over a quarter of total demand. Further down the line we see more examples of potential waste (e.g. internal requests at 3.3% and abandoned or sales calls at 1.4%). If those responsible for acting on the system had the luxury of being able to address these latter causes of waste, then by all means they should do so, but Pareto analysis tells us that, in this case, the biggest levers for success are in tackling the areas towards the left hand side of the chart.

Therefore, to release maximum capacity, effort should be concentrated on reducing the 'big hitters' first, perhaps by ensuring that victims of crime are provided with contact details of the officer dealing with their case from the outset, as well as making sure that they receive regular updates about progress. This would immediately reduce the single largest type of demand. You will also notice that there are other themes within the chart that are not core policing activity (e.g. mental health and civil disputes). Here, careful consideration should determine whether this type of demand is appropriate in the first place (think back to Waste Type One in Chapter Seven, i.e. the things a system or process shouldn't become involved with at all). Obviously there are occasions where officers should become involved in mental health incidents but there are many others where the police are not the most appropriate lead agency. Proactive risk management, professional judgement and evidence-based prioritisation should be applied to differentiate the two.

Taken in its purest sense, it could be argued that the quickest wins will result from tackling only the themes that comprise the top 80%, even at the expense of others to the right hand side of the 80/20 break point. There is a danger to this, however; worthwhile, albeit low-volume, themes can be ignored. This is where a mature assessment of benefits and risks becomes necessary. Those interpreting the chart must ensure that they do not concentrate purely on the numbers – an understanding of the narrative behind the data is always essential. To illustrate this, have a look at the chart below:

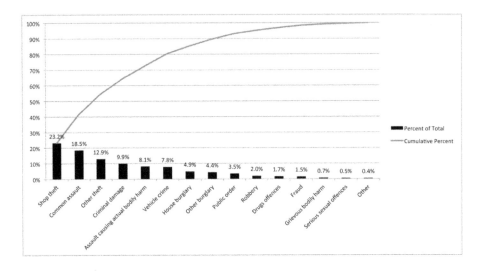

Figure 10.4: Pareto chart – Crime types

This chart depicts the relative proportions of different crime types in our hypothetical police division. At one end of the scale are the big hitters of shop theft and common assault (i.e. the lowest possible level of assault, where there is no injury). These two offence types account for 41.7% of total recorded crime. At the other end of the scale are the much more serious, yet relatively infrequent, offence categories of grievous bodily harm and serious sexual offences. If one were to prioritise where to take action following this Pareto analysis, the temptation might be to concentrate on the 'volume' offences at the expense of the more serious offences which make up only a fraction of a per cent of the total.

Clearly this would be wrong. Whilst the police should strive to reduce things like shop theft and common assault, there is also a strong duty to address the more serious crimes. Imagine if serious sexual offences were treated as a low priority on the basis of them being at an 'acceptably low level' numerically speaking. There is no acceptable level for this type of crime and police managers must prioritise action based on threat, risk and harm, rather than purely numbers. The alternative is a nightmare world where only the 'low hanging fruit' are targeted - prioritisation based on what is easy, rather than what is right. Pareto analysis can be a useful tool for identifying where the bulk of opportunities lie for making significant changes but, as ever, the data must be interpreted by a human mind and action must always be compatible with purpose.

Nevertheless, when data are intelligently interpreted within the overall context, Pareto analysis can be a very powerful tool for shining a bright light on where the greatest opportunities for improvement lie. It is also an effective technique for identifying waste and for encouraging evidence-based prioritisation, thereby earning itself a place in the box of what I consider to be useful tools.

IT – Friend or Foe?

IT (or Information Technology) is an interesting one. Some people would like you to believe that it is the answer to all an organisation's woes. I have seen organisational change programmes where the overall system design appears to be based solely around the IT. By definition, it will have been designed against something other than purpose and will, therefore, be a recipe for disaster (and probably an expensive disaster at that). An all-singing, all-dancing IT 'solution' is a sure-fire way of wrecking the system.

IT has its place, but its role should always be to *support* a system or process, rather than shape it. When applied in the right setting and right proportions, IT can be a fantastic tool, capable of enhancing existing processes. Spitzer provides the following examples of the benefits of well-integrated IT:

> For instance, technology can measure *more*, more quickly; it can automate data collection; reduce data handling errors; perform intricate analytics (including modelling 'what if' scenarios); enable simulation and predictive modelling…[5]

This list sums up some of the advantages of effective IT systems; note, however, that it does not include the word '*interpret*'. Only a human can interpret the information that an IT system produces. This is why it is so important that data is overlaid with narrative when attempting to understand measures or performance information. A machine can speed things up and produce accurate information, but it cannot *understand* it.

Incorporating IT into systems can *enhance* the system or process, but it mustn't *become* the system or process. IT does not make a bad system

---

5   Spitzer (2007) p.163

good – if the wrong measures are being used in the first place, or the overall design of the system is somehow dysfunctional, IT will not change this. It cannot make the wrong things right. Proceed with caution.

Optimise! Optimise! Optimise!

It sounds like the deranged battle cry of a demented Dalek, but actually it's the key to maximising efficiency and minimising waste.

Conventional management practice tends to focus on ensuring outputs are produced within specifications. For example, say you wanted to have an item delivered and you were given a delivery slot of between 2pm and 4pm. Sure, this is better than waiting at home all day, but what you really want is for the delivery to be as close to, say, 3pm as possible. This would allow you to plan your day better and allow you time to get on with other stuff. In these circumstances, 3pm is the optimum, or *nominal*, delivery time. From the delivery company's perspective, the entire range of possible delivery times between 2pm and 4pm are treated as though they are equal to each other (i.e. 2.01pm, 3pm, or 3.59pm are all classed as 'within specification'). In contrast, from the customer's perspective, having to rush back home by 2pm or hang around until 4pm, are entirely different to the ideal of a delivery occurring at 3pm.

Henry Neave[6] provides a couple of further examples that demonstrate how deviation from the nominal (optimum) value corresponds to a progressive increase of waste. This is in sharp contrast with the notion of arbitrary specification limits that attempt to delineate 'acceptable' values from 'unacceptable' ones. The first is the notion of a metal socket being manufactured to comply with design specifications relating to the size of its diameter:

> The truth of the matter is that, the closer the diameter is to the nominal, the better the socket is. And the further away it is, the worse it is. There are no sudden *steps* from good to bad, or from bad to worse. The seriousness of errors increases continuously as we move further and further away from the nominal.[7]

---

6   Neave (1990) pp.170-172
7   *ibid* p.170

The second example relates to room temperature, and is summarised below:

For the sake of argument, let's say that the ideal room temperature in an office fitted with a thermostat is 70° Fahrenheit. Do you think many people would notice if it was 71° one day, or 69° the next? Probably not. What about 73° or 67°? Maybe. How about 65° or 75°? A few people in the room may feel a little too cool or a bit too warm. What if the thermostat goes really bonkers and outputs temperatures of 55° or 85°? (Or worse still, 40° or 100°?) People will definitely notice these extremes and it will affect their work. As the temperature change moves further away from the nominal, the more pronounced the effect.

Suppose that with the best will in the world, the engineer who designed the room's thermostat wanted to avoid temperature extremes, so built it to specifications that limited temperature fluctuations. What would they be? Perhaps +/- 5°? Whilst these settings might prevent the most extreme fluctuations from occurring and thereby driving room temperature to the realms of discomfort, they do not acknowledge that there is a difference between 65° and 75°. These specifications treat all possible temperatures within this range as being acceptable, rather than recognising that 70° is actually the nominal value.

As Neave puts it:

> Whichever interval you choose, say 65°-75°, the facts remain that: Temperatures near 65° or 75° are not as suitable as temperatures near 70°; and you're not going to be able to tell the difference between 74.9° and 75.1°, so it just doesn't make any sense to class 74.9° as satisfactory and 75.1° as unsatisfactory.[8]

The contrast between specifications and progressive waste caused by deviation from the nominal value is perhaps best illustrated by using diagrams. In *Figure 10.6* below, we see how specification limits attempt to determine the invisible line between good and bad.

---

8   *ibid*, p.172

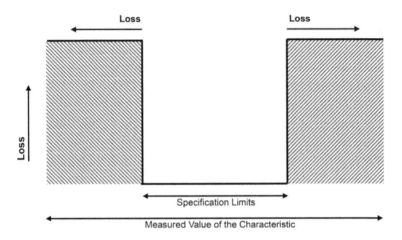

Figure 10.5: Step loss diagram

The diagram highlights the weakness of the assumption that there is a sudden step from good to bad; it treats everything within the limits as equally acceptable, and everything outside of them as unacceptable. This is not an accurate depiction of how loss occurs – the reality is that the further we move from the nominal value, the greater the loss. It does not occur instantaneously as some invisible line is crossed. This Step Loss model would suggest that there is a definable dividing line between acceptable and unacceptable, and that a value immediately outside of the specification is as undesirable as another value a thousand miles past it. This proposal ignores reality because it assumes that an incremental continuum of values does not exist.

A much more accurate way to depict economic (and other types of) loss is to illustrate it using a parabolic loss model,[9] as below:

---

9   Perhaps the most famous diagram used to depict gradual loss is the Taguchi Loss Function; the parabolic loss model is a simplified version of this. For more, see Deming (1994) pp.217-219 and Neave (1990) pp.173-176; 181-192

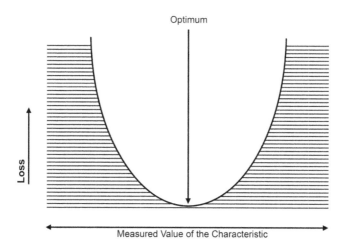

Figure 10.6: Parabolic loss diagram

Without attempting to go through any complicated mathematics relating to how the model is calculated (mainly because they go above my head), by simply looking at this diagram it immediately becomes obvious that loss increases incrementally as we move further away from the nominal value (i.e. the optimum). This model rejects the notion that there is a sudden step from good to bad and is therefore a much more accurate representation of how deviation from the nominal value creates incremental loss, or waste.

Returning to the delivery example to illustrate this, the customer's nominal value would be for the delivery to arrive at 3pm. The specification limits are for the delivery to occur between 2pm and 4pm. This would suggest to the delivery company that any time between these hours is equally acceptable, whereas the customer knows that 3pm is best for them, so the closer the delivery driver can get to 3pm, the better. As the delivery time moves away from the nominal value, it slips into the grey area on the diagram; therefore loss (perhaps measured in the customer's time) increases.

Below is a linear version of 'loss' that I devised to illustrate how loss increases when there is a delay in the police response to an incident.

Efficiency Loss Diagram

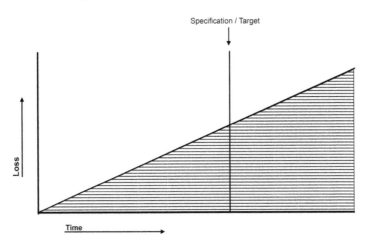

Figure 10.7 Linear efficiency loss diagram

As time passes, loss increases, which could mean that criminals get away, property is damaged, people are hurt, or the situation somehow escalates. It's pretty obvious to most people that if the police get to an incident quickly there is a better chance of resolving it effectively. This efficiency loss diagram includes the inevitable arbitrary response time target, where every value to the left of the specification is perceived as equally acceptable, and everything to its right as unacceptable. The grey shaded area of loss refutes this assumption, clearly demonstrating how loss is incremental and there is no sudden step from good to bad.

To explore these concepts further, I have added some reference points and timings to the diagram and displayed the adapted version below:

Efficiency Loss Diagram - Response Times

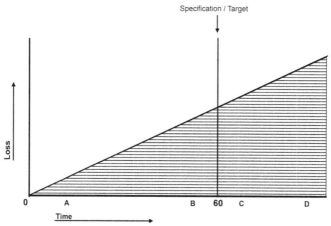

Figure 10.8: Linear efficiency loss diagram – Response times

Here, we challenge the assumption that every value prior to the response time target of 60 minutes is acceptable, and every value thereafter is equally unacceptable. (A 60-minute response time target is most usual for matters deemed a 'priority' but not an 'emergency'). The specifications approach proposes that arrival times 'A' and 'B' are of equal benefit, but, as the diagram shows, this is not the case. Loss continues to increase as time passes and has no regard for arbitrary targets or cut-off points. In the same way, once the target time has been breached, loss continues incrementally. There is no sudden step. Also, there is not a lot of difference between the degree of loss encountered at arrival time 'B' and arrival time 'C', despite them being positioned marginally either side of the target time. Why is one okay whilst the other isn't? It's bonkers isn't it? Clearly, arrival time 'D' is most undesirable, but is most likely to occur because of system conditions – setting an arbitrary response time target will not change this fact.

You may recall that my theory about targets involves the assertion that no numerical target is immune from causing dysfunctional behaviour. Response time targets are no different, and unfortunately lend themselves to generating the temptation for arrival times to be recorded just before the cut-off point, even if the officer is still a few minutes away. As we saw in Chapter Six, examples of 'fiddling' police and ambulance response times emerged as a result of the pressure to meet targets.

Another way in which response time targets can trigger dysfunctional behaviour is when they cause control room operators to delay the despatch of officers because there is still plenty of time before the time limit is reached; this tends to occur when there are other jobs closer to the expiry time. A new incident may be placed behind another that is already 50 minutes old, simply to avoid the older job missing the target time. The control room operator anticipates that an officer will be available to go to the newer job perhaps in 30 or 40 minutes time – this means that both incidents can be resourced ahead of the 60 minute target time, albeit in the region of arrival time 'B' on the diagram for both.

So, an incident which may well be resolvable with a speedy police response becomes neglected in favour of another where there would be no significant benefit in deploying officers at arrival time 'B' rather than at arrival time 'C'. The opportunity for effectively resolving the newer incident has been reduced or may be lost. It is the pressure to comply with the target that causes this behaviour.

A dysfunctional behaviour caused by this type of target occurs when the target time has been missed. Due to the 'step' mentality towards loss, once an incident passes the target time, there is no incentive to arrive quickly anymore – it's already a total loss. Operators may put such an incident on the 'back burner' in favour of sending resources to other incidents that are approaching the target time. Whilst *Figure 10.8* is explicit in demonstrating that loss continues to grow after the target has been breached, the specifications approach actually treats an arrival after 61 minutes as being equal to an arrival after three hours. There is no perceived advantage in ensuring a resource has arrived by arrival time 'C' any more so than if no one gets there until arrival time 'D', or later.

Although loss is depicted as occurring in a nice straight line in these diagrams, this would rarely be the case in real life. In some cases, the only opportunity to resolve an incident might well be within the first five minutes (e.g. offenders are still at the scene). In others, it may be possible to resolve the incident satisfactorily for some time afterwards, but if left too long, the potential for sudden escalation could become a factor. This is why it is so important to rely upon the judgement of frontline professionals when determining the most appropriate response. A one-size-fits-all arbitrary response time target is incapable of making such assessments, because it cannot absorb variety.[10]

---

10   Seddon (2008) pp.62-63

The following diagrams feature a couple of variants of *Figure 10.8* and relate to different types of incident which cause different patterns of loss. Each is briefly explained afterwards.

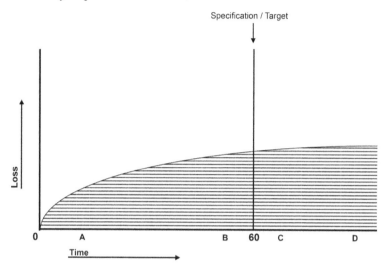

Figure 10.9: Efficiency loss diagram – Response times (Loss slope 1)

In this example, the type of loss has a relatively low impact, but increases most drastically in the first few minutes after the event. After that, the loss slope does not increase significantly over time. This type of incident could be a shoplifting case, where the offender is only present in the area for a few minutes after the theft has been committed. If officers have not arrived by arrival time 'A', the offender may only be located as a result of slower-time enquiries, such as through the recovery of CCTV footage or witness evidence. In such cases, if officers cannot be deployed whilst the offender is in the immediate vicinity, there is no great advantage in aiming to arrive just ahead of the response time target.

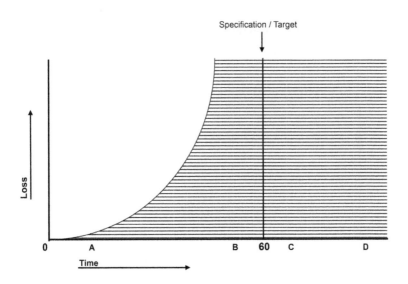

Figure 10.10: Efficiency loss diagram – Response times (Loss slope 2)

In this case, loss increases exponentially after a few minutes and reaches a critical level well ahead of the response time target. This variant of the diagram could relate to an argument in the street that suddenly escalates, resulting in a stabbing. It is therefore imperative that officers arrive quickly to diffuse the situation before it gets out of hand. We looked at such an example in Chapter One where, because of a slow police response, the opportunity to resolve what began as a relatively low-level incident was missed. This type of curve demonstrates the benefits of adopting a default position of sending officers to incidents as soon as possible rather than being guided by target times.

In all the examples, nominal value translates as being the most effective response that the caller can experience. Usually this means the police get to the incident quickly and resolve it successfully. In cases where a caller does not require an early attendance, the response time target is particularly redundant and could actually encourage an unnecessarily quick response at the expense of other more urgent matters that require attention.

As I pointed out in Chapter Six, I argue that the solution is to scrap response time targets. Operators should use their professional judgement to ascertain whether or not a situation is an emergency which requires an urgent response. If it is, send officers using blue lights and sirens – they will get there as quickly as they can, regardless of any target. If it isn't an emergency, the aim should be to get there at the most appropriate time, in line with the caller's nominal value. Usually this will be as quickly as possible; to do so minimises loss and optimises service delivery. Response times should still be measured, but only to aid understanding of the system and identify opportunities for improvement. There is absolutely no benefit in setting arbitrary numerical targets in this situation (or anywhere else) – they make people do the wrong things and cause loss to accumulate.

Systems and processes pertaining to the deployment of police resources should focus on doing what is necessary to achieve nominal (optimum) value for the caller. Affording frontline officers and staff the latitude to exercise professional judgement, evidence-based prioritisation and proportionate risk management is a superior approach that far outstrips conventional operating models, which are incapable of absorbing variety. Only a flexible and intuitive approach to incident management and despatch will effectively achieve purpose in this area of policing. The theory surrounding optimisation, along with an understanding of loss functions, can help make this possible.

Road Rage

Have you ever been driving along a motorway when the traffic grinds to a halt? If you're like me, you sit there pulling your hair out, checking the clock and flicking impatiently through radio channels, as you sit helplessly in an endless line of traffic. Eventually, it starts to move slowly. At last, you break through the 10mph barrier and before long you are travelling along as normal, wondering what it was that caused the tailback. But there's nothing there! No road works, no broken down vehicles, no nothing.

This phenomenon always used to baffle me. Naturally, I could understand why a traffic accident or adverse weather conditions would cause delays and I could also get my head around why three lanes of traffic being squeezed into two at road works would generate congestion (i.e. flow is restricted so traffic slows down). I could even appreciate why drivers gravitating towards the overtaking lane whilst leaving the inside lanes relatively empty causes crowding and slows the overall pace. But stationary traffic caused by some invisible blockage? Nope.

Then one day, I discovered that the answer lies in understanding and managing variation and capacity. It's all about flow.[11]

---

11   For more on flow, see Seddon (2003) pp.16-17

If you are familiar with the concept of 'managed motorways' you will be accustomed to variable speed limits, painted chevrons on the road surface and the occasional use of the hard shoulder as an extra lane at peak times. Managed motorways employ these techniques to improve flow and, interestingly, this often involves restricting the speed limit to much less than the usual 70 miles per hour. The reason behind this is that uneven flow (caused by vehicles 'bunching up' and sudden changes in speed) causes blockages and hampers progress. Furthermore, by monitoring traffic flow on the camera network, operators can assess the volume and rate of traffic flow and make a judgement about how well (or otherwise) the motorway lanes are coping with demand. This is equivalent to interpreting data on an SPC chart – the practice highlights signals and allows the operator to anticipate what will happen should the motorway continue to operate within the same parameters.

If traffic is particularly heavy, or if a lane is closed, it is reasonable to assume that flow will become 'bumpy', due to an uneven and irregular pace (i.e. *'Mura'*); in the worst cases, flow may completely grind to a halt. Whilst it would be nice for everyone to trundle along at 70mph, the limitations of the system (i.e. only having three available lanes) prevent this from occurring efficiently in times of heavy demand. Therefore, if the motorway operator reduces the speed limit to 50mph, this controls the traffic flow more effectively and reduces unevenness.

It may at first be frustrating for drivers to be forced to slow down, but the counterintuitive truth is that by altering this system condition (i.e. speed), they will get from 'A' to 'B' faster by travelling at a slower, yet more consistent pace. This is because there has been a reduction in speed variation. The alternative is the free-for-all where traffic keeps stopping and starting due to vehicles bunching up, driving too closely, braking suddenly and changing lanes; this triggers a chain reaction which leads to erratic flow, stoppages and ultimately a longer end-to-end time.

Ideally, it is best to increase the capacity of a process to meet predictable demand, rather than control the flow through it, but this is not always possible when dealing with large infrastructures like the motorway network. Nevertheless, by studying predictable demand, certain sections of motorway (such as parts of the M6 and M42 in the West Midlands, and the M25 around London) have been redesigned and now operators can routinely open up the hard shoulder as an extra lane during peak times. This increases capacity and improves flow.

Another traffic-related analogy is that of the traffic island (or 'roundabout'), a commonplace feature of traffic management in the UK. Traffic moves round the island in a circular clockwise motion, until each vehicle leaves at the appropriate exit. The concept is a near-perfect model of self-regulation, as long as incoming flow is relatively consistent from all directions. It is a simple model that reduces unnecessary waiting, batching and queuing.

Contrast this with a road junction that is controlled by automatic traffic lights. Queues build up until vehicles are sent across the junction in batches. Even when a particular entrance to the junction is quiet, vehicles that could potentially pass through safely are often held by a red 'stop' light, resulting in unnecessary delays. In contrast with the principles of roundabouts, delays and waste are often the unintentional by-products of this automated method.

Get In The Queue

The examples we have just looked at highlight the benefits of managing variation and/or increasing capacity. When emphasis is shifted from attempting to manage *cost* (in this example the costs would be measured in time and inconvenience) to managing *flow*, costs go down and efficiency increases. As Seddon puts it, 'Focus on flow and costs will fall, focus on costs and costs will rise'.[12]

A useful theory that helps us see how flow can be improved is that of *queuing theory*.[13] The first person to develop a viable queuing theory was French mathematician S. D. Poisson, who used statistical approaches to predict the probability of desired outcomes. His work led to the creation of formulae that can be used to calculate the optimum amount of resources required to handle predictable demand at the most efficient rate. Further queuing theories were subsequently developed by Danish mathematician A. K. Erland, which aid understanding of different types of queues.

Queuing theory can be as simple or as complicated as you want it to be. I know which I prefer. In simple terms, it assists system design by identifying the rate at which flow moves along processes. An obvious example would be a queue of people at a Post Office counter. If the average transaction takes five minutes and a new customer arrives every five minutes, then this process is optimised to deal with demand at the rate it arrives. Conversely,

---

12   Seddon (2008) p.71
13   See: Gross and Harris (1998); Hall (1991)

if a new customer predictably arrives every four minutes, then whilst the first customer is being served, the second one arrives and a queue begins to form.

This imbalance between capacity and demand has a cumulative effect and the queue itself grows and causes exponential delays. If demand continues at the same rate, it will be impossible for the person at the counter to ever catch up. The consequences become progressively worse with no prospect of equilibrium being restored. The table below shows the queuing times for customers in this scenario.

Customer No.	Arrival time	Queuing Time
1	0 mins	0 mins
2	4 mins	1 min
3	8 mins	2 mins
4	12 mins	3 mins
5	16 mins	4 mins
6	20 mins	5 mins

Figure 10.12: Queuing times

By the time 20 minutes have elapsed, four customers will have been served and the fifth and sixth customers will be in the queue. The sixth customer will have to wait the full five minutes it takes to serve the fifth customer; during this time the seventh customer will have arrived and the queue will continue to build up in this way.

By using queuing theory to understand flow, we are able to establish how much capacity is needed to service predictable demand. Ideally, if capacity can be matched to predictable demand, this will result in a perfect flow through this stage of the process; i.e. one in, one out, with no queuing.

Where it is not possible to increase capacity, the other option is to take steps to manage flow more effectively. This could involve scheduling (as long as it achieves purpose for the customer or service user), or tactics such as those seen in the traffic examples. In all cases, queuing theory offers a clear and practical approach to identifying and removing blockages, as well as reducing failure demand and sub-optimisation.

A Quick Summary

Hopefully this chapter has proved to be a practical resource. Remember that tools have no brain – the techniques described can only ever be useful if they are applied in the correct setting, at the right time and with due regard to the overall context. Simply focusing on waste removal without questioning the process will not help you build a better system. Merely speeding up or shortening a process that shouldn't be there in the first place is a waste of time. In a similar vein, blindly relying on IT misses the point. A bad process that becomes automated is just an automated bad process.

Overall, it is imperative to understand that whilst tools can be useful in the right circumstances, they do not change management thinking.

CHAPTER ELEVEN

Fertile Ground

This chapter will explore the conditions that are necessary for systems thinking philosophy to flourish within organisations by focusing on two key areas:

1. The assumption implicit in the Principal-Agent model (and therefore conventional management practice) that good performance is contingent on workers being subject to control mechanisms, coercion and extrinsic motivators. This was explained in some detail in Chapter Five.

2. The importance of organisational culture and context; how a systems ethos generates an environment that overcomes the obstacles caused by traditional management devices.

The essence of my proposal is that the combination of self-motivated workers and a trust-orientated environment creates a culture that is conducive to systems thinking and results in a more effective organisation.

Gardening Tips

Up to this point we have looked at various techniques for improving systems, as well as a whole host of things to avoid. We have seen how understanding variation provides the key to dramatic performance improvement and learnt that by simply removing waste we can instantly create capacity. We have discussed how numerical targets distort outputs and cause irreparable damage. We have explored the dangers associated with tampering, and looked at different tools that can aid diagnostics. You have been shown examples of these things in action in a policing context, and may well be thinking about how they could be applied in your workplace.

Here's the rub: none of these approaches will work if your organisation's culture and management ethos is incompatible with systems thinking philosophy. For the techniques to work and for the systems approach to become truly embedded, management at the very top of the organisation must genuinely and overtly support it. Without this endorsement, systems thinking will not take root. It is not enough to leave it to middle or junior managers to try to implement – this simply will not bring about transformation at the organisational level.

Systems thinking is not a gimmick. It is not a set of tools. It is not a quick fix solution. You can't just pick it up off the shelf and apply it, or delegate someone to apply it for you. You have to live and breathe it. Your organisation must provide fertile ground for it to grow, in the same way as you would if you were growing a flower. You might plant the very best seed in the ground and water it every day, but no matter how carefully you attend to it, if it is planted in the wrong type of soil it won't grow (or it may begin to grow but then wither and die). The correct type of nourishment is essential.

This chapter will explore how these essential 'nutrients' present in an organisation's 'soil' propagate an explosion of colourful systems thinking flora, but first I want to point out something interesting about the 'seeds'. The people (the seeds) who choose to work in particular organisations have qualities within them that can make the organisational aspirations of managers easier to attain (at less cost). Characteristics of wanting to make a difference, or serving the community are found particularly amongst frontline public services workers.

Have a look at these quotes:[1]

"I get the greatest satisfaction in helping people."

"I wanted to put something back and make a difference."

"I want to serve the people in the area where I was born and bred."

"Taking criminals off the street still gives me great satisfaction and motivation - knowing I've made that area a little bit safer for other people."

"I joined the police to help people."

"I joined the police as I just love locking up the bad guys!"

"I wanted to belong to an organisation that would protect the weak and the vulnerable."

---

1   Comments made by Constables, Sergeants and Inspectors, of between 4 and 24 years' service, during research conducted by the author.

"I get great satisfaction in giving someone an excellent service."

"I joined the police to combat what I considered to be wrong with society and to make a difference to as many people's lives as possible."

"I joined the police due to the old cliché that I wanted to make a difference."

These are responses from serving police officers who were asked the question, "Why did you join the police?" Many who participated in the research immediately followed up their statement with sentiments to the effect that they thought their reasons would be perceived as 'corny' or 'clichéd'. Having joined the police for similar reasons, I know that there is nothing corny or clichéd about wanting to help people or make a difference – I also recognise that the reasons given by these officers are absolutely heartfelt.

Now rewind to Chapter Nine where we talked about purpose. We are reminded of the section on police purpose statements, such as the famous motto of the LAPD – "To protect and to serve" – that simple slogan sticks in the mind because it goes straight to the core of what the police are all about. (It's not a 124-page strategic plan – just a core concept that attunes self-motivated workers with organisational purpose.) Now consider how well-aligned that stated corporate aim is with the innate motives that guided these people to the police service in the first place.

The questions I'd pose are:

- Do we appear to have a group of people who have gravitated towards the role, and are in natural alignment with organisational purpose?

- Did this group opt for the role because they want to make a difference, to help others, to protect, to serve, to stop people from doing bad things?

- Could these individuals be driven by an internal desire to do the right thing for the sake of others; a group of people who are already compelled by strong intrinsic motivation?

If this group is representative of the majority of police officers, then what a great starting point for any police recruiting department! If certain types of people are drawn towards public service because of a sense of vocation and innate altruism, then perhaps a significant proportion of police officers, fire-fighters, nurses, doctors, teachers, social workers (and so on) are in those very roles today because of unwitting self-selection. It should be very easy for managers to work with a group of people who are already predisposed to organisational purpose. All the recruiting department needs to worry about when putting applicants through the selection procedure is whether they meet the necessary standards of education, fitness, aptitude, etc.

And once someone successfully joins an organisation and shows competence in a particular role, managers should afford them the latitude to get on with their work without undue interference. For example, I am confident that my neighbourhood team Sergeants know their respective areas and respond appropriately to crime patterns and public concerns – I don't need written plans from them about their intended operational activity nor do I hold them to account against targets. I know that there is no need to force them into alignment with organisational purpose through control mechanisms and coercion.

You'd think this would be obvious, but looking at how the traditional Western style of management operates, it seems we go to great lengths to recruit the right people, then impose unnecessary controls and counterproductive management practices all over them. This not only stops them from doing the job they joined to do but also damages morale, increases waste and drives up costs. Why do we do this?

Time for a Bit of Theory

I believe that there are many deep-seated cultural, societal and psychological reasons that explain why organisations default to this traditional mode of management. I sense a genuine fear of 'letting go' that stems from an ingrained lack of trust. Managers worry that unfettered workers will run amok, ignoring organisational purpose in favour of the self-serving behaviours characteristic of the untrustworthy agent operating within the Principal-Agent model.

There is a compelling alternative to the Principal-Agent model, one which propagates organisational trust, builds better relationships and encourages the fertile environment necessary for systems thinking to thrive. This alternative philosophy is an established theory derived from the fields of psychology and sociology, called Stewardship Theory. The Principal-

Steward model is predicated on trust and empowerment.[2] The underlying assumption is that the steward (i.e. the worker) is intrinsically motivated to work towards organisational purpose and can therefore be afforded a degree of trust and autonomy. A helpful definition of stewardship is as follows:

> ...the willingness to be accountable for the well-being of the larger organisation by operating in service, rather than in control, of those around us. Stated simply, it is accountability without control or compliance.[3]

Acceptance of the possibility of workers behaving as stewards instantly renders redundant the traditional obsession of regulating the workforce, through directives, incentives and other controls. It fundamentally shifts the starting point from one where managers assume workers are lazy, incompetent or untrustworthy to one where it is acknowledged that they care about their work and want to do their best. Systems thinker and governance expert, Dr. Jim Armstrong, argues this point, identifying the importance of trust within the stewardship disposition:

> Unlike in agency theory, where controls are emphasised, it is better to maximise the autonomy, authority and discretion of organisations under stewardship leadership since they can be trusted.[4]

Experts in the field of behavioural psychology argue that this is because under the Principal-Steward model, "...pro-organisational, collectivistic behaviors have higher utility than individualistic, self-serving behaviors".[5] They strive to achieve the aims of the organisation because they elevate them above their own interests and want to do a good job through "...trust, reputational enhancement, reciprocity, discretion and autonomy, level of responsibility, job satisfaction, stability and tenure, and mission alignment".[6]

These features of stewardship are entirely compatible with the sentiments expressed by the police officers who took part in the research carried out for this book; i.e. acting in the service of others is the primary motivator for performing the role.

---

2   See: Block (1993); Davis, Donaldson and Schoorman, F.D. (1997a); Van Slyke (2007)

3   Block(1993) p.20

4   Armstrong (1997) p.22

5   Davis, Donaldson and Schoorman (1997) p.24

6   Van Slyke (2007) p.165

The notion of stewardship is also consistent with the thrust of much of Sir Ronnie Flanagan's Review of Policing[7] and the HMIC report, *Leading from the Frontline*,[8] where arguments were presented in support of increased utilisation of street-level discretion,[9] as well as devolved decision-making and frontline leadership. As discussed in Chapter Seven, these reports highlighted the prevalence of risk aversion and unnecessary bureaucracy within policing, along with the associated consequences. Both reports proposed that solutions lay in greater application of professional judgement by frontline officers, along with increased autonomy and latitude for frontline leaders.

Motivation

Writer and researcher Dan Pink proposes that the secret to good organisational performance lies in people's innate desire to direct their lives, learn and create new things, and experience a sense of achievement.[10] He argues that intrinsic motivation drives the human desire for attainment in the following key areas:

- Purpose

- Mastery

- Autonomy.

Purpose goes right to the heart of every system, as well as the most upstream point of any process (see Chapter One), i.e. 'Why does the system exist?' 'What is its aim?' If workers can see how their efforts contribute towards purpose this gives them a sense of psychological ownership and personal achievement.[11] Conversely, if they are forced to perform tasks that are disconnected from purpose, this can demoralise them and harm productivity (e.g. having to conform to meaningless internal reporting requirements).

Mastery is about bettering oneself and can apply as much to hobbies as it does to one's work. Why do amateur musicians or sportspeople spend so

---

7   Flanagan (2008)

8   HMIC (2008)

9   For an exploration of the exercise of discretion by frontline officials, including how their practical application of policy contributes towards the political process, see Michael Lipsky's proposal of 'street-level bureaucracy':Lipsky, M. (1980)

10   Pink (2009)

11   See Wasserman (2006)

much time, money and effort on their pastimes? Because people want to get better at the things they enjoy. It's intrinsically, rather than financially, rewarding. Consider how much more productive workers are when they are doing a job they love. Their main motivation isn't the money (although pay is important of course – see below); they are driven by the desire to better themselves and to contribute their skills to benefit the system. Mastery enhances reputation and credibility. Psychiatrist, Dr. David Krueger goes so far as to propose; "The experience of mastery of being effective may well be the most powerful motivating force in an individual's work."[12]

Autonomy is inextricably linked to trust – a key theme that runs through systems thinking. Trust leads to trust – and as managers realise that the vast majority of workers want to positively contribute towards purpose, they see that it is safe to afford them autonomy. Devolved responsibility, professional judgement and frontline empowerment lead to stronger relationships and a more effective system. Pink suggests that organisational design, rigid hierarchies and traditional management norms are barriers which stifle the innovation that autonomy generates. He proposes that allowing the workforce genuine freedom to suggest fresh ideas and test new methods is far more beneficial than constraining them with prescriptive policy or doctrine. Simply remove the barriers and see what people come up with.

Money, Money, Money

Sometimes people scoff when I suggest that money isn't the primary motivational factor for work. They argue that they have mortgages, food and drink to pay for, and that if they didn't get paid to work they wouldn't be able to afford any of those things. I respond that they are absolutely right but that money isn't usually the *main* motivator. Think about it. Money, rewards or other material compensations do not explain why a police officer wants to work unsociable hours and deal with an array of unpleasant and frightening situations when there are much more palatable (and safer) occupations out there. There are situations where money is a more obvious motivator than a sense of achievement, Pink suggests that financial incentives are more relevant in work situations where payment is directly linked to units produced (e.g. £1 per sack of potatoes filled). Piece-workers may be encouraged to complete more units of product if

---

12   Krueger (1992) p.11

they know they will receive more pay, but this type of lever does not work in more complex situations.

Indeed, such an incentive can cause dysfunctional behaviour – how many times have salespeople tried to pressure you into buying something you don't need or want? That's because they often work under incentive schemes that determine how much they are paid – usually according to the number of units sold. The primary objective becomes how many units they can sell, rather than what the customer's actual needs are. Given the latitude to be more creative and freed from such artificial drivers for activity, I suspect that these salespeople would come up with fresh approaches and tailor their efforts to match customers' needs. This would lead to happier customers, a more even flow and increased sales.

The argument is just as relevant at the punitive end of the traditional manager's 'motivational' armoury. Comparison against targets, league tables, admonishing people for failure, etc. are meant to improve performance by motivating workers. Actually, they are completely futile. True motivation comes from within – it cannot be contrived by third parties and imposed on others. 'Carrot and stick' motivation is blunt and transactional – it simply doesn't tap in to the real reasons why people want to do a good job.

Pink recounts an amusing but depressing perspective on transactional attempts at motivating people:

> What's frustrating, or ought to be frustrating... is that when we see these carrot-and-stick motivators demonstrably fail before our eyes - when we see them fail in organisations right before our very eyes - our response isn't to say: "Man, those carrot-and-stick motivators failed again. Let's try something new." It's, "Man, those carrot-and-stick motivators failed again. Looks like we need more carrots. Looks like we need sharper sticks." And it's taking us down a fundamentally misguided path.[13]

More Perspectives

The notion of an empowered workforce that contributes towards purpose whilst striving for constant personal improvement is entirely compatible with Deming's desire to instil "joy in work". He observes that workers

---

13   Pink (2011)

are more productive when they operate in an environment where they are happy and able to take pride in what they do. He is also clear about whose responsibility it is to ensure this environment exists. In his own words:

> Management's job is to create an environment where everybody may take joy in his work.[14]

To further cement the argument that people are driven by intrinsic motivation rather than merely financial or other extrinsic incentives, it is also worth considering Maslow's well-known hierarchy of needs,[15] which classifies factors that drive human motivation. A version of this is reproduced below:

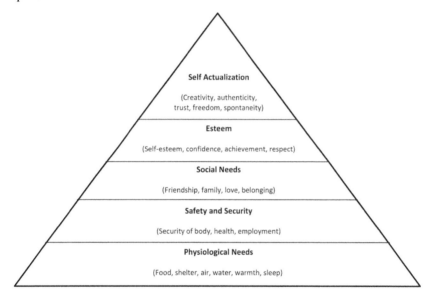

Figure 11.1: Maslow's Hierarchy of Needs

The pyramid illustrates Maslow's proposal that people require a variety of stimuli to light that inner fire of motivation. These range from basic needs such as food and shelter, to 'higher order' needs such as trust, freedom and creativity. The needs positioned toward the base of the pyramid are those that are necessary to live – so it is possible to associate them with extrinsic motivators. For example, if you had no food it's fair to say that remuneration for even the most mundane job would motivate you to work.

---

14   Neave (1990) p.198
15   Maslow (1970) (Note: there are various versions of the pyramid; some contain slightly different text and more categories. This version is shown as being indicative).

As we move up through the layers, we meet the complex intangibles, such as states of mind and relationships. Whilst these are not strictly necessary for day-to-day survival, they are the components of inner richness. Maslow was clear that people needed a balance of the elements across all levels of the pyramid if they were to lead fulfilled and psychologically healthy lives.

An organisation that encourages trust and self-esteem gives workers the opportunity to satisfy their higher order needs, thereby generating enhanced productivity. Affording workers a greater degree of autonomy and the opportunity to improve their skills (mastery) is a much greater motivator than paying them a little bit more for working faster, or threatening them with a critical staff appraisal.

Under the trust-orientated Principal-Steward model there is the powerful combination of having staff who are predisposed towards purpose *and* liberated to operate in an environment that is conducive to their higher order needs.

Theory X and Y

In 1960, Douglas McGregor[16] published his Theory X and Theory Y. Theory X most closely resembles the Principal-Agent model and the assumption that an individual will act opportunistically and needs to be controlled and coerced through a mix of incentives, inspection and sanctions. In contrast, Theory Y assumes that individuals naturally want to do a good job; they welcome responsibility and will exercise self-direction. This is consistent with the concepts of stewards being trustworthy and intrinsically motivated to achieve the goals of their organisation.

Stewardship – At a Glance

As we have seen, many of the main features of Stewardship Theory are diametrically opposed to the traditional ethos of management. Whilst it is proposed that the position on trust is at the core of each model, the table below summarises the main differences:

---

16   McGregor (1960)

Agency Theory	Stewardship Theory
• Mistrust	• Trust
• Goal incongruence	• High convergence; goals shared
• Theoretical assumptions are derived from economics	• Theoretical assumptions are derived from psychology and sociology
• Control-orientated management philosophy	• Involvement-orientated management philosophy
• Rational, selfish behaviour	• Pro-organisational behaviour
• Use of rewards and sanctions to foster goal alignment (transactional, extrinsic)	• Empowerment, personal responsibility and autonomy (intrinsic motivation)
• Monitoring, audit and inspection	• Shared values, culture and norms
• Focus on outputs	• Focus on outcomes

Figure 11.2: Principal-Agent versus Principal-Steward

These contrasting features are drawn from existing literature[17] but I propose that the following characteristics are also key differences between the two theories, and they bear particular relevance to the policing context:

Agency Theory	Stewardship Theory
• Contractual organisational loyalty	• Vocational, self-selection
• Policy-based and doctrine-led decision-making	• Professional judgement
• Permissions culture	• Devolved responsibility
• Risk averse, retrospective blame for error	• Risk aware, proportionate risk management
• Anti-systemic	• Pro-systemic

Figure 11.3: Principal-Agent versus Principal-Steward

Overall, the stewardship disposition emphasises pro-systemic behaviours that foster trust and goal convergence for greater personal and organisational effectiveness.

---

17   See: Donaldson and Davis (1991); Davis, Donaldson and Schoorman (1997a); Armstrong (1997); Van Slyke (2007) '

Get Real

As the tables above illustrate, there are fundamental differences between conventional management practices and the alternative systems-orientated philosophy of management. It might seem as if they are permanently fixed and mutually exclusive but, because the real world imposes influences which are sometimes incompatible with the neat world of theory, there can sometimes be a degree of overlap.

For a start, it is accepted that it would be naïve to optimistically trust everyone unconditionally in every circumstance. Likewise, it is acknowledged that proportionate inspection can be entirely appropriate for higher risk areas of activity. It would also be foolish to disregard technical competence in favour of unrestricted autonomy. (You wouldn't let an unqualified person fly a jumbo jet would you?)

Nevertheless, a default starting position of trust is a good one – even investing a small degree of autonomy in someone from the outset can pay dividends. Consider this point made by Professor Russell Hardin of New York University: "...the gains from trust far outweigh the savings from mistrust."[18]

In the same vein, Professor David Van Slyke of Syracuse University suggests that interfaces which begin from the principal-agent position may evolve into hybrid principal-steward relationships, based on accumulating positive interactions between the parties. This increases levels of trust over a period of time.[19]

Stewardship is not simply about cutting everyone loose to do their own thing either. Some members of staff may seek a higher level of direction from managers because clear instructions and parameters make them feel secure. And not everyone will be a great innovator. Managers need to recognise the different skills and abilities within their teams and ensure that people have the opportunity to play to their strengths. The richness of teams (and systems) often lies within these differences, and managers should capitalis e on this and ensure that everyone is afforded the latitude to grow as individuals and complement each other in the quest to attain organisational purpose.

Furthermore, it may be that there can be multiple concurrent principal-agent *and* principal-steward relationships occurring at many levels within

---

18   Hardin (2006) p.23
19   Van Slyke (2007)

the same organisation It is entirely feasible that these relationships can involve different agent or steward configurations at different times, despite involving the same people. Circumstances may also dictate the mode of interaction that is most appropriate at the time. This proposition is alluded to by Donaldson and co-authors in a separate paper:

> We believe that principals in organisations are likely to have agency relationships with some managers and stewardship relationships with others.[20]

Others agree that principal-agent and principal-steward relationships can co-exist in the same organisation at the same time, and that such relationships are not necessarily fixed – "...today's 'agent' may be tomorrow's 'steward', or vice versa".[21]

These observations point towards a flexible form of stewardship which sits more neatly in real-life organisational interrelations. Therefore, I propose that Agency Theory and Stewardship Theory can be presented as a single overlapping theoretical construct, in the form of a continuum that demonstrates a gradation of agency and stewardship characteristics. (See *Figure 11.4*, below):

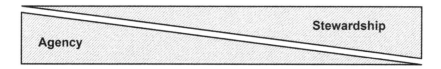

Figure 11.4: Agency – Stewardship Continuum

This model recognises the distinctiveness of each theory, whilst taking into account the multiple nuances of the Agency/Stewardship balance that can arise in local contexts and individual relationships. It represents an adaptive and entirely pragmatic mode of stewardship that blends theory with operational reality. It is proposed that a flexible (yet stewardship-biased) approach eclipses conventional agency-orientated management practice, and harnesses workers' intrinsic motivation. By shifting the balance away from the far bottom left corner of the model and towards the stewardship axis, managers will unleash the true potential of their workforce.

---

20   Davis, Donaldson and Schoorman (1997b) p.612
21   Albanese, Dacin and Harris (1997) p.611

Climate Change

So, one of the conditions necessary for systems thinking to flourish in organisations is the acceptance of the Stewardship model as a template for interrelationships. Managers must first acknowledge that people are primarily intrinsically motivated. The next step is to mould the system's operating environment to complement stewardship principles.

A simple pictorial representation featuring key components of systems thinking organisations can be seen in the form of the 'Joiner Triangle',[22] devised by management expert, Dr Brian Joiner. This is reproduced below:

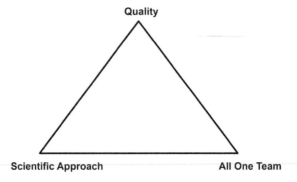

Figure 11.5: The Joiner Triangle

The triangle focuses on three crucial elements of effective systems thinking organisations. 'Quality' speaks for itself, whilst 'Scientific Approach' reminds us of the importance of evidence-based decision-making, understanding variation and the practice of intelligent data interpretation. Perhaps most relevant to this section, however, is the 'All One Team' header, as this is the corner of the triangle most directly relevant to organisational culture.

In line with the 'whole system' viewpoint, Joiner's 'All One Team' ethos is about fostering a culture of trust and cooperation between individuals and departments. In parallel with the other points of his triangle, this element seeks to build a solid foundation for the effective spread of the systems approach throughout the organisation. It is particularly powerful because it encourages trust-based relationships and stewardship principles to blossom within the culture of the organisation. Joiner describes his 'All One Team' concept as follows:

---

22   Joiner (1994) p.11

Believing in people; treating everyone in the organisation with dignity, trust and respect; working toward win-win instead of win-lose for all stakeholders…[23]

The reference to 'win-win' reminds us of the importance of avoiding sub-optimisation. By ensuring that individuals and departments complement each other rather than compete against one another, the focus will be on mutual purpose rather than the need to protect particular interests at the expense of the overall system. A culture of cooperation is an essential ingredient of a pro-systemic organisation and this can only occur in the right organisational environment.

Performance management expert, Dr. Dean Spitzer highlights the importance of context and writes about how organisational climate is a critical influencing factor in an organisation. He defines this term as:

…the prevailing 'atmosphere' of the organisation, the social-psychological environment that profoundly influences all behaviour, and it is typically measured by employee's perceptions. The climate is what best 'defines' the organisation to employees.[24]

Spitzer suggests that these defining environmental factors are wide-ranging and include the following:[25]

- The extent of formality (hierarchical structure) versus informality

- Inward-looking versus outward-looking

- Past-focus versus future-focus

- Trust versus distrust (and cynicism) of employees

- Open versus closed communication

- Task-focus versus people-focus

- Controlling versus collaborative decision-making

- Meritocratic rewards versus entitlement

- Change versus rigidity

- Risk taking versus risk aversion.

---

23   *ibid* p.11
24   Spitzer (2007) p.57
25   *ibid* p.57

You will immediately recognise that some of these themes overlap with subject matter already touched upon – for example, risk aversion has been identified as an unfortunate trait of modern day policing; the 'trust versus mistrust' theme underpins stewardship philosophy; the 'past-focus versus future-focus' topic bears particular relevance to the importance of presenting and interpreting performance data so as to aid prediction (see Chapters Two and Three). Indeed, Spitzer argues that performance management is the defining feature that influences the character of organisations more than any other.

Spitzer also emphasises the benefits of open communication and collaborative decision-making. This is consistent with Moynihan's proposals for a dialogue-based approach to performance management that focuses on narrative and context.[26] Furthermore, the environmental conditions pertinent to Spitzer's organisational climate concept reflect elements of a comparative summary of organisational characteristics drawn up by Seddon[27] (see the table below).

Command & Control Thinking		Systems Thinking
• Top-down, hierarchy	**Perspective**	• Outside-in, system
• Functional	**Design**	• Demand, value and flow
• Separated from work	**Decision-making**	• Integrated with work
• Output, targets, standards: related to budget	**Measurement**	• Capability, variation: related to purpose
• Contractual	**Attitude to customers**	• What matters?
• Contractual	**Attitude to suppliers**	• Cooperative
• Manage people and budgets	**Role of management**	• Act on the system
• Control	**Ethos**	• Learning

26   Moynihan (2008)
27   Seddon (2008) p.70

Command & Control Thinking		Systems Thinking
• Reactive, projects	**Change**	• Adaptive, integral
• Extrinsic	**Motivation**	• Intrinsic

Figure 11.6: Command & Control versus Systems Thinking

The table draws attention to many of the counterintuitive principles of systems thinking, such as integrating decision-making into the work. This concept alone is a world away from the traditional management position and drives home the fact that the approach is a fundamentally different way of *thinking*, as opposed to a few tweaks here and there, or the application of a set of tools.

Deming's System of Profound Knowledge

It would be very remiss of me to omit coverage of Deming's System of Profound Knowledge and his 14 Points.[28] Without intending to go into great depth (I thoroughly recommend hearing it from the man himself by reading the relevant sections in his books *Out of the Crisis* and *The New Economics*), it is important to appreciate the sheer power of his theories. These elements of Deming's work fit perfectly with everything else in this book and are particularly relevant to anyone seeking to imbue their organisation with a pro-systems climate.

Deming outlines his System of Profound Knowledge as having four components, all related to one another:

- Appreciation of a system
- Knowledge about variation
- Theory of Knowledge
- Psychology

He assures us that we need not be "…eminent in any part nor in all four parts in order to understand it and to apply it,"[29] but cautions against viewing the various elements of the theory in isolation because they are

---

28   For more on the System of Profound Knowledge and Deming's 14 Points see: Deming (1986) pp.18-96; Deming (1994) pp.92-115; Neave (1990) pp.39-55. (Please note that the precise wording of the headers of the 14 Points can vary depending on which source is used. Deming continually developed his points and this is reflected in the literature. I have used the wording from Deming 1986.)
29   Deming (1994) p. 93

all interdependent. We have already encountered these pillars in various parts of this book – in particular, Chapter One explored the concept of a system, whilst Chapters Two and Three looked at variation. For this reason I don't intend to cover old ground. Chapters Two and Three also touched upon the third element of the System of Profound Knowledge – 'Theory of Knowledge'.

Deming argues that knowledge is built on theory:

> The theory of knowledge teaches us that a statement, if it conveys knowledge, predicts future outcome…[30]

And,

> Rational prediction requires theory and builds knowledge through systematic revision and extension of theory based on comparison of prediction with observation.[31]

Deming contends that the effective use of accumulated knowledge is conditional on it being understood in conjunction with theory. His point is that scientific evaluation of data enhances our ability to predict the future behaviour of processes, (e.g. by plotting performance data in an SPC chart) and this generates a mandate for action. This subsequent action may involve revising or extending the relevant theory, based on observations of how the data behave. Deming also makes the important distinction between 'knowledge' and 'information', suggesting that 'information' is merely akin to a raw material, such as the words in a dictionary, whereas 'knowledge' is about understanding and applying that information.

Psychology forms the fourth pillar of the System of Profound Knowledge. It requires us to understand people, relationships, interactions and critical factors, such as the drivers for motivation, self-esteem and organisational trust. We have touched upon some psychology in our explorations of Stewardship and Agency theories and seen how it is relevant to every activity within any system that involves human beings. A basic appreciation of psychology provides a firm grounding for understanding how the other parts of the System of Profound Knowledge fit together and complement each other.

---

30   *ibid* p.102
31   *ibid* p.102

14 Points

Deming devised (and continually developed) his 14 Points for Management, which were intended to summarise some of the main points of his philosophy. It is not my intention to go through them individually or in great detail, but simply to draw attention to those that are particularly relevant to the topics covered in this book. I recommend further study of the original source material – it is highly relevant to the public and private sectors alike.

The first of the 14 Points is *'Create constancy of purpose for improvement of product and service'*. This focuses us on the aim of the system – i.e. purpose – as well as upon the principle that we should always strive to continually improve the system and the product or service it produces. It also emphasises consistency and discourages short-termism. Point One is linked to Point Five – *'Improve constantly and forever the system of production and service'*, which encourages continuous review, evaluation and improvement, as in the Check – Plan – Do model we looked at in Chapter Nine.

The notion of continuous improvement applies as much to personal development as it does to system design; this sentiment is echoed in Point Thirteen – **'***Institute a vigorous program of education and self-improvement'*. This investment enhances the workforce's skill base, resulting in performance improvement and the opportunity for workers to strive for mastery. We have seen the benefits this brings in terms of enhanced alignment with purpose, loyalty and trust.

Point Three – *'Cease dependence on mass inspection'* reminds us of the wrongheaded approach to quality management that we examined in Chapter Seven, whilst Point Nine – *'Break down barriers between staff areas'* highlights the dangers of a system design that relies upon functional specialisms (i.e. silos), as explored in Chapter One and elsewhere.

Other points of particular relevance are Point Eight - *'Drive out fear'* and Point Ten – *'Eliminate slogans, exhortations and targets for the workforce'*. These points hint at the destructive nature of traditional top-down management practices, and press for the genesis of an organisational climate free from the coercive tools associated with command and control organisations. The topics covered in Chapters Five and Six resonate most strongly with these points. Finally, Point Fourteen – *'Take action to accomplish the transformation'*, reminds us that organisational transformation is everyone's responsibility, but that success depends on intervention and overt support from the most senior management.

Get Changed

As you now know, the transformation that Deming calls for can only come about through the application of knowledge, along with a healthy appreciation of theory. Often, however, organisational change programmes are reliant on one-size-fits-all methodology, or are devoid of the scientific approach necessary for sustained transformation. It can also be tempting for managers to focus on rearranging the functional aspects of the system without paying due regard to the human elements. Professor Keith Grint of Warwick University estimates that approximately 75 per cent of change programmes seem to fail[32] and suggests that this is partly due to the mistaken assumption that "...all types of change were susceptible to the same type of change programme when, in fact, change is often radically different".[33] He also points out the importance of "...relationships over structures, and of reflecting rather than reacting..."[34]

When implementing change programmes, aside from the (I hope) obvious themes of designing the system against demand and having a clearly articulated purpose to work towards, managers need to consider cultural and climatic aspects of the transformation. The breaking down of hierarchies, departmental affiliations and other traditional organisational norms will not be easy. There will be egos and relationships to contend with, as well as fear, cynicism and suspicion. Unlike the simplistic Unfreeze – Change – Refreeze models of change proposed by psychologist Kurt Lewin,[35] changing the culture of an organisation will usually be a non-linear, multi-layered, long-term challenge.

Those driving such a transformation should avail themselves of change management theories, such as the organisational change principles proposed by Professor Vivien Lowndes of the University of Nottingham. Lowndes argues that local context, internal power relations, and even the possibility of resistance must always be factored into the transformation programme. This is particularly relevant when attempting to instil systems thinking principles, as so much of the philosophy is counterintuitive. When people are exposed to a philosophy that is way out of their comfort zone,

---

32   Grint (1995)
33   Grint (2010) p.184
34   *ibid* p.185
35   Lewin (1947)

emotions as extreme as outright denial or a refusal to engage may well be anticipated. Managers and colleagues should watch for this and make a determined effort to ease people through the transformation process in a cooperative and non-threatening way.

The change programme, if conducted in line with the Check – Plan – Do cycle, should be a learning process that fosters continuous improvement and lends itself to adaptation where necessary. Proper evaluation is also important, along with the understanding that any change programme involving cultural transformation should be organic and iterative, as opposed to having a predetermined 'end date' or rigid 'milestones' set in advance. Adherence to these principles should place managers in the strongest possible position for invoking a programme of transformation that leads to the conditions necessary for systems thinking to thrive.

A Brief Summary So Far

Once the concept of workers as stewards is accepted, along with the associated theoretical positions on trust and motivation, organisations can take a first step to transforming management thinking. When this is coupled with an organisational climate that fosters pro-systemic and pro-stewardship principles, it will generate the fertile environment necessary for the systems philosophy to thrive.

A Short Pub Tale

Next, we move from the intense world of academic theory to the practical world of the local pub. Here's a short story.

I was standing at the bar in a busy local pub recently, not far from a woman who was waiting to order food whilst her disabled adult son sat a few feet behind her at their table. He seemed somewhat distressed to be separated from his mother and kept calling across to her. She told him she wouldn't be long but was clearly becoming uncomfortable. So, when a waitress walked past she politely asked her if it was okay if her food order could be taken at the table.

The waitress appeared to be more uncomfortable than the woman and her initial response was, "I'm really sorry but it's company policy that food orders have to be taken at the bar". The woman replied, "Ok, don't worry about it then. Thanks anyway". The waitress could have left it at that, but she didn't. She realised that whilst she had instinctively complied with policy, her response wasn't helpful. She told the woman that she would ask the manager.

As luck would have it, the manager walked past at that moment and the waitress posed the question. The manager responded instantly, "Of course you can. No problem at all". I could see the relief on the woman's face, as well as that of the waitress, and they returned to the table where son and mother were reunited. The waitress began to take their food order and all was well. Although it was contrary to usual procedure, no one else waiting to place food orders at the bar seemed to mind. It was clearly the right thing to do. The waitress knew it was the right thing to do. She wanted to help, but didn't have the authority. The manager knew it was the right thing to do. She also wanted to help. It was obvious really.

The episode made me wonder why this company's organisational climate seemed to restrict this type of low level decision-making. Why not simply trust waiters and waitresses to make such decisions without having to refer them upwards, or seek permission before being able to help? Had the manager been unavailable at that moment, the situation could have been painfully drawn out. Let's face it; if a member of waiting staff made the wrong decision in similar circumstances, what harm could be done?

The lesson for managers is this – in these sorts of low risk circumstances your staff will probably make the same decision as you would anyway. What's more, it will probably be the right decision. Why not just let them do it? It's usually pretty safe.

From Pubs to Policing

Police overtime is a particularly good example of this 'pub theory' in action. Wherever I have worked it has always been standard practice for the Inspector to authorise overtime. This applies even when he or she wasn't there when a particular officer worked the extra hours. Usually the officer's Sergeant forwards the overtime claim to the Inspector, advising that it is a legitimate claim and that the additional hours recorded are correct. The Inspector signs the overtime sheet and the officer's claim is processed.

This procedure always struck me as a little odd, not to mention bureaucratic. When faced with such overtime claims, it quickly dawned on me that the procedure causes delays by inserting an unnecessary stage into the process; furthermore, if a Sergeant has already verified that a claim is legitimate then what is the value in a second layer of checking? Don't we trust our Sergeants?

I could count on one hand the number of overtime claims that I have had cause to question (and then it's usually just because the handwriting is illegible). If someone dishonestly applied for overtime they were not entitled to then they would commit a criminal offence and risk losing their job. If an officer's Sergeant (who works closest with them) submits a claim to me, then 99.9% of the time my function under this policy is purely to rubber-stamp the application based on the fact that the Sergeant has endorsed it.

If I am relying on the word of the Sergeant, then why shouldn't he or she be able to authorise the overtime? Have I ever disagreed with an overtime claim endorsed by a Sergeant? No. They tend to make the same decision that I would. Do I trust my Sergeants to allocate overtime fairly and submit officers' claims accurately? Of course I do. Furthermore, I practice what I preach; in my current role as Sector Inspector I have made it known that I am happy for all overtime claims to be authorised by my Sergeants. Guess what – the overtime budget hasn't spun out of control, there has been no mass fraud, and the process is much faster and more efficient. Funds are used appropriately and effectively, plus my sector's budget has never been overspent. People tend to behave responsibly when they are trusted.

Obviously in policing many situations involve a greater degree of risk than in the pub and overtime examples above. I am not suggesting that there should be a big free-for-all where every worker is afforded *carte blanche* to make whatever decisions they want, regardless of their level of expertise. One of my roles is as a PSU (Police Support Unit) Commander. I run a team of three Sergeants and 21 Constables in public order and crowd control situations. Sometimes this involves wearing riot helmets and carrying shields, and performing some pretty dangerous work in violent and hostile situations.

Every officer who is deployed as part of a PSU has to undergo yearly public order training, plus the PSU Commander has to be conversant with an array of tactics and commands. No one would suggest that a non-specialist should be able to assume the role of PSU Commander (or make decisions on their behalf) without the necessary qualifications and experience. It would be a recipe for disaster, with officers and members of the public being put at risk. Likewise, you wouldn't allow a hospital cleaner to make clinical decisions on behalf of a brain surgeon. I'd also argue though that you shouldn't allow a brain surgeon to make decisions about the hospital cleaning schedule. The cleaners know their role better than anyone else.

The examples above highlight the importance of trust and devolved responsibility within sensible and flexible boundaries. Those in the work know the work better than anyone else, and should be trusted to make decisions within their area of expertise. In matters of relatively low risk, staff should be empowered to make straightforward decisions. In areas of greater risk, or situations that require a degree of expertise to make an informed decision, such as during a riot or in relation to proposed brain surgery, then it's appropriate that the relevant expert makes the decision.

I argue (and have consistently found) that, as a manager, if you practise devolved responsibility it pays dividends. Loyalty flourishes and trust thrives. Waste is also cut out of the process by removing unnecessary layers of checking. The organisational climate defaults towards a stewardship disposition and the whole system benefits.

Who's to Blame?

Usually those whom you trust to make decisions on your behalf will make the right decision, but sometimes human beings make mistakes. If and when this happens, it should be taken as an opportunity for learning – if someone makes a decision that turns out to be the wrong one, despite the fact that they made it in good faith based on the information known to them at the time, then it is counterproductive to retrospectively criticise them. Someone who tries to do the right thing but is subsequently castigated if something goes wrong will be discouraged from taking the initiative in future.

Think of any recent national scandal or service failure. Now picture the media reaction, along with the typical response of managers. What type of scenario usually ensues? What sorts of comments are made in the press? What kinds of demands are made of those at the centre of the mess?

The first thing that springs to mind is this sort of predictable litany:

"*How* could this be allowed to happen?"

"*Who* allowed this to happen?"

"This must *never* happen again!"

(The italics are there for a reason, which I'll explain in due course).

These statements are usually followed by senior figures limply trotting out phrases such as:

"We are determined to learn the lessons".

"We have introduced new policies to prevent a reoccurrence".

"A small number of individuals were responsible for this unacceptable situation and disciplinary proceedings have been commenced against them".

Sound familiar? Of course it does. Any banking scandal, social services failure, police mistake or medical error tends to run its course with these sorts of accusatory pronouncements ringing throughout. The most junior parties involved (i.e. those who scuttle about somewhere at the bottom of the organisational food chain) often take the hit, before everything is certified as being okay again by those at the top.

But is it really a people problem, and do these reactions actually reduce the likelihood of a reoccurrence? Professor James Reason of the University of Manchester argues that there are two main approaches to the problem of human error: the person approach and the systems approach.[36] The dominant tradition of apportioning blame to individuals is indicative of the person approach; i.e. whenever something goes wrong the assumption is that a person must have erred, been negligent or just been otherwise bad. Usually, an identifiable individual will subsequently be named as the transgressor and must shoulder the blame. Conversely, the systems approach suggests that whilst human beings are fallible and sometimes make mistakes, the overriding cause of organisational failings is rooted firmly in the design of the system.

Reason suggests that the person approach is ingrained, not least because "Blaming individuals is emotionally more satisfying than targeting institutions".[37] Without attempting to get into any deep psychology over that statement, just consider how much easier it is to personalise blame instead of expressing dissatisfaction towards a faceless institution or similar entity. How many times do you see football managers or CEOs of large companies coming under personal pressure to resign following

---

36   Reason (2000)
37   *ibid* p.768

a scandal or other perceived failure? There seems to be a media-fuelled appetite for blood on such occasions, even though it is entirely possible that the person being targeted was not aware of the precise circumstances that led to the problem. Whether it's the overall boss, the departmental head, team leader, or a smattering of underlings that ultimately take the hit, as long as there's a human face at the end of the inquisition, the accusers tend to walk away feeling vindicated.

Perpetuating the personal approach is the notion of people as free agents who are masters of their own destiny when it comes to decision-making (remember the "It's the people!" disagreement in Chapter Three?). The argument goes that because someone has chosen a particular course of action that ultimately led to disaster, it must have been that person's fault for not selecting an alternative option.

The problem with the person approach is that (as Reason puts it), "… by focusing on the individual origins of error it isolates unsafe acts from their system context".[38] He argues that mistakes tend to fall into recurrent patterns that reflect flaws in the system. Anyone can make mistakes, even the 'best' people, and the impact of these mistakes is magnified if the system is incapable of 'catching' these occasional human errors. Weaknesses in system design not only exacerbate the effect of such mistakes, but can even increase the likelihood of them occurring the first place.

Active Failures and Latent Conditions

Nevertheless, individual mistakes and failures can and do happen for a variety of reasons, such as fatigue, lack of training, work being rushed, lapses of concentration and so on. These types of mistake are categorised as *active failures*. In contrast, the other (greater) contributory factors present in almost all adverse events are known as latent conditions. Latent conditions are systems characteristics which increase the likelihood of errors occurring. These can be related to organisational practices, policies, structures or culture, amongst others. For example, a worker operating under pressure to meet a production target may be tempted to rush his or her work. When defective items are produced, this occurs because of a combination of active failures on the part of the worker (i.e. work was rushed, poor attention to detail, etc.), and the latent conditions that encouraged corner-cutting and inattention to quality (e.g. target-driven performance management).

---

38   *ibid* p.769

For example, research into Local Authority Children's Services departments in the UK found evidence of latent conditions affecting the way individual workers performed their duties on the front line.[39] The research found that frontline staff were constrained by restrictive one-size-fits-all policies and procedures, which left little or no room for them to use their professional judgement to identify risk or to prioritise their workload. The system design generated huge amounts of unnecessary bureaucracy and smothered local context in favour of arbitrary targets and managerial control. These operating conditions increased the likelihood of errors, either as a result of directly affecting working practices or by causing "…elevated stress levels and fatigue".[40]

Latent conditions can lie dormant within a system for years and are responsible not only for provoking active failures, as in the example above, but also for undermining the system's natural defences against threat and risk. This creates 'holes' in the system's defence mechanisms which, if aligned at the time an active failure occurs, can spell catastrophe. An analogy is that of several slices of Swiss cheese being lined up next to each other to represent various systems conditions[41] (e.g. processes, operating models, safeguards, policies, organisational culture, etc). Generally, if the slices are placed next to each other in a random order, then it would be unlikely that there would be holes all the way through the row of stacked slices.

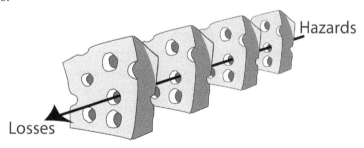

Figure 11.7: The Swiss cheese model

If the holes represent weaknesses present throughout the system (i.e. latent conditions) there will be occasions where some holes become

---

39   Broadhurst, *et al.* (2010)

40   *ibid* p.356

41   Note: Reason introduces the Swiss cheese analogy *(ibid* p.769), but refers to the slices as 'defensive layers'. I have extended this concept to include all systems conditions, not merely those installed for protective purposes. The principles of the model remain the same however.

momentarily aligned and a 'tunnel' can be seen through all the slices. This is where latent conditions create a situation of heightened risk.

Most of the time, individual latent conditions (or holes) can exist in systems without causing adverse consequences. This is because on those occasions when a problem slips through the net in one part of the system, systems conditions or safeguards in other parts of the system automatically curb the risk before it combines with other latent conditions to cause serious consequences. However, when a set of circumstances or variables conspire to produce a configuration where the holes in the system suddenly line up, then the potential for a problem to slip right through presents itself.

The catalyst for a major organisational failing is often a relatively low-level mistake by an individual – an active failure. What follows tends to be a witch-hunt for the individual rather than a search for the latent conditions present within the system that made the calamity possible. This is the wrong way to go about it – not only is it the equivalent of shutting the stable door after the horse has bolted, but it is damaging to the individual and does nothing to actually prevent a reoccurrence. This is why even after someone has been vilified following a serious organisational failure, similar events will tend to reoccur at some point in the future. When a similar catastrophic event does happen again, the usual reaction is to once more blame another individual, thereby leaving dangerous latent conditions untouched. Lessons, it seems, have not been learned.

Apart from targeting individuals so that personal blame can be apportioned for organisational failures, the traditional reaction tends to be centred on the premise that tighter controls, more restrictive policies and more draconian sanctions will force an improvement. This notion is firmly based on the mistrust-orientated Principal-Agent model once again, along with entrenched organisational risk aversion. It brings with it all the adverse consequences of preferring risk avoidance to proportionate risk management. Furthermore, it still fails to address the latent conditions that are causing the problems.

Chemical Leak

Consider the following example that demonstrates the futility of pressing on with blaming individuals whilst ignoring latent conditions:

A major leak of harmful environmental pollutants occurs at a hypothetical chemical plant. The usual uproar ensures:

"*How* could this be allowed to happen?"

"*Who* allowed this to happen?"

"This must *never* happen again!"

The chemical company responds by launching an 'investigation' that sets the blame squarely at the feet of a small group of workers who 'failed to follow the correct procedures'. They are immediately sacked and replaced with others. No other action is taken. Now, assuming that the company continues to operate under the same system design and working practices, how likely is it that there will be a reoccurrence? What about if they replaced all their employees? Well, the fact is that another leak is still just as likely as it ever was. As soon as those holes in the Swiss cheese line up again, on a day where a hapless human being also 'fails to follow the correct procedure', then... Bam!! Back to square one. Different workers, same result.

The person approach to error management, along with the shallow and risk-averse reactions it encourages, does not offer a solution to the problem. Simply blaming individuals or attempting to plug organisational gaps by stuffing them full of new policies or disciplinary procedures will always be a spectacular and costly failure. If systems conditions are ignored when attempting to mitigate future organisational failings, the term 'never happen again' should be replaced with 'almost certainly *will* happen again'.

How to Do It Properly

Effective error management involves "...limiting the incidences of dangerous errors and – since this will never be wholly effective – creating systems that are better able to tolerate the occurrence of errors and contain their damaging effects".[42] The greatest opportunities for building organisational defences against errors lie in developing an effective system design from the outset, based on the principles that we have explored so far. This necessitates a deep understanding of the system as a whole, along with its stated purpose, interdependencies and prevailing culture.

A system comprising disconnected or competing functional silos will always be more susceptible to those dangerous latent conditions that increase the likelihood of serious organisational failings. Likewise, an organisational culture dominated by the principal-agent disposition will

---

42   Reason (2000) p.769

further increase vulnerability. The risk is additionally intensified by the application of traditional management devices such as target-driven performance management or disproportionate audit and compliance functions.

A dysfunctional system, such as that described above, lends itself to the suppression of innovation and openness, in favour of technical compliance and self-protection. Many examples of this type of organisational climate were found during the research conducted into error management in Children's Services, as described below:

> The prevailing performance culture is also not conducive to honest and reflective feedback. Workers are too busy responding to the relentless targets, and, in a culture in which individuals are held accountable for error, and 'heads roll' in response to unfavourable audits, everyday errors will inevitably be kept quiet.[43]

The evidence points time and time again to latent conditions being the primary contributory factor in serious organisational failings, rather than the individual. Organisational learning is stifled in an environment where blame is commonplace because workers will feel uneasy about reporting mistakes or 'near-misses'. The result is that opportunities to learn about potential vulnerabilities in the operating model are missed and emergent risks remain unplugged. When these systems characteristics are combined with a managerial culture that favours tampering in preference to measured, evidence-based decision-making, the organisational conditions that ensue are ideal for guaranteeing failure after failure after failure.

The antidote to this malaise is to adopt a fundamentally different management perspective on failures. Those who are in the work know best where systems weaknesses lie and should be encouraged to highlight them so that solutions can be devised. Managers must welcome this and interpret it as an opportunity to improve the system, not as an indication of failure or weakness.

Such openness can only thrive in a system where dialogue is encouraged amongst those who operate within it. (Remember the point about being prepared to argue with the boss at the start of the book?) Receptiveness to new ideas and a willingness on the part of management to hear what

---

43   Broadhurst, *et al.* (2010) p.366.
See also: Reason (2000); Munro (2005); Fish, Munro and Bairstow (2008)

might be a little unpalatable will throw a bright light on dangerous latent conditions, which if left unchecked could fester and grow to become a real threat.

If They Can Do It...

Reason cites high reliability organisations – "systems operating in hazardous conditions that have fewer than their fair share of adverse events"[44] – as being exemplars of how behaviours typically associated with a trust-based organisational climate can act as a kind of inbuilt barrier against serious organisational errors. The types of organisations that fall into this category include nuclear aircraft carriers and air traffic control systems – long-term research has shown they consistently avoid serious errors and effectively maintain safety, even in high pressure or crisis situations.[45]

The key to this success is in fostering a culture of trust and responsibility amongst all staff, as well as maintaining a systems perspective on error management. Effective error management is reliant upon those at the 'sharp end'; it is imperative that there exist a clear sense of purpose, in addition to an ethos of trust. This encourages a sense of constant alertness, so that staff will automatically scan for risk and flag up potential vulnerabilities. Errors are analysed from a systems perspective so that learning can be gleaned and put to good use, rather than blaming an individual and carrying on as before. As Reason puts it:

> Instead of isolating failures, they generalise them. Instead of making local repairs, they look for system reforms.[46]

The practice of frontline workers exercising professional judgement and initiative is an excellent recipe for dealing with variety or unexpected developments. Frontline flexibility and trust, along with "…freedom and responsibility within a framework"[47] (a phrase coined by business writer Jim Collins), aid decision-making and go a long way to absorbing variation. A worker who relies upon a clearly articulated and understood organisational purpose as an internal compass does not usually go too far wrong.

---

44   Reason (2000) p.770
45   See: Weick (1987); Weick, Sutcliffe and Oldfield (1999)
46   Reason (2000) p.780
47   Collins (2001) p.125

I therefore argue that effective error management relies upon two key elements:

1. Intrinsic systems design features that either prevent the emergence of adverse latent conditions, or which mitigate their effect, and

2. A workforce that is attuned to purpose, operating within an organisational environment conducive to dialogue, trust and devolved responsibility.

This is why reacting to serious organisational failings should be less about *who* allowed something to happen and all about *how* it happened.

Commander's Intent

To ensure purpose is attained, the Army relies upon a concept known as Commander's Intent. Commander's Intent is simply a clearly-articulated goal (or purpose) that specifies the high-level aim of an operation. It tells participants *what* to do, not *how* to do it. At the highest level, Commander's Intent could be communicated as, *"Drive the enemy out of area 'X' and secure the land taken"*. As the order descends through the ranks, the overriding aim remains the same, but frontline officers are afforded the autonomy to devise specific tactics to achieve the aim. Every activity undertaken at every level occurs in direct pursuit of the overarching Commander's Intent. Each individual soldier has a part to play. They understand their role. Machine gunners, tank crews, engineers and medics all have different responsibilities, but all are performing roles crucial to achieving the Commander's Intent. Systems thinking in a warzone!

The advantage of Commander's Intent is that it is adaptable in the face of adversity, as well being a straightforward concept to grasp. Colonel Tim Kolditz, the head of the behavioural sciences division at West Point (United States Military Academy for prospective officers), says, "You can lose the ability to execute the original plan, but you never lose the responsibility of executing the intent".[48] This results in effective ground-level decision-making by frontline soldiers who are 'in the work' as it were, and who know what to do to achieve the objective.

Commander's Intent removes any temptation to cling to policies written by someone higher up the ladder; ground-level participants have

---

48   Heath and Heath (2008) p.26

to *interpret* the broad directive and devise suitable tactics. It encourages decision-making instead of hesitation, thereby promoting proportionate risk management over risk aversion. In a dynamic or rapidly developing situation, there is no place for hesitancy or avoidance of risk. Indeed, former US Secretary of State and retired four-star US Army General, Colin Powell warns: "Procrastination in the name of reducing risk actually increases risk."[49]

Every officer must know the capabilities of the system within which they are operating (e.g. number of troops available, levels of skill, experience and training), along with the latent conditions that could adversely affect their efforts to achieve the aim (e.g. fatigue, defective equipment, lack of ammunition). The simplicity and clarity of Commander's Intent encourages innovation in what many might consider the ultimate command and control organisation.

Commander's Intent – The Policing Context

The same principles tend to apply when policing public disorder situations. A Gold/Silver/Bronze command structure is established, with a clear overarching purpose articulated from the top, such as 'To prevent crime and disorder and keep the Queen's peace' at a high-profile football match, or 'To allow demonstrators to march peacefully between location A and location B'. As this stated intent descends to the ground-level commanders, a greater level of detail about tactical options emerges, which ultimately translates into what the bobbies on the ground actually do. As a Police Support Unit (PSU) Commander, I might order my PSU to clear a street of rioters or protect a strategically important junction, but in the back of my mind I'm thinking, *"Everything I do here is to keep the Queen's peace"*. The core reason of why we are on the streets at that time is understood by all of my PSU officers.

My experience of public order deployments is that they are something we tend to do quite well, certainly in my force. I rarely have senior officers leaning over my shoulder telling me what to do. I've never been measured against any targets in a major disorder situation; neither have I been instructed to produce written plans about how I'm about to deal with the 150 football hooligans that have just come around the corner wearing face coverings, intent on causing us harm.

---

49   Taken from Colin Powell's '18 Lessons of Leadership,' (Lesson 15)

Dear Father Christmas…

Imagine if the Commander's Intent logic could be transplanted into everyday policing. It would instantly render many of the devices of conventional management practice obsolete. I can picture it now:

- No targets.

- No meaningless comparisons against the wrong measures.

- No detailed instructions that prescribe how the bobby on the street performs straightforward tasks.

- No tampering by management, because responsibility would lie with those who understand the work.

- No requirement for local Sergeants and Inspectors to conform to prescriptive menu-driven tactics in response to local issues that they best know how to deal with.

- No obligation for frontline officers to report huge amounts of information about routine policing activity to satisfy management's desire to see that their plans are being followed to the letter.

The benefits would be enormous:

- A more responsive, adaptive and flexible mode of operational policing at ground level.

- Greater trust and responsibility, leading to stronger relationships between individuals and departments.

- A more systems-orientated organisation, where common goals are clearly articulated and understood.

- An attuned workforce that operates in an organisational environment where dialogue is valued and innovation flourishes.

- A greater opportunity to learn from others within the organisation, leading to improved processes.

- Instant reduction of waste and an increase in capacity, derived simply from stopping doing the wrong things.

- A more robust error management culture, where system design and staff empowerment combine to identify and mitigate adverse latent conditions.

I've actually done this in real life at a sector level and it works.[50]

Final Thoughts

In this chapter, we have explored the advantages of an organisational climate that liberates self-motivated workers who are intrinsically aligned to purpose. We have seen how an innate sense of purpose drives workers to prosper under stewardship conditions. We have examined alternative models of trust, devolved responsibility and error management, and seen how these approaches can reap immense benefits for both the organisation and its employees. When an organisation adopts a pro-stewardship disposition, the resulting cultural transformation generates the fertile environment necessary for systems thinking to take root.

---

50   Guilfoyle (2012b) pp.33-45. This text describes the systems-orientated methods I implemented within a large sector of Wolverhampton Local Policing Unit between October 2010 and July 2012, during my time as the Sector Inspector there.

CHAPTER TWELVE

Management Thinking Won't Change Itself

Nearly done. You've made it to the final chapter, but this is really just the beginning of the journey. We have covered the main tenets of systems philosophy; the 'whole system' viewpoint, the importance of interdependencies, purpose, using the right measures to understand the evidence base, and how data inform method. We have looked at the dysfunctional behaviours caused by targets and seen how tampering, binary comparisons, sub-optimisation and internalised competition drive waste into the system and impair service delivery. We have explored evidence that demonstrates how conventional management practice has been responsible for restricting innovation and generating an organisational environment that discourages trust and autonomy. We have stared into the management abyss and discovered all the things that I didn't know about when I devised my well-intentioned crime assessment method, years ago.

But it's not all bad news is it? Once you are able to recognise the wrong things that occur in organisations and systems, you can stop them from happening. That's a start, and at least it will stop your organisation from going backwards. The next step is to start doing the *right things* so that it can accelerate forwards and really begin to achieve purpose. In contrast to the horrors of the dysfunctional management practices which we have examined using theory, evidence and examples, we have also explored systems-orientated alternatives that eclipse the traditional approaches. These too have been presented using theory, evidence and examples that are relevant to the police service and beyond.

We have learnt that the key to understanding any system or process is the intelligent interpretation of data. We have discovered the opportunities that are unlocked by understanding predictable demand and variation and the application of Statistical Process Control. We have examined how having the *right measures, measured right* aids understanding of the system and identifies opportunities for improvement. We have applied simple models that help identify and remove waste, determine evidence-based responses and priorities, strengthen the system and foster continuous improvement. We have seen how a stewardship disposition harnesses the power of intrinsic motivation and generates an organisational climate where trust, autonomy and frontline professional judgement lead to cohesive relationships and better service delivery.

So now it's time to draw it all together and issue a rallying cry to go and put these approaches into practice. We will begin to do this using the diagram below – *'Theory of an Effective System'*, which is my attempt at bringing together the main elements of the systems approach in a clear, simple model that shows how the different elements fit together.

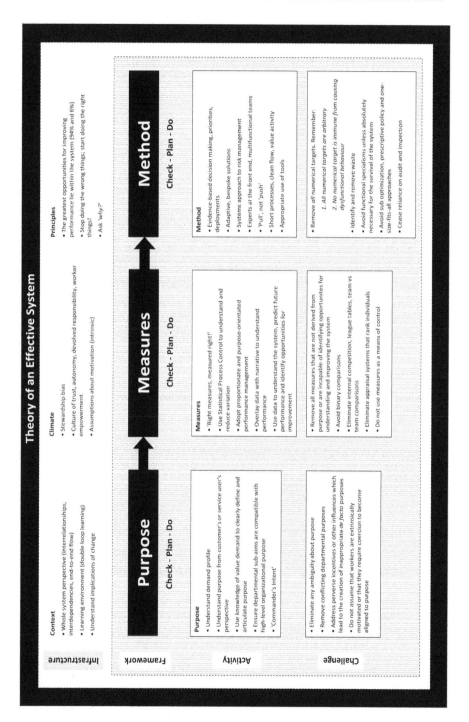

Figure 12.1: Theory of an Effective System

The 'Theory of an Effective System' diagram is an attempt to encapsulate the hypotheses presented throughout this book. At its heart are the dual frameworks of the Purpose – Measures – Method model and the 'Check –Plan – Do' cycle. Check – Plan – Do is a continuous cycle at each stage of Purpose – Measures – Method , and a combination of the two propagates a learning ethos throughout the system; this is a prerequisite for continuous improvement. Underneath this central framework are specific principles that generate essential activities, as well as identify areas to challenge or avoid. Adherence to these principles will result in a system that is geared towards achieving purpose whilst simultaneously reducing waste.

Around all of these elements is the overall organisational environment, with its three pillars of Context, Climate and Principles. The points under these headers determine the cultural disposition of the system and apply to every principle that sits in the three columns beneath Purpose – Measures – Method. When the principles are adopted within the optimal cultural environment, then a thriving and effective system will be achieved.

The model cannot define absolutely every aspect of an effective system, but I hope it acts as a useful focal point for the main theories and practices that are endorsed throughout the book. By way of highlighting key elements of what we have studied, I will now present salient points in summary form. These can be cross referenced with the 'Theory of an Effective System' diagram above, as well as with the relevant chapters, should you need to refresh your memory in more depth.

Systems and Processes

- Adopt a 'whole system' perspective (think of the human body analogy I used in Chapter One). Every part of the system is relevant to every other part of it. Systemic interrelationships and interdependencies must be acknowledged and understood in order to avoid sub-optimisation.

- Appreciate the importance of theory. As Deming reminds us:

    Theory is a window into the world. Theory leads to prediction. Without prediction, experience and examples teach nothing. To copy an example of success, without understanding it with the aid of theory, may lead to disaster.[1]

---

1   Deming (1994) p.103

- Remember that opportunities for improving performance lie within the system. (Deming, of course, talked about the 94%/6% split – the reality is that exact proportions are often impossible to quantify and will vary from system to system.) Management bears the responsibility to work on the system in order to improve performance. There is no point focusing solely on the workers (6%) and trying to squeeze every drop of performance out of them if the system (94%) is not improved. The very best workers can still only ever operate within the parameters dictated by the system.

- When designing (or fixing) the system, always start by getting knowledge about demand. Understand the system's demand profile and be certain about what value demand looks like. When this is known, purpose should become clear. Ensure that it is incontrovertibly articulated and understood by everyone in the system.

- Try to keep processes as short as possible. Identify blockages, delays, bottlenecks and unnecessary stages, then remove them. Keep flow as even as you can. Allow the customer or service user to pull value from the system – don't push it at them.

- Put expertise at the front end. Deal with demand as it presents itself – don't classify it, batch it, shift it around a bit or diarise it to be dealt with later. In other words, "Deal with today's problem today!" Effective operating models avoid functional specialisms unless they are absolutely necessary for the survival of the system (e.g. Counter Terrorism Unit).

- Always consider processes from an end-to-end perspective. Learn to appreciate that it is often necessary (but counterintuitive) to enlarge the part of the system or process that comes into contact with the customer or service user. Whilst this might at first appear expensive, it will reduce end-to-end time and cost by eliminating rework and failure demand, and there will be no need for stages further down the line because purpose was met at the initial point of transaction. Remember that short-term savings usually cause greater costs in the long term. To remind you of this notion, see *Figure 1.2* in Chapter One.

- Appropriate use of tools can help you understand and improve your system (e.g. by removing waste) but they are not a solution in their own right.

Purpose – Measures – Method

- Adopt a 'helicopter view' when seeking to define purpose and always understand it from the point of view of the customer or service user. Keep it simple. (Remember LAPD's *To Protect and to Serve* motto?) Use the definition to help identify priorities and ensure that any departmental sub-aims are totally compatible with the overriding organisational purpose.

- Apply the philosophy of 'Commander's Intent' (see Chapter Eleven) to ensure alignment with purpose, whilst affording frontline leaders the latitude to devise their own tactics dynamically.

- Determine purpose-derived measures that tell you how the system is operating. Use them to learn about the system, predict how it will continue to perform into the future, and identify opportunities for improvement. Put them in the hands of the workers and ensure they are at the heart of constructive dialogue. Never use the data from measures as a beating stick, to make comparisons between teams or to populate league tables. This will generate internal competition, demoralise staff, introduce perverse *de facto* purposes and cause dysfunctional behaviour that damages the system. This is not a threat – it's a promise.

- Remove all measures that are not derived from purpose, or are incapable of identifying opportunities for improving the system.

- Overlay data with the narrative about performance to understand *why* stuff happens. Build a proportionate and focused performance management function at the very heart of the system and use the data it produces as an evidence base that provides the mandate to act (or not act).

- Remember the mantra – '*Right measures, measured right*'.

- Ensure that method is directly related to purpose. Give yourself the best possible chance of achieving purpose by assessing the evidence base before undertaking activity (unless immediate action is required, such as in incidences of spontaneous disorder.) Ensure that the response to the evidence base is proportionate and subject to continuous review, so as to foster organisational learning. (Refer to the Evidence-Based Response Model from Chapter Four, *Figure 4.5.*)

- A proportionate, evidence-based response will reduce waste and encourage intelligent prioritisation, rather than the common management responses of tampering and knee-jerk reactions. *Do not react* if the evidence base does not indicate that a response is necessary or viable.

- Assess the cost/benefit balance (see Chapter Seven), i.e:
  - o Does the value of the activity outweigh the anticipated costs involved?
  - o Does the likely outcome justify the resources invested in the activity?

- Constantly review methods and remove priorities when they go out of date. Avoid the pain caused by overloading workers with multiple conflicting priorities and the chaos associated with the 'Policy Roulette Wheel' (see Chapter Four).

- Design your methods around the customer or service user's needs, to generate adaptive, bespoke solutions. One-size-fits-all does not work.

- Accept that there may be a degree of risk (there certainly is in policing) and *manage* it, don't *avoid* it!

- Don't rely on inspection. As Harold Dodge warns: "You can not inspect quality into a product".[2]

- Do the right thing and the figures will look after themselves. This applies to performance, budgets; everything. Conversely, as John Seddon points out: "…cost management actually increases costs".[3] In the same way, if it is not done properly, performance management makes performance *worse*.

---

2   Deming (1986) p.29
3   Seddon (2003) p.101

- So, to summarise Purpose – Measures – Method:
  - o Ensure that *purpose* is explicit and understood
  - o Ensure that the right *measures* are derived from purpose, used insightfully
  - o Ensure the data from measurement are used to initiate a *method* that is justified by the evidence base.

Check – Plan – Do

- Check is the most important stage of the cycle. Get it right! *Get knowledge* before attempting to change anything.

- Check involves learning about all of the following:

  1. *Purpose:* What is the purpose of this system?

  2. *Demand:* What are the types and frequencies of demand?

  3. *Capability*: What is the system predictably achieving?

  4. *Flow*: How does the work work?

  5. *Understanding system conditions*: Why does the system behave in this way?

  6. *Management thinking*: Underlying assumptions about how the work is managed.

- Plan can be summarised as *identifying levers for change, making adjustments to the system and devising appropriate measures that will inform method.*

- Do is about *initiating the planned action and monitoring its effect, using the purpose-derived measures specified during the Plan stage.*

Variation

- Pay heed to Deming's wise words: "Life is variation. Variation there will always be, between people, in output, in service, in product".[4]

---

4   Deming (1994) p.98

- Use Statistical Process Control (SPC) to understand variation. This will enable you to understand the capability of the system and identify any patterns that might be present in the data. Once the degree of variation is known, managers can begin to take action to reduce it. A reduction in variation equates to increased efficiency and effectiveness.

- Look for signals and respond appropriately to them. Understand the difference between signals and noise.

- Don't forget that the vast majority of variation comes from the system, not the person. As Brian Joiner puts it:

  > One necessary qualification of anyone in management is to stop asking people to explain ups and downs (day to day, month to month, year to year) that come from random variation.[5]

- Have regard to Mistake One and Mistake Two:
  o *Mistake One:* To react to an outcome as if it came from a special cause, when actually it came from common causes of variation.
  o *Mistake Two:* To treat an outcome as if it came from common causes of variation, when actually it came from a special cause.

- Always interpret data in context and look beyond the numbers. Remember Lloyd S. Nelson's observation:

  > The most important figures needed for management of any organisation are unknown and unknowable.[6]

And Einstein's sign:

> Not everything that counts can be counted, and not everything that can be counted counts.[7]

---

5   Joiner 28th July 1992. Cited in Deming (1994) p.216
6   *ibid* p.20
7   For this and other Einstein quotes see:
    http://rescomp.stanford.edu/~cheshire/EinsteinQuotes.html

- Never make binary comparisons. Why? Because they're rubbish.

- Always ask, "Compared to what?" It will drive you and others mad but it's worth it.

Waste

- Remember that the easiest and most cost effective way of improving capacity is to simply stop doing the wrong things – BUT – when it comes to building an effective system, waste removal is not the whole story!

- Identify and remove waste (e.g. inappropriate demand, handovers and bottlenecks, rework, failure demand, unnecessary or disproportionate thirst for reports, plans, meetings, tasks, or internalised requirements that do not benefit the service user, or help achieve purpose). Use the waste model presented at *Figure 7.5* in Chapter Seven to help identify waste and how it enters the system, then devise ways of eradicating it.

- Why not print off my 'Rules for Meetings' and place them prominently on the wall of wherever you most regularly hold meetings, or even incorporate them into agendas? I've found that reminding people of the three simple rules at the start of a meeting keeps everyone focused and ensures that their time (and mine) is not wasted. Here they are again:

  1. There must be a clear purpose to the meeting.

  2. The number of attendees and length of the meeting must be proportionate to what it seeks to achieve.

  3. There must be clear decisions and outcomes that everybody understands and acts upon when they leave the room.

Targets

- All numerical targets must be removed. This might sound radical (and maybe even a bit scary) but it is absolutely essential. Once targets are out of the way, performance will improve!

- The core of my theory on targets is this:
  - All numerical targets are arbitrary.
  - No numerical target is immune from causing dysfunctional behaviour.

- The only 'target' worth striving for is perfection, all of the time. Often, the constraints of the system, external factors and real life will prevent you from achieving 100% success, but doing your best is far superior to only aiming for 13.7% (or whatever arbitrary target has been set this year). At the very least, plotting progress using purpose-derived measures will allow intelligent interpretation of performance and perhaps uncover opportunities to improve the system.

- Don't get priorities, measures and targets mixed up! Remember:
  - Priorities are important (when evidence based).
  - Measurement (when done properly) is necessary.
  - Numerical targets are bad.

Organisational Climate

- Understand the structural and environmental conditions that determine how the system operates.

- Generate an organisational climate conducive to:
  - Stewardship principles
  - Trust
  - Autonomy
  - Devolved responsibility
  - Professional judgement
  - Frontline empowerment.

- Recognise the existence and power of intrinsic motivation. Don't assume that workers are primarily extrinsically motivated or require coercion to become aligned to purpose.

- Adopt a systems approach to error management. Don't assume it's a people problem when something goes wrong; instead, examine the system to expose the latent conditions that exacerbate active failures, and then work on them to reduce the likelihood of a reoccurrence.

- Acknowledge and understand the implications of change.

- Challenge conventional wisdom through double loop learning – ask *"Why?"*

Overall

- When redesigning any system, follow this straightforward two-part strategy:

  1. Stop doing the wrong things.

  2. Start doing the right things.

- Understand that unless the organisational climate provides fertile ground for systems thinking approaches to thrive, it will be impossible to successfully achieve the transformation you seek.

Does It Work Though?

You may well be thinking, "All this theory is great, but does it work in real life?" Or perhaps, "These principles are good for private industry/manufacturing/somewhere else, but can they actually drive transformation in a policing environment?" The answer to both these questions is a resounding "Yes". From my own personal experience I can tell you that the systems approach eclipses conventional management practice in every way. Even when systems thinking can only be practised by individual managers in pockets around an organisation, it still remains a superior alternative to the conventional approach.

In October 2010 I took over a large sector in Wolverhampton, West Midlands, and set about applying the very principles that are laid out in this book.[8] I was faced with a range of challenges, including

---

8   For a more comprehensive narrative regarding my practical application of the systems approach in Wolverhampton, see: Guilfoyle (2012b) pp.33-45

- Officers subject to individual performance targets

- Performance culture predicated on the wrong measures (e.g. number of arrests, detections, intelligence submissions)

- Data presented using binary comparisons and team vs team comparisons

- A strong culture of reporting detail about daily activity to management

- Written plans required for everything

- Limited autonomy for the seven team Sergeants

- Confusion over priorities

- Knee-jerk reactions to isolated incidents

- Teams working in silos

- Low morale

- Risk aversion

- Huge strain on capacity caused by excess workload.

This combination of factors had the effect of generating an unduly bureaucratic and restrictive organisational climate, where the exercise of professional judgement and devolved responsibility were severely constrained. It also meant that staff were uncertain about what purpose really was and this led to impaired service delivery. On the positive side, it was obvious to me that my workforce of around 70 police officers and PCSOs just wanted to get on with the job of helping people and preventing and detecting crime, in what was a very busy and demanding area to police.

I set about stopping the 'wrong things', so that the frontline workers could concentrate on the 'right things'. It was clear to me that much of the officers' existing workload did not constitute value activity – so a review of demand and working practices (i.e. Check) was conducted, which clarified what they should be concentrating on (i.e. purpose). Purpose was defined as, "Active offender management, providing an excellent service to the public, and doing the right thing."

In other words, this meant locking up or disrupting criminals, helping people and doing it well. Protecting and serving, if you like. A purpose statement like that is about as clear as it gets and this enabled those working in the sector to keep this broad 'Commander's Intent' in mind at all times, so as to guide their own activity.

Other immediate action that I took was as follows:

- All targets were abolished.

- Measures that counted numbers of arrests, etc. were scrapped.

- Team versus team comparisons, internal competition and the use of binary comparisons were stopped.

- The requirement for routine activity to be reported to me was abandoned.

- Plans were only required where it was necessary and proportionate to produce them (e.g. when planning a series of coordinated dawn raids).

- SPC was used to analyse data.

- Team Sergeants were afforded autonomy and the existing culture of permissions was broken down. An emphasis on proportionality, devolved responsibility, local decision-making and the application of professional judgement at the front line was also asserted.

- Proportionate risk management and evidence-based decision-making was actively encouraged.

- Teams were encouraged to work across boundaries to support each other.

- Non-value activity was identified and removed.

These steps had the effect of immediately creating capacity. We had stopped doing the wrong things and started doing the right things. The extra capacity, as a result of removing waste, rapidly began to 'snowball' into more capacity because the workforce was liberated to concentrate on purpose. The effect was that outstanding offenders were quickly arrested, resulting in fewer offences in our area, a reduced workload, more capacity to conduct preventative work, and so on. By January 2011 there was sufficient additional capacity to create a multi-functional proactive team and this gave us greater opportunities to target emerging threats and sector priorities (evidence-based ones, of course). This team supported the seven geographical neighbourhood policing teams and provided an enhanced degree of responsiveness and flexibility to the sector.

The impact of the systems approach was staggering. Team Sergeants reported that they enjoyed the newly invested trust they were experiencing. The use of SPC meant that, for the first time, sector staff could actually see what the capability of the system was, as well as identify when to respond to signals. Opportunities for improvement were quickly recognised and acted upon. Evidence-based responses became the norm. Dialogue about performance was encouraged and framed in a format that fostered learning. The net result was that purpose-orientated activity occurred effectively within a system framed by a trust-based organisational climate.

Measures – Actual and Aspirational

I would have liked to have introduced alternative measures that are derived from purpose. These could include total end-to-end time for investigations, proportion of incidents dealt with at the first point of contact, or the number of handovers within an ongoing enquiry. These measures would aid understanding of the system and identify opportunities for improvement. *Right measures, measured right.* But, the introduction of such measures at a sector level was not possible, so I tended to loosely track the crime rate to establish the effect of the systemic changes. Even this produced interesting reading:

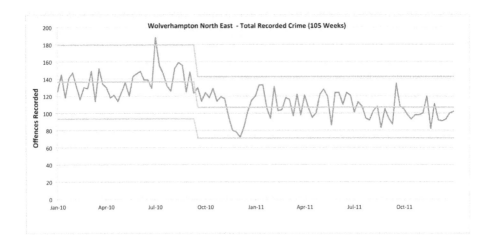

Figure 12.2: Total recorded crime data

The above chart displays a downwards step change and sustained reduction in variation from the point the changes were introduced in October 2010.

Furthermore, the chart below tracks serious acquisitive crime (i.e. house burglaries, robberies and vehicle crime), and shows an initial decrease at the same point in time, as well as a further downwards step change and reduction in variation that coincides with the inception of the proactive team at the end of January 2011.

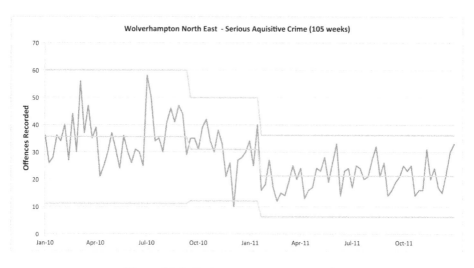

Figure 12.3: Serious acquisitive crime data

Notwithstanding that there are external factors affecting crime rates, along with the fact that this is just one type of measure, there does appear to be a correlation between the systemic changes implemented on the sector and the crime rate. Certainly, officers on the sector will talk about a culture change and fresh clarity of purpose, as well as some great stories about catching criminals and what it feels like to be trusted to get on with their jobs.

Other indicators also suggest that the systems approach had a measurable, tangible effect; for example, the total volume of ongoing investigations being conducted by officers reduced from a long-term average in excess of 300, to less than 200. Over time this decreased further and eventually settled at around 130. Anecdotally, the average end-to-end time for investigations also shortened. Furthermore, the list of outstanding offenders wanted on warrant or subject to being recalled to prison was reduced from a long-term average of between 15-20 to zero within a matter of weeks. All this meant additional capacity was created and the public experienced a better service.

The transformation on my sector occurred as a result of my unilateral localised intervention. There were areas that I would have liked to have influenced more, but which were outside of my control.

I hope that transformation to systems thinking principles can occur across the whole organisation. As I write, there is a discernible appetite for the systems approach developing within several police forces around the country. I believe senior management want to deliver the best police service possible, and all it takes is for someone to grasp the nettle.

Dealing With Doubt

As you embark upon your systems thinking journey it is inevitable that you will be confronted by doubters. These will be a mix of the 'La la la, I'm not listening' types, who flatly refuse to listen to evidence, along with the curious but uncertain. They will have questions for you. Some will instinctively defend conventional management practices because they are so entrenched that hardly anyone ever questions their logic. Some will never have heard of any alternative. You will notice repetitive themes emerging in the criticisms you may face.

You will need to be patient. It's very hard for people to hear that something that is trusted unconditionally actually harms the organisation and the people in it. They believe that targets do drive performance. They think that extensive policies and written plans make a positive difference. They may feel uncomfortable or threatened by what are, to them, completely alien ideas.

It won't always be easy, especially if you are trying to influence managers who refuse to accept the evidence. Reactions might be similar to those you could anticipate if you told a room full of children that there's no Father Christmas. It can be especially frustrating if you are able to demonstrate that the systems approach works by pointing to actual, tangible evidence, relevant theories and concrete examples, and they still can't hear it. I recall expressing such frustrations to a friend, who told me of a proverb from the bible that goes, "A prophet is not without honour, but in his own country".[9] In the same vein, I found this quote recently from writer Aldous Huxley:

> The vast majority of human beings dislike and even dread all notions with which they are not familiar... Hence it comes about that at their first appearance innovators have generally been persecuted, and always derided as fools and madmen.[10]

---

9 King James Bible, Mark 6:4
10 Huxley (1927)

One Inspector who took part in the research for this book told me the following:

> *"I find myself feeling like a managerial pariah. I know of one other Chief Inspector who is inclined to tell people that he has seen the Emperor nude. It doesn't make you popular with your bosses".*

Be prepared then. You might well be dismissed as a fool, crackpot or some sort of subversive 'organisational terrorist'. If so, just plough on in the knowledge that you are doing the right thing.

On the other hand, it's very rewarding when you see a light bulb go on when something you say suddenly makes sense – the "Oh yeah!" moment.

No One Said It Was Going to be Easy

So there you have it – a few thoughts on how I believe policing can be improved through the application of systems thinking principles. A lot of it goes against the grain. A lot of it is counterintuitive. For some managers, a lot of it will be difficult to swallow at first. What is certain, however, is that those who dare to try to implement this alternative way of thinking will require unfaltering courage in their convictions. As Professor Betsy Stanko of the University of London and the Metropolitan Police observes:

> ...the question remains as to whether any one individual within the police profession can swim against the traditional tide of doing things.[11]

I can't help but wonder how many individuals in individual departments in individual police forces around the world want to try to swim against the tide. If you are one of those people, my advice to you is *just do it*. Influence the parts of your job you can influence. Influence those around you. Influence upwards. Do the right thing. Make a difference.

Driving Test

I started with a story and I'm going to finish with one.

I used to get really frustrated if a driver in front of me braked whilst negotiating bends in the road. When I did my police driving course I was taught that you never brake on a bend as it reduces the tyres' performance

---

11   Rowson, Lindley and Stanko (2012)

and can affect overall control of the vehicle. (You're meant to set up an approach with the appropriate speed and gear before you go into the bend, so that you have better control of the vehicle and improved tyre grip. You then accelerate as you come out of the bend.)

I didn't know this before I did the police driving course. So, why would the drivers in front of me know? They've probably never come off the road from braking on a bend, so this would simply reinforce the impression that there's no reason to adapt their driving style. Braking also provides a degree of comfort and the illusion of greater control.

If a driver knew there was a better way to negotiate bends, he or she would probably be doing it already. This is exactly the same as management thinking. If a manager has only ever known how to apply targets, used binary comparisons, and relied on prescriptive policy, lengthy meetings and written plans, why would he or she be looking for another way of managing?

The answer is that these managers probably won't be, especially if they have worked their way up through their organisation doing just that, and seen everyone around them doing it as well. To be fair to these managers, if they have never been shown that there is a better way they will keep doing things in the same fashion, oblivious to the damage it causes. Their management norms provide the same sort of false comfort as unnecessary braking and, to them, there appears to be no logical reason why they would want to challenge those norms or alter the way they do business.

This means that someone else *has to*: management thinking won't change itself. As Deming said:

> *We've got some big changes to make, and you're going to have to make them.*
>
> *Who else will do it?*[12]

---

12   Neave (1990) p.xvi

Bibliography

Ackoff, R.A. (2004) 'Transforming the Systems Movement.' Third International Conference on Systems Thinking in Management. (ICSTM '04) Conference paper: 26th May 2004. Philadelphia

Albanese, R.M., Dacin, T. and Harris I.C. (1997) 'Agents as Stewards.' *The Academy of Management Review*, 22(3):609-611

Alberti (2009) *A Review of the Procedures for Emergency Admission and Treatment, and Progress against the Recommendation of the March Healthcare Commission Report.* London: HMSO

Argyris, C. and Schön, D. A. (1974) *Theory in Practice: Increasing Professional Effectiveness.* San Francisco, CA: Jossey-Bass

Argyris, C. (1976) *Increasing Leadership Effectiveness.* New York: Wiley

Armstrong, J. (1997) *Stewardship and Public Service.* Ottawa: Public Service Commission of Canada

Baker, R. S. and Sexton, J. D. (2000) *Aldous Huxley: Complete Essays 1926-1929.* Lanham, Maryland, MD: Ivan R. Dee, Inc

Barratt, D. (2007) 'Targets "Force Police to Make Ludicrous Arrests".' *The Independent.* [Online] http://www.independent.co.uk/news/uk/crime/targets-force-police-to-make-ludicrous-arrests-448921.html

Bekke, H.A., Perry, J.L. and Toonen, T.A. (eds.) (1996) *Civil Service Systems in Comparative Perspective.* Bloomington, IN: Indiana University Press;

Bevan, G. and Hood, C. (2006) 'What's Measured is What Matters: Targets and Gaming in the English Public Healthcare System' *Public Administration* 84,(3): 517-538

Bicheno, J. (2008) *The Lean Toolbox for Service Systems.* Buckingham: PICSIE Books

Bird, R. (2008) 'Indicators, Targets and the Decline of Education.' [Online] http://www.teachingexpertise.com/articles/indicators-targets-and-the-decline-of-education-3160

Bird, S. M., Cox, D., Farewell, V. T., Goldstein, H., Holt, T. and Smith, P. C. (2005) 'Performance Indicators: Good, Bad and Ugly.' *Journal of the Royal Statistical Society* (A), 168(1):1-27

Block, P. (1993) *Stewardship: Choosing Service Over Self Interest.* San Francisco: Berrett Koehler

Bommer, W. H., Johnson, J. L., Rich, G. A., Podsakoff, P. M. and McKenzie, S. B. (1995) 'On the Interchangeability of Objective and Subjective Measures of Employee Performance: a Meta-Analysis.' *Personnel Psychology,* 48(3):587-605

Bouckaert, G. and van Dooren, W. (2003) 'Performance Measurement and Management' in Bovaird, A and Loffler, E. (Eds.) *Public Management and Governance.* London: Routledge

Boyne, G. A. and Chen, A. A. (2006) 'Performance Targets and Public Service Improvements'. *Journal of Public Administration Research and Theory*, 17:455-477

Brindle, D. (2012) 'Why Headline Goals Have Taken Over From Top Down Targets.' Guardian Professional. [Online] http://www.guardian.co.uk/public-leaders-network/2012/jan/17/headline-goals-top-down-targets?CMP= 17th January 2010

British Transport Police. (2008) 'London Underground/DLR Policing Plan 2008-2009.' [Online] http://www.btp.police.uk/pdf/FOI_publications_ LondonUndergroundDLRpolicingplan_0809.pdf

Broadhurst, K., Wastell, D., White, S., Hall, C, Peckover, S., Thompson, K., Pithouse, A. and Davey, D. (2010) 'Performing "Initial Assessment": Identifying the Latent Conditions for Error at the Front-Door of Local Authority Children's Services'. *British Journal of Social Work*, 40(2):352-370

Caers, R., Du Bois, C., Jegers, M., De Gieter, S., Schepers, C. and Pepermans, R. (2006) 'Principal-Agent Relationships on the Stewardship-Agency Axis'. *Nonprofit Management and Leadership*, 17(1):25-47

Capon, N., Farley, J. and Hubert, J. (1987) *Corporate Strategic Planning*. New York: Columbia University Press

Centre for Crime and Justice Studies (2007) *Ten Years of Criminal Justice Under Labour – An Independent Audit*. London: Centre for Crime and Justice Studies

Chief Secretary to the Treasury. (1998a) Modern Public Services for Britain: Investing in Reform. Comprehensive Spending Review: New Public Spending Plans 1999–2002. London: HMSO

Chief Secretary to the Treasury. (1998b) Public Services for the Future: Modernisation, Reform, Accountability. Comprehensive Spending Review: Public Service Agreements 1999–2002. London: HMSO

Clarke, J. (2003) 'Scrutiny through inspection and audit' in Bovaird, A and Loffler, E. (eds.) *Public Management and Governance*. London: Routledge. pp.153-154

Colin-Thomé, D. (2009) *A Review of Lessons Learnt for Commissioners and Performance Managers Following the Healthcare Commission Investigation.* London: HMSO

Collins, J. (2001) *Good to Great*. London: Random House Business Books

Collins, N. (2011) 'Police Force Replaces "Targets" With 'Milestones'. [Online] http:// www.telegraph.co.uk/news/uknews/law-and-order/8548858/Police-force-replaces-targets-with-milestones.html 1st June 2011.

Copperfield, D. (2012) *Wasting More Police Time*. Croydon: Monday Books

Crace, J. (2007) 'Rose-Tinted Memoirs.' [Online] http://www.guardian.co.uk/ education/2007/jun/12/schools.education

Crawford, J. (2003) *Managing Transformation Actually Means Transforming Management*. Ampthill: The Deming Forum

DAC Working Party on Aid Evaluation. (2001) 'Results Based Management in the Development Cooperation Agencies: A Review of Experience.' [Online] http://www.oecd. org/dataoecd/17/1/1886527.pdf (p.7)

Davis, J. H., Donaldson, L. and Schoorman, F.D. (1997a) 'Toward a Stewardship Theory of Management'. *Academy of Management Review*, 22(1): 20–47

Davis, J. H., Donaldson, L. and Schoorman, F.D. (1997b) 'The Distinctiveness of Agency Theory and Stewardship Theory'. *Academy of Management Review*, 22(1): 611–3

De Bruijn, H. (2002) *Performance Measurement in the Public Sector*. London: Routledge

Deming, W. E. (1986) *Out of the Crisis*. Cambridge, MA: MIT Press

Deming, W. E. (1994) *The New Economics for Industry, Government, Education* (2nd Ed) Cambridge, MA: MIT Press

Department of Health (2010) 'A&E Clinical Quality Indicators Implementation Guidance.' [Online] http://www.dh.gov.uk/prod_consum_dh/groups/dh_digitalassets/@dh/@en/@ps/documents/

Donaldson, L. (1990) 'The Ethereal Hand: Organizational Economics and Management Theory.' *Academy of Management Review*, 15(1):369–381

Donaldson, L., and Davis, J. (1991) 'CEO Governance and Shareholder Returns: Agency Theory or Stewardship Theory.' *Australian Journal of Management*, 16:49-64

Donaldson, L and Schoorman, F.D. (1997). 'Toward a Stewardship Theory of Management'. *Academy of Management Review*, 22(1):20–47

Drucker, P. F. (1954) *The Practice of Management*. New York: Harper & Brothers

Eterno, J. A, and Silverman, E. B. (2012) *The Crime Numbers Game: Management by Manipulation*. Boca Raton, FL: CRC Press

Etzioni, A. (1964) *Complex Organisations*. New York: Holt Rinehart and Wilson

Fesler, J. W., and Kettl, D. F. (1991) *The Politics of the Administrative Process*. New Jersey: Chatham House Publishers

Fish, S., Munro, E. and Bairstow, S. (2008) *Learning Together to Safeguard Children: Developing a Multi-Agency Systems Approach for Case Reviews*. Report. London, SCIE

Flanagan, R. (2008) *The Review of Policing – Final Report*. London: HMSO

George, M. L., Rowlands, D. T. and Kastle, B. (2004) *What is Lean Six Sigma?* New York: McGraw-Hill Professional

Goldstein, H. and Spiegelhalter, D. (1996) 'League Tables and Their Limitations: Statistical Issues in Comparisons of Institutional Performance.' *Journal of the Royal Statistical Society*, A. 159:385-443

Greenwood, C. (2010) 'Theresa May Axes Police Performance Targets.' (The Independent). [Online] http://www.independent.co.uk/news/uk/home-news/theresa-may-axes-police-performance-targets-2013288.html

Grint, K. (1995) *Management: A Sociological Introduction*. Cambridge: Polity Press

Grint, K. (2010) 'Wicked Problems and Clumsy Solutions: the Role of Leadership.' in Brookes, S. and Grint, K. *The New Public Leadership Challenge*. Basingstoke: Palgrave Macmillan (pp.169-186)

Gross, D., and Harris, C. M. (1998) *Fundamentals of Queuing Theory*. New York: John Wiley & Sons

Guilfoyle, S. J. (2012a) 'On Target? Public Sector Performance Management: Recurrent Themes, Consequences and Questions'. *Policing: A Journal of Policy and Practice* 6 (3): 250-260

Guilfoyle, S. J. (2012b) 'What Works and What Matters.' In Pell, C. and Seddon, *Delivering Public Services That Work. Volume 2*. Axminster: Triarchy Press (pp.33-45)

Goodhart, C.A.E. (1975) 'Problems of Monetary Management: The UK Experience.' *Papers in Monetary Economics*. (Volume I), Reserve Bank of Australia

Hall, R. W. (1991) *Queuing Methods: For Services and Manufacturing*. Englewood Cliffs, NJ: Prentice Hall

Hardin, R. (2006) 'The Street-Level Epistemology of Trust.' In Kramer, R.M. (Ed.) *Organizational Trust: A Reader*. Oxford: Oxford University Press

Haughey, D. (2012) 'Pareto Analysis Step By Step.' [Online] http://www.projectsmart. co.uk/pareto-analysis-step-by-step.html

Healthcare Commission (2009) *Investigation into Mid-Staffordshire NHS Foundation Trust*. London: HMSO

Heath, C. and Heath, D. (2008) *Made to Stick*. London: Random House Books

Heinrich, C. J. (2008) 'Advancing Public Sector Performance Analysis.' *Applied Stochastic Models in Business and Industry*, 24:373-389

Heinrich, C. J. and Marschke, G. (2010) 'Incentives and Their Dynamics in Public Sector Performance Management Systems.' *Journal of Policy Analysis and Management*, 29(1):183-208

Henderson, M. (2012) Using the Tools of Science to Improve Social Policy. *The Guardian*. [Online] http://www.guardian.co.uk/society/2012/may/13/scientific-method-test-public-policy

HMIC (2008) *Leading From The Frontline*. London: HMSO

Home Office (2002) P*olice Reform Act*. London: TSO

Home Office (2008) *Improving Performance – A Practical Guide to Improving Police Performance Management*. London: HMSO

Home Office (2011a) *The National Standard for Incident Recording* – NSIR 2011. [Online] http://www.homeoffice.gov.uk/publications/science-research-statistics/research-statistics/ crime-research/count-nsir11?view=Binary

Home Office (2011b) *Counting Rules for Recorded Crime*. London: HMSO

Hood, C. (1991) 'A Public Management for All Seasons?' *Public Administration*, 69(1):3-19

Hood, C. (1996) 'Exploring Variations in Public Management Reform of the 1980s'. In Bekke, H.A., Perry, J.L. and Toonen, T.A. (eds.) *Civil Service Systems in Comparative Perspective*. Bloomington: Indiana University Press

Hood, C. (1998) *The Art of the State: Culture, Rhetoric and Public Management*, Oxford: Oxford University Press

Hood, C. (2006) 'Gaming in Targetworld: The Targets Approach to Managing British Public Services.' *Public Administration Review*, 66(4):515-521

Hood, C. and Dixon, R. (2010) 'The Political Payoff from Performance Target Systems: No-Brainer or No-Gainer?' *Journal of Public Administration and Theory*, 20(2):281-298

Hughes, O.E. (2003) *Public Management and Administration*, 3rd. Ed. Basingstoke: Palgrave Macmillan

Huxley, A. (1927) *Proper Studies*. New York: Doubleday, Doran

Jackson, P. M. (2011) 'Governance by Numbers: What Have We Learned Over The Past 30 Years?' *Public Money and Management*, 31(1):13-26

Jacob, B. A. (2005) 'Accountability, Incentives and Behavior: Evidence from School Reform in Chicago.' *Journal of Public Economics*, 89(5-6):761-796

James, O. (2004) 'The UK Core Executive's Use of Public Service Agreements as a Tool of Governance.' *Public Administration*, 82(2):397-419

Jennings, E. T., and Haist, M. P. (2004) 'Putting Performance Measurement in Context.' *In The Art of Governance: Analyzing Management and Administration.* Ingraham, P. W. and Lynn, L. E. (eds.) Washington, DC: Georgetown University Press

Jensen, M. C., & Meckling, W. H. (1976) 'Theory of the Firm: Managerial Behavior, Agency Costs and Ownership Structure'. *Journal of Financial Economics,* 3(1):305-360

Joiner, B. (1994) *Fourth Generation Management.* New York: McGraw-Hill

Juran, J. M. (1962) *Quality Control Handbook.* New York: McGraw-Hill

Juran, J. M., and Gryna, F. M. (1970) *Quality Planning and Analysis.* New York: McGraw-Hill

Kassim, H. and Menon, A. (2003) 'The Principal-Agent Approach and the Study of the European Union: Promise Unfulfilled?' *Journal of European Public Policy,* 10(1):121 – 139

Koch, R. (2001) *The 80/20 Principle: The Secret of Achieving More With Less.* London: Nicholas Brealey Publishing

Kotler, P., Lee, N., and Farris, P. (2008) *Marketing Strategy from the Masters* (3rd Ed.). Upper Saddle River, New Jersey:Pearson Education, Inc

Krueger, D. W. (1992) *Emotional Business.* San Marcos, CA: Avant Books

LAPD (2012) 'To Protect and to Serve.' [Online] http://www.joinlapd.com/motto.html

Lapsley, I. (1999) 'Accounting and the New Public Management: Instruments of Substantive Efficiency or a Rationalising Modernity?' *Financial Accountability & Management,* 15:201–207

Latzko, W. J. and Saunders, D. M. (1995) *Four Days with Dr. Deming.* Reading, MA: Addison-Wesley

Leapman (2007) 'Leaks Reveal Police Target Soft Touches to Meet Detection Rates.' *The Telegraph.* [Online] http://www.telegraph.co.uk/news/uknews/1550045/Leaks-reveal-police-target-soft-touches-to-hit-detection-rates.html

Ledbury Community Portal (2010) [Online] http://www.ledburyportal.co.uk/portal/index.php?option=com_content&view=article&id=3402:4000-inappropriate-999-calls&catid=1:latest&Itemid=279

Lewin, K. (1947) 'Group Decision and Social Change'. In Newcomb, T. and Hartley, E. (eds.) *Readings in Social Psychology.* New York: Holt

Lipsky, M. (1980) *Street-level Bureaucracy; Dilemmas of the Individual in Public Services.* New York: Sage

Loa Tzu (or Laozi), Chapter 58 of the *Tao Te Ching* (1993). Cambridge, MA: Hackett

Longman, H. (2011) 'A&E: Is There a Better Way?' [Online] http://www.patient-access.org.uk/userfiles/file/A&E%20-%20is%20there%20a%20better%20way%20HL%20v3.pdf

Loveday, B. (2000) 'Managing Crime: Police Use of Crime Data as an Indicator of Effectiveness.' *International Journal of the Sociology of Law,* 28:215-237

Loveday, B. (2005) 'Performance Management: Opportunity or Threat to Public Services?' *The Police Journal,* 78(2):97-102

Lowndes, V. (1999) 'Management Change in Local Governance.' In Stoker, G. (ed.) *The New Management of British Local Governance.* Basingstoke: Palgrave

Malkin, B. (2008) 'Emergency Services Reveal Silliest 999 Calls.'*The Telegraph.* [Online] http://www.telegraph.co.uk/news/uknews/1577098/Emergency-services-reveal-silliest-999-calls.html

Maslow, A. H. (1970) *Motivation and Personality.* New York: Harper & Row

McGregor, D. (1960) *The Human Side of Enterprise.* New York: McGraw-Hill

McLaughlin, E., Muncie, J. and Hughes, G. (2001) 'The Permanent Revolution: New Labour, New Public Management, and the Modernization of Criminal Justice.' *Criminology and Criminal Justice,* 1(3):301-318

Micheli, P. and Neely, A. (2010) 'Performance Measurement in the Public Sector in England: Searching for the Golden Thread.' *Public Administration Review,* July/August 2010, 592-600

Monro (2008) 'Police Focus on Minor Crimes to Meet Targets.' *The Times* [Online] http://www.timesonline.co.uk/tol/news/uk/article4033441.ece

Moynihan, D. P. (2008) *The Dynamics of Performance Management.* Washington DC: Georgetown University Press

Munro, E. (2005) 'A Systems Approach to Investigating Child Abuse Deaths'. *British Journal of Social Work,* 25, 531–46

Neave, H. R. (1990) *The Deming Dimension.* Knoxville,TN: SPC Press

Neyroud, P. and Disley, E. (2007) 'The Management, Supervision and Oversight of Criminal Investigation.' In Newburn, T. (Ed.) *Handbook of Policing.* Cullompton: Willan Publishing

Niles, R. (2012) 'Standard Deviation' [Online] http://www.robertniles.com/stats/stdev.shtml

Ohno, T. (1988) *Toyota Production System: Beyond Large-Scale Production,* New York: Productivity Press

Pearce, J. L., Stevenson, W. B. and Perry, J. L. (1985) 'Managerial Compensation Based on Organizational Performance: A Time Series Analysis of the Effects of Merit Pay.' *Academy of Management Journal.* 28(2):261-278

Pell, C. and Seddon, J. (2012) *Delivering Public Services That Work. Volume 2,* Axminster: Triarchy Press

Perry, J. L. and Porter, L. W. (1982) 'Factors Affecting the Context for Motivation in Public Organizations'. *Academy of Management Review,* 7(1):89-98

Perry, J. L. and Wise, L. R. (1990) 'The Motivational Bases of Public Service'. *Public Administration Review,* 50(3):367-373

Phillips, M. (2007) 'A Small Slice of Cucumber and the Target Culture that is Crippling Britain.' *Daily Mail.* [Online] http://www.dailymail.co.uk/news/article-455163/A-small-slice-cucumber-target-culture-crippling-Britain.html

Pidd, M. (2005) 'Perversity in Public Service Performance Measurement.' International *Journal of Productivity and Performance Management,* 54(5/6):482-493

Pink, D. H. (2009) *Drive: The Surprising Truth About What Motivates Us.* New York: Riverhead Books

Pink, D. H. (2011) 'Daniel Pink on Motivation.' *The Washington Post.* [Online] http://www.washingtonpost.com/wp-dyn/content/article/2011/01/08/AR2011010800379.html

Pollitt, C. (1999) *Integrating Financial Management and Performance Management.* Paris: OECD/PUMA

Pollitt, C. and Bouckaert, C. (2000) *Public Management Reform.* Oxford: Oxford University Press

Powell, C. '18 Lessons of Leadership.' (Lesson 15) [Online] http://govleaders.org/powell2.htm

Rainey, H. G. (1982) 'Reward Preferences Among Public and Private Managers: In Search of the Service Ethic.' *The American Review of Public Administration,* 16(4):288-302

Reason, J. (2000) 'Human Error: Models and Management.' *British Medical Journal,* 320, 768-770

Rothstein, R. (2008) 'Holding Accountability to Account.' National Center on Performance Incentives. Working Paper 2008 – 04. Nashville: Vanderbilt

Rowson, J., Lindley, E. and Stanko, B. (2012) *Reflexive Coppers: Adaptive Challenges to Policing.* London: RSA

Scherkenbach, W. W. (2001) *The Deming Route to Quality.* Chalford: Management Books 2000 Ltd

Schick, A. (1998) *A Contemporary Approach to Public Expenditure Management.* Washington: World Bank Institute

Seddon, J. (2003) *Freedom from Command and Control.* Buckingham: Vanguard

Seddon, J. (2008) *Systems Thinking in the Public Sector.* Axminster: Triarchy Press

Seddon (2011) 'Universal Credit: A Brilliant Idea Guaranteed to Fail.' [Online] http://www.universalcredit.co.uk/category/universal-credit-a-brilliant-idea-guaranteed-to-fail

Seddon (2012) 'Check – Plan – Do' [Online] http://www.systemsthinking.co.uk/2-2-1.asp

Silverman, R. (2012) 'Help! I've Been Bitten by a Hamster.' The Telegraph. [Online] http://www.telegraph.co.uk/news/uknews/law-and-order/9482692/Help-Ive-been-bitten-by-my-hamster-emergency-services-reveal-inappropriate-999-calls.html

Smith, P. C. (1990) 'The Use of Performance Indicators in the Public Sector' *Journal of the Royal Statistical Society,* 153(1):53-72

Shewhart, W. (1939) *Statistical Method from the Viewpoint of Quality Control.* Washington, DC: The Graduate School, US Department of Agriculture

Spitzer, D. R. (2007) *Transforming Performance Measurement: Rethinking the Way We Measure and Drive Organizational Success.* New York: Amacom

Stevens, D. E. and Thevaranjan, A. (2010) 'A Moral Solution to the Moral Hazard Problem.' *Accounting, Organizations and Society,* 35(1):125–139

South Wales Police (2010) 'Almost 14,000 Less Victims of Crime in South Wales.' [Online] http://www.south-wales.police.uk/en/content/cms/news/almost-14000-less/

Surrey Today (2012) [Online] http://www.thisissurreytoday.co.uk/Surrey-Police-reveals-999-calls-s-spider-living/story-15029855-detail/story.htm

Taylor, F. (1911) *The Principles of Scientific Management.* New York: Harper & Row

Tendler (2007) 'We Are Making Ludicrous Arrests Just to Meet our Targets.' *The Times.* [Online] http://www.timesonline.co.uk/tol/news/uk/crime/article1790515.ece

Tubb, G. (2012) 'ASBOs to be Axed in Blitz on Bad Behaviour.' *Sky News.* [Online] http://uk.news.yahoo.com/police-forced-act-anti-social-behaviour-014912664.html

Van Slyke, D. M. (2007) 'Agents or stewards: Using theory to understand the government-nonprofit social service contracting relationship.' *Journal of Public Administration Research and Theory,* 17(2):157-187

Walsh, J. P., Seward, J. K. (1990) 'On the Efficiency of Internal and External Corporate Control Mechanisms'. *Journal of Management Review,* 15(1):421-458

Wasserman, N. (2006) 'Stewards, Agents, and the Founder Discount: Executive Compensation in New Ventures'. *Academy of Management Journal,* 49(1):960–976

Weber, M. (1930) *The Protestant Ethic and the Spirit of Capitalism.* London: Allen and Unwin

Weber, M. (1947) *The Theory of Social and Economic Organisation.* New York: Oxford University Press

Weick, K. E. (1987) 'Organizational Culture as a Source of High Reliability,' *California Management Review,* 1987, 29:112-127

Weick, K. E. (1995) *Sensemaking in Organizations.* Thousand Oaks, California: Sage

Weick, K. E., Sutcliffe, K. M. and Oldfield, D. (1999) 'Organizing for High Reliability: Processes of Collective Mindfulness.' *Research in Organizational Behaviour,* 1999, 21:23-81

West Midlands Police (2008) 'Crime Recording and Proportionate Investigation Pilot.' Review document. Unpublished. pp. 41-42

West Midlands Police Authority. (2008a) 'Strategic Policing Plan 2008-2011.' [Online] http://www.west-midlands-pa.gov.uk/documents/main/1/strategic_policing_plan_2008-2011_june_2008.pdf (p.2

West Midlands Police (2012) 'What We Do – Counter Terrorism Unit.' [Online] http://www.west-midlands.police.uk/crime-reduction/tackling-terrorism/index.asp

West Midlands Police (2012a) 'Walsall Sees Dramatic fall in Crime With More Than 1,600 Fewer Victims.' [Online] http://www.west-midlands.police.uk/np/walsall/news/newsitem.asp?id=7883

Western, S. (2007) *Leadership: A Critical Text.* New York: Sage

Wheeler, D. (1998) *Avoiding Man-Made Chaos.* Knoxville, TN: SPC Press

Wheeler, D.J. (2000) *Understanding Variation: The Key to Managing Chaos.* (2nd Ed.) Knoxville, TN: SPC Press

Whitehead, T. (2010) 'Police Accused of Fiddling Response Times.' *The Telegraph.* [Online] http://www.telegraph.co.uk/news/uknews/law-and-order/7324855/Police-accused-of-fiddling-response-times.html

Wright, S. (2007) 'Nicked for Throwing a Cream Bun: Police Dossier of Dubious Offences.' *Daily Mail.* [Online] http://www.dailymail.co.uk/news/article-454889/Nicked-throwing-cream-bun-police-dossier-dubious-offences.html

Womack, J. P. and Jones, D. T. (2003) *Lean Thinking.* New York: Free Press

About The Author

Simon Guilfoyle is a serving Police Inspector and systems thinker. He is passionate about doing the right thing in policing. Having studied the works of W. Edwards Deming and associated authors he has applied their theories in everyday policing and found that the systems approach consistently leads to improved performance, lower costs and a better service to the public.

He writes and lectures on the benefits of incorporating systems thinking principles into policing, and has spoken at several national events. He also acts as an independent systems advisor to UK police forces and other agencies.

In 2011, Simon graduated from the University of Birmingham with a Masters Degree with distinction in Public Administration and, in 2012, attained a Professional Graduate Certificate in Education from Canterbury Christchurch University. He is currently studying for a PhD at Warwick University's Business School, exploring how police performance management can be enhanced through the application of systems principles.

In 2012, his article, 'On Target? Public Sector Performance Management: Recurrent Themes, Consequences and Questions', was published in the Oxford University Press journal, *Policing: A Journal of Policy and Practice*. In the same year, he also authored a chapter in *Delivering Public Services that Work (Vol 2)*, published by Triarchy Press.

Simon is a member of the Society of Evidence Based Policing and a Fellow of the RSA. He regularly posts blog entries on systems thinking, policing and everyday life on his blog site *www.inspguilfoyle.wordpress.com* and can be found on Twitter at @SimonJGuilfoyle. Join the conversation using #intelligentpolicing.

He can be contacted via email at simon.guilfoyle@ymail.com

About The Publisher

Triarchy Press is an independent publishing house that looks at how organisations work and how to make them work better. We explore the most promising practices in this area and look, in particular, for writers who can provide a bridge between academic research/theory and practical experience. We aim to stimulate ideas by encouraging real debate about organisations in partnership with those who work in them or research them.

We have published many books by authors from a Systems Thinking background. These include:

Management f-Laws, Differences that make a Difference ,Memories and *Systems Thinking for Curious Managers,* all by Russell Ackoff

Systems Thinking in the Public Sector by John Seddon

Delivering Public Services that Work (Vol 1) by Peter Middleton and John Seddon

Delivering Public Services that Work (Vol 2) by Charlotte Pell and John Seddon

Growing Wings on the Way by Rosalind Armson

Erasing Excellence by Wellford Wilms

Managers as Designers in the Public Services by David Wastell

The Search for Leadership: An Organisational Perspective by William Tate

The Decision Loom by Vincent Barabba

To find out more, buy a book, write for us or contact us, please visit

www.triarchypress.com

Index

REVIEWS

"This book could be game changing for the police service. Systems thinking theory can be viewed as complex and challenging, but not for Simon Guilfoyle. In this book he provides a comprehensive and cohesive explanation of the theory based on years of research and his practical experience of applying systems thinking in a policing context.

This book provides you with everything you need to know to introduce systems thinking in your workplace, and to convince others to do so too!"

Irene Curtis

(President of the Police Superintendents Association of England & Wales)

"Traditionally, policing has been 'managed by default': officers are deployed with little heed paid to what they should do and how they should do it. They are usually just left to 'just get on with it'! However, there is much that the police do that they share with other organisations. Suspects need to be admitted into custody, interviewed, fingerprinted, whilst elsewhere witnesses may need to be identified and interviewed. This may entail a more or less complex array of officers and civil staff performing different, but interlocking activities. How can such routine activities be organised and managed better than they are?

Simon Guilfoyle thinks he has the answer. This comes not just from a theoretical approach developed far from the streets where real officers must work, but from a fusion of theory and practical (but reflective and thoughtful) experience of policing. Simon Guilfoyle is both an academic and a practitioner, holding the rank of Inspector in the West Midlands Police in which he has served for 18 years.

Written in an accessible and engaging style this book will provoke as well as inspire its readers. Those readers should not only be other police officers, but anyone with a professional interest in policing."

P.A.J. Waddington

Professor of Social Policy

Hon. Director, Central Institute for the Study of Public Protection,
The University of Wolverhampton

"Simon Guilfoyle's book is the ultimate antidote to the tick-box culture that has spread through our public services like a computer virus in recent decades. However, whereas others merely point out the absurdities and distortions that may derive from unthinking application of performance targets but have no credible alternative, Guilfoyle has shown that the problem is targets not measurement. To demonstrate this, Guilfoyle takes the reader on a fascinating journey through the various techniques of managing quality from Deming onwards, showing how statistical process control can, through analysis of variations, tell us far more than targets which distort whatever they are intended to measure.

What makes Guilfoyle's book different is that these concepts and theories are not only presented with a wealth of practical examples from policing and other fields, but the author's approach is itself developed from experience gained over many years as an operational police officer working and managing in one of the UK's most challenging urban environments. The book is thus no armchair polemic or technocratic discourse, but a set of principles, theories and techniques that have been tried and tested over years. What it shows is that there is no substitute for applying intelligence to the problem of quality in public service delivery, and that the shortcut that performance indicators appear to offer is an illusion that can have devastating consequences.

Guilfoyle's book presents complex theories and techniques in a clear and engaging style that is accessible without being simplistic and is ideally suited to use on training courses as well as being an ideal textbook for public sector management. Although the book is primarily concerned with policing, its message and methods will be both relevant and revelatory for students of any field of public service and for public managers at any stage of their career."

Dr Adrian Campbell
Head of Masters in Public Administration (MPA) programme,
School of Government and Society, University of Birmingham

"Simon is a 21st century police officer. He really cares about improving how the police perform their duties. His insights into Systems Thinking and Performance Measurement within UK Policing has developed a cult following within most of the national forces. This book distils and makes

accessible Simon's acumen, expertise, empathy and mass of experience and conveys it humorously and articulately to show police officers, both frontline and commanding, that by applying these principles they can make the world a better place."
Dr. Mark Johnson
Associate Professor of Operations Management,
Assistant Dean (Executive Education).
Systems Editor, International Journal of Physical Distribution and Logistics Management, Warwick Business School, University of Warwick

"Simon Guilfoyle's Intelligent Policing will rightly attract the attention of police leaders and the policed public throughout the country. By describing his own experience, the lessons he draws should inspire every public service manager.

Management is a simple activity that with the best of intentions most managers constantly make more difficult. But by thinking of organisations as systems, and focusing on purpose, demand and capacity, they give themselves the means of keeping it simple (not easy!). The good news is that using these principles managers can transform performance, morale and public perception by doing less of the bad stuff and more of the good. And not just at the top – at every level in the organisation. He did it – so can you."
Simon Caulkin
Writer and Management commentator

"Targets, MBO, cost-cutting and other misguided management behaviour is demotivating officers, destroying performance and eroding public confidence. In his book, Guilfoyle offers a comprehensive and compelling alternative that should be on every Senior Officer's agenda."
Hazel J Cannon, Director of The Deming Forum

"This book tears the faltering heart out of the way things have always been done and replaces it with a super-sleek, ultra refined approach that will leave many senior management chilled to their very bones!

Inspector Simon Guilfoyle encourages managers, most of whom are stuck in a world of performance targets and knee-jerk priorities, to ditch their current belief systems and adopt a 'systems thinking' approach to their work. A proportionate, measured response will always reap far greater rewards than one born from uninformed management interference based on insufficient and inappropriate data.

A real eye-opener for those who currently seek to prove their worth through the presentation of skewed statistics and re-invention of old policy. Bin the targets, acknowledge that there are some acceptable risks and empower your staff….just a few of the changes that might actually make a difference. I just hope that there are some out there who are brave enough to take up the challenge…"

Minimum Cover, The Police Officer Blog
http://minimumcover.wordpress.com/